Theatre, Performance and Commemoration

CULTURAL HISTORIES OF THEATRE AND PERFORMANCE

The Bloomsbury series of *Cultural Histories of Theatre and Performance* recognizes that historical knowledge has always been contested and revised. Since the turn of the twenty-first century, the transformation of conventional understandings of culture created through new political realities and communication technologies, together with paradigm shifts in anthropology, psychology and other cognate fields, has challenged established methodologies and ways of thinking about how we do history. The series embraces volumes that take on those challenges, while enlarging notions of theatre and performance through the representation of the lived experience of past performance makers and spectators. The series' aim is to be both inclusive and expansive, including studies on topics that range temporally and spatially, from the locally specific to the intercultural and transnational.

Series editors:
Claire Cochrane (University of Worcester, UK)
Bruce McConachie (University of Pittsburgh, USA)

George Farquhar: A Migrant Life Reversed
David Roberts
The Polish Theatre of the Holocaust
Grzegorz Niziołek
A Century of South African Theatre
Loren Kruger
Alternative Comedy: 1979 and the Reinvention of British Stand-Up
Oliver Double
Soviet Theatre during the Thaw: Aesthetics, Politics and Performance
Jesse Gardiner

Forthcoming titles

Performing Modernity: Culture and Experiment in the Irish Free State, 1922–1937
Elaine Sisson
Theatre with a Purpose: Amateur Drama in Britain 1919–1949
Don Watson
German Amateur Theatre and Social Change in the Early Nineteenth Century
Meike Wagner

Theatre, Performance and Commemoration

Staging Crisis, Memory and Nationhood

Edited by
Miriam Haughton, Alinne Balduino P. Fernandes
and Pieter Verstraete

methuen | drama
LONDON · NEW YORK · OXFORD · NEW DELHI · SYDNEY

METHUEN DRAMA
Bloomsbury Publishing Plc
50 Bedford Square, London, WC1B 3DP, UK
1385 Broadway, New York, NY 10018, USA
29 Earlsfort Terrace, Dublin 2, Ireland

BLOOMSBURY, METHUEN DRAMA and the Methuen Drama logo are trademarks of
Bloomsbury Publishing Plc

First published in Great Britain 2023

Copyright © Miriam Haughton, Alinne Balduino P. Fernandes, Pieter Verstraete
and contributors, 2023

Miriam Haughton, Alinne Balduino P. Fernandes and Pieter Verstraete have asserted
their right under the Copyright, Designs and Patents Act, 1988, to be identified
as Editors of this work.

For legal purposes the Acknowledgements on p. xiv constitute an extension
of this copyright page.

Cover design: Ben Anslow
Cover image: Still from *Medicated Milk*. Director and Performer – Áine Stapleton.
(Photo © José Miguel Jiménez)

All rights reserved. No part of this publication may be reproduced or transmitted
in any form or by any means, electronic or mechanical, including photocopying,
recording, or any information storage or retrieval system, without prior
permission in writing from the publishers.

Bloomsbury Publishing Plc does not have any control over, or responsibility for,
any third-party websites referred to or in this book. All internet addresses given in this
book were correct at the time of going to press. The author and publisher regret any
inconvenience caused if addresses have changed or sites have ceased to exist,
but can accept no responsibility for any such changes.

A catalogue record for this book is available from the British Library.

Library of Congress Cataloging-in-Publication Data
Names: Haughton, Miriam, editor. | Fernandes, Alinne Balduino P., editor. |
Verstraete, Pieter, editor.
Title: Theatre, performance and commemoration : staging crisis, memory and nationhood /
edited by Miriam Haughton, Alinne Balduino P. Fernandes and Pieter Verstraete.
Description: London ; New York, NY : Methuen Drama, 2023. |
Series: Cultural histories of theatre and performance | Includes index.
Identifiers: LCCN 2022045960 | ISBN 9781350306769 (hardback) |
ISBN 9781350306790 (paperback) | ISBN 9781350306783 (ebook) |
ISBN 9781350306776 (epub)
Subjects: LCSH: Drama–Political aspects. | Theater and society. |
Memorials–Political aspects. | Anniversaries–Political aspects.
Classification: LCC PN1643 .T48 2023 | DDC 306.4/848–dc23/eng/20221031
LC record available at https://lccn.loc.gov/2022045960

ISBN: HB: 978-1-3503-0676-9
ePDF: 978-1-3503-0678-3
eBook: 978-1-3503-0677-6

Series: Cultural Histories of Theatre and Performance

Typeset by Newgen KnowledgeWorks Pvt. Ltd., Chennai, India

To find out more about our authors and books visit www.bloomsbury.com
and sign up for our newsletters.

Contents

Notes on Contributors ix
Acknowledgements xiv
Foreword: *Speculating on ceremony* xv
    Rebecca Schneider

Introduction: Theatre, performance and commemoration 1
    Alinne Fernandes, Miriam Haughton and Pieter Verstraete

Part 1 Commemorative Practices: Performing the Contradictions of Our Present

1. Unruly remembering: Great War anti-heroes and national narratives in Northern Ireland 19
    Tom Maguire

2. *My Revolution Is Better Than Yours*: Remembrance, commemoration and counter-memory of May 1968 37
    Jorge Palinhos and Karel Vanhaesebrouck

3. Dancing the emigratory experience: Challenging the boundaries of (imagined) communities and (invented) traditions 51
    Christel Stalpaert

4. Representations of transition, memory and crisis on stage in *Punto y coma* (Ready or Not) by Uruguayan dramatist Estela Golovchenko 65
    Sophie Stevens

Part 2 Disruptive Lessons: Thinking through the Affects of Memory

5. Know thy enemy: Wajdi Mouawad on history, memory and reconciliation at *La Colline* 81
    Yana Meerzon

6. From difficult pasts to present resonance: Performances of memory and commemorative gestures in contemporary Vienna 97
    Vicky Angelaki

7   Dancing impossible histories: Commemoration, memory and trauma in screendance   111
    Aoife McGrath

Part 3 Challenging the Nation/the State: Performing Affective Critiques

8   Performing/mourning Marikana as affective critique of a nation in crisis   129
    Miki Flockemann

9   Resonances of mnemonic community: Turkey's Kurdish Question in European opera   143
    Pieter Verstraete

10 Post-colonial imaginations: Afro-Asian dialogues in the past and the present   159
    Bishnupriya Dutt

Index   171

Contributors

EDITORS

Alinne Fernandes is Senior Lecturer in English and Translation and Coordinator of Núcleo de Estudos Irlandeses (NEI), a research cluster on Irish Studies, at the Universidade Federal de Santa Catarina, Florianópolis, Brazil. NEI is currently sponsored by the Irish DFA Emigrant Support Programme. She completed her PhD in Translation and Dramaturgy at Queen's University Belfast in 2012, during which she developed a methodological framework for theatre translation. In 2017, her translation of Marina Carr's *By the Bog of Cats...* was published as *No Pântano dos Gatos...* (2017) with an introduction by Marina Carr and notes on her extensive study on the play. She has published articles on theatre translation and Irish drama in international peer-reviewed journals such as *Research in Drama Education, Journal of Romance Studies, Quaderns: Revista de Traducció, Cadernos de Tradução* and *Ilha do Desterro*. She has co-edited two journal special issues, *Ilha Do Desterro* (71.2, 2018) and *Cadernos de Tradução* (2023). Besides Carr's play, Fernandes has translated and worked as dramaturge on the production of several plays for performance and staged readings, such as Mary Raftery's *No Escape*, Esteve Soler's *Contra el Progreso*, W. B. Yeats and Lady Gregory's *Cathleen ni Houlihan* (with Maria Rita Viana) and Patricia Burke Brogan's *Eclipsed*, as well as directed several rehearsed readings. Fernandes is a member of the Irish Society for Theatre Research (ISTR).

Miriam Haughton is Director of Postgraduate Studies in Drama, Theatre and Performance at the University of Galway, Ireland, and vice-president of the Irish Society for Theatre Research (ISTR). She is the author of *The Theatre of Louise Lowe* (forthcoming 2024) and *Staging Trauma: Bodies in Shadow* (2018). Miriam is also co-editor of the collections *Legacies of the Magdalen Laundries: Commemoration, Gender and the Postcolonial Carceral State* (2021) and *Radical Contemporary Theatre Practices by Women in Ireland* (2015). Her research has appeared in *Contemporary Theatre Review, Modern Drama, New Theatre Quarterly, Performance Paradigm, Mortality, Irish Studies Review* and *Cadernos de Letras* and *Feminist Encounters*. She has co-edited two journal special issues, *Ilha Do Desterro* (2018) and *Irish Theatre International* (2014) and published essays in multiple collections. Miriam is Director of the Feminist Storytelling Network (FSN), a supporting member of the National Women's Council of Ireland (NWCI), and co-chair of the IFTR 2020–1 conference at NUI Galway, 'Theatre Ecologies'.

Pieter Verstraete is Assistant Professor in Media, Arts & Culture (Media and Cognition) at the University of Groningen and a Marie Curie-Sklodowska Fellow at the Institute for Theatre Studies of FU Berlin with the research project, 'Exiled Lives on the Stage' (acronym ExiLives). His research splits into two strands: One is on intermedial practices in theatre with a particular emphasis on sound, voice and listening in contemporary music theatre. The second concerns political and social issues, mainly playing out in the realm of Turkey–Europe relations, which includes debates on interculturalism, (post)migration, democracy, nationalism, performative protest and exile. Publications include various works on sound, voice and aurality in *Performance Research* (2010), *Theatre Noise* (2011), *The Legacy of Opera* (2013), *Disembodied Voice* (2015), *Journal of Sonic Studies* (2017). His texts on Turkey were published by IPC-Mercator (2013), the *Jahrbuch Türkisch-Deutsche Studien* (2014), *Praksis* (2016), *Performance Matters* (2019), *Textures* (2019), *TRI* (2019) and *Documenta* (2021). He is also co-editor of the books *Inside Knowledge: (Un)doing Ways of Knowing in the Humanities* (2009) and *Cathy Berberian: Pioneer of Contemporary Vocality* (2014).

AUTHORS

Vicky Angelaki is Professor in English Literature at Mid Sweden University (Department of Humanities and Social Sciences). She was previously based in the UK for a number of years (Birmingham City University, University of Birmingham and University of Reading). Major publications include the monographs, *Theatre & Environment* (2019), *Social and Political Theatre in 21st-Century Britain: Staging Crisis* (2017), *The Plays of Martin Crimp: Making Theatre Strange* (2012), the edited collection, *Contemporary British Theatre: Breaking New Ground* (2013; 2016) and the special issue of *Contemporary Theatre Review* titled 'Dealing with Martin Crimp' (2014). She co-edits the series Adaptation in Theatre and Performance (with Kara Reilly). Her next monograph will be *Martin Crimp's Power Plays: Intertextuality, Sexuality, Desire* (2023). She is currently working on the research project 'Performing Interspaces: Social Fluidities in Contemporary Theatre', funded by the Riksbankens Jubileumsfond (Sweden).

Bishnupriya Dutt is Professor of Theatre and Performance Studies in the School of Arts and Aesthetics, Jawaharlal Nehru University, Delhi, India. Previously she was at the Department of Journalism and Mass Communication at University of Calcutta (1989–99). Her area of research includes colonial and post-colonial histories of theatre, feminist readings of Indian Theatre and contemporary performative practices and popular culture. She has also been a theatre actor and director in India. Her recent publications include *Gendered Citizenship: Performance and Manifestation* (co-edited with Reinelt and Sahai) (2017), 'Protesting Violence: Feminist Performance Activism in Contemporary India' (2017), 'Protesting Through Gestures: Maya Rao in Dialogue with Dance and Theatre' (2017), 'Performing Resistance with Maya Rao: Trauma and Protest in India' (*CTR* 2015), *Engendering Performance, Indian Woman Performers in Search of an Identity* (2010) and *Unsafe Spaces of Theatre and Feminism in India* (*TRI* 2012).

Miki Flockemann is Extraordinary Professor in the Department of English at the University of the Western Cape, South Africa. Her primary research interest is the aesthetics of transformation. Her publications include those on comparative studies of diasporic writings from South Africa, the Americas and the Caribbean in journals such as *Kunapipi, Tulsa Women's Studies, Ariel, Journal of Commonwealth Literature, MaComere* and *English in Africa*. She has published on aesthetic trends in South African theatre in journals such as *South African Theatre Journal, Journal for Theatre and Drama* and *Contemporary Theatre Review*. Book chapter contributions include those in *The Routledge Reader in Gender and Performance* (1998), *The Routledge Reader in Post-Coloniality and Performance* (2000) and *Performing Migrancy and Mobility in Africa: The Cape of Flows* (2015) and *Making Space: Three Decades of Magnet Theatre* (2016). Her most recent publication is a chapter in *New Directions in Diaspora Studies* (2018).

Tom Maguire is Professor of Contemporary Drama and Performance at Ulster University. He teaches in undergraduate and postgraduate programmes and supervises research students in Drama and in Museums and Cultural Heritages. He is a co-investigator in two major projects, *Future Screens NI* and *Museums, Crisis and Covid-19*. He is chair of the Board of the International Theatre for Young Audiences Research Network and an editor on the Young Asian Shakespeares edition of the Asian Shakespeare Intercultural Archive. He serves on the Peer Review College of the AHRC and on the editorial board for *About Performance*. He is chair of the Board of Big Telly Theatre Company and a board member of Young at Art, Belfast. He published *Making Theatre in Northern Ireland: Through and beyond the Troubles* in 2006 and *Performing Story on the Contemporary Stage* in 2016 and has contributed to a wide range of edited collections and international peer-reviewed journals. He has edited *Heritage After Conflict: Northern Ireland* (2018) with Elizabeth Crooke.

Aoife McGrath (BA(Hons), TCD, PhD, TCD) is a lecturer in Drama at the School of Arts, English and Languages, Queen's University, Belfast. After a professional dance career in Germany and Ireland, Aoife worked as a choreographer, dance critic and as dance advisor for the Irish Arts Council. Recent publications include work on: dance and affect; improvisation and feminism; dance, modernity and politics; and creativity in contemporary re-imaginings of traditional Irish dance. Aoife's book publications include her monograph, *Dance Theatre in Ireland: Revolutionary Moves* (2013) and co-edited collection (with Emma Meehan, CDaRE, Coventry), *Dance Matters in Ireland: Contemporary Processes and Practices* (2018). Aoife is co-convenor of the Choreography and Corporeality Working Group of the IFTR (with Philipa Rothfield, La Trobe, Australia, and Prarthana Purkayastha, Royal Holloway, UK), an executive committee member of the Irish Society for Theatre Research, a member of the board of directors of Dance Limerick, and a performer/choreographer member of Dance Ireland.

Yana Meerzon is Professor of Theatre Studies, Department of Theatre, University of Ottawa. Her research interests are in drama and performance theory, theatre of exile and migration, cultural and interdisciplinary studies. Her book publications include *A Path of the Character: Michael Chekhov's Inspired Acting and Theatre Semiotics* (2005) and *Performing Exile – Performing Self: Drama, Theatre, Film* (2012). She has also co-edited several collections, such as *Performance, Exile and 'America'* (with Silvija Jestrovic, 2009); *Adapting Chekhov: The Text and Its Mutations* (with J. Douglas Clayton, 2012); *History, Memory, Performance* (with David Dean and Kathryn Prince, 2015); *Routledge Companion to Michael Chekhov* (with Marie-Christine Autant-Mathieu, 2015); and a special issue of *Theatre Research in Canada*, a journal on theatre and immigration (2015). Currently, she is working on a new book project *On Self and Encounter: Constructing Subjectivity in the Age of Cosmopolitanism*.

Jorge Palinhos is a playwright, dramaturge and researcher based in Portugal. His research at CEAA-ESAP and CITAR-UCP focuses on space and performance and power and action in contemporary drama. Some of his works have been presented in Portugal, Spain, France, Belgium, Netherlands, Germany, Switzerland, Serbia, Brazil and the United States. He has a PhD in Cultural Studies, and teaches Contemporary Drama and Dramaturgy at the Higher Film and Theatre School in Lisbon, and Game Writing at the University of Applied Sciences of Bragança, besides being a member of the editorial board of the journal *Aniki*.

Christel Stalpaert is Full Professor Theatre, Performance and Media Studies at Ghent University, Belgium, where she is a director of the research centres, S:PAM (Studies in Performing Arts and Media) and PEPPER (Philosophy, Ethology, Politics and Performance). Her main areas of research are the performing arts, dance and the new media at the meeting point of philosophy. She has contributed to many journals such as *Performance Research*, *Text & Performance Quarterly*, *Contemporary Theatre Review* and *Dance Research Journal* and edited works such as *Deleuze Revisited: Contemporary Performing Arts and the Ruin of Representation* (2003), *No Beauty for Me There Where Human Life Is Rare: On Jan Lauwers' Theatre Work with Needcompany* (2007), *Bastard or Playmate? Adapting Theatre, Mutating Media and the Contemporary Performing Arts* (2012) and *Unfolding Spectatorship. Shifting Political, Ethical and Intermedial Positions* (2016). She is editor-in-chief of *Documenta, Studies in Performing Arts and Film*.

Sophie Stevens is a Leverhulme Early Career Fellow in the School of Literature, Drama and Creative Writing at the University of East Anglia. Her research project investigates the work of Latin American women dramatists in order to explore links between activism, performance, digital networking and translation. Between 2017 and 2020, she worked as a post-doctoral researcher on Language Acts and Worldmaking, a flagship project funded by the Arts and Humanities Research Council as part of the Open World Research Initiative. Her work has been published in *Symposium: A Quarterly Journal in Modern Literatures* and *The Mercurian: A Theatrical Translation Review*. She has also contributed to the Language Acts and Worldmaking book series published by John Murray Press. Her monograph *Uruguayan Theatre in Translation: Theory and Practice* was published in 2022. She is a theatre translator and practitioner and member of the Out of the Wings Theatre Collective. She has presented English translations at the Out of the Wings Festival (Omnibus Theatre), New Spanish Playwriting Festival (Cervantes Theatre) and CASA Latin American Theatre Festival (Southwark Playhouse).

Karel Vanhaesebrouck is a professor and chair of theatre studies at the Université Libre de Bruxelles, where he teaches courses in the MA programme 'Arts du spectacle vivant' and acts as a director of the research centre CiASp | Centre de recherche en Cinéma et Arts du Spectacle. He also teaches theatre history and cultural history at the theatre school RITCS (Brussels) and ESACT (Liège). His scholarly work has been published in journals such as *Poetics Today, Image & Narrative, Contemporary Theatre, Critique, Théâtre/Public, TDR/The Drama Review* and many others. His research interests are situated at the intersection of cultural history and performance studies, ranging from the on-stage representation of violence to the analysis of rehearsal processes of present-day artists. Vanhaesebrouck occasionally works as an author and a dramaturge, mostly but not exclusively in documentary theatre.

Acknowledgements

The editors would like to thank the contributors of this volume for their commitment to and engagement with the collection as it slowly emerged; thanks also to Methuen Bloomsbury for their enthusiasm and guidance, in particular, to Series Editors Claire Cochrane and Bruce McConachie, and Ella Wilson for her tireless support. We would also like to thank our colleagues for their encouragement, and our universities, the University of Galway in Ireland, Universidade Federal de Santa Catarina in Brazil, Freie Universität Berlin and Rijksuniversiteit Groningen. We are most grateful to Irish artist Áine Stapleton for permission to use an image from her feature film *Medicated Milk* for the cover of this book, as it speaks provocatively to the intersections of commemoration and performance, and the body as a site of memory, nationhood, crisis and potential.[1] Most of all, we are grateful to the artists who bravely create work that inspires, questions and pays tribute to the past in all its complexity. Theatre and performance are acts of community formation as well as artistic encounter, and the crises of health, nationhood and indeed memory of recent years remind us that without access to community we find ourselves in darkness. As the humanitarian and environmental crises gather pace, and the outbreak of war threatens the sanctity of human life, we must continue to create and inspire, question and reflect and, above all, remain connected. In the five years it took to create this book, we ourselves have experienced new life, death, migration, exile and loss during a pandemic that has been way too long, but here we stand. So, last but not the least, we would like to thank our partners and families, Holly, Mario and Pete, Andrey, Arthur and Tom and Görkem, who have also endured it all with us.

Note

1. To read about *Medicated Milk* or Stapleton's work, see: https://www.ainestapleton.com/.

Foreword: *Speculating on ceremony*

Rebecca Schneider

What are we doing when we gather bodies, objects, sounds and gestures together on stage, on screen, in procession, moving or standing still in order to make claims to commemoration? What happens when times touch or fold, cross or bleed? When one place becomes another place, what takes place? None of these questions is easily answered and obviously would vary depending on the 'we' involved – kin, comrade, friend, enemy, nation, celebrant or dissident. Are bodies moulded in reiterative or ceremonial postures in order to recall what we might otherwise forget? Or, do we play the past across our stages, screens, bodies, eyes and ears in order to forestall a future that we fear might threaten tradition, identity, security, or some sedimented set of so-called norms? Do we participate in commemoration in order to, as Robin Wall Kimmerer put it regarding Indigenous ceremony, 'remember to remember' (2013: 5)? Or do we hide behind (by casually passing by) a commemorative monument on stolen land in order to not have to acknowledge the complicated pasts some genres of 'we' are heir to?[1]

The essays in this book do not let such questions rest. Rooted in disparate global sites, commemoration is explored here in relation to the idea of 'nation', sensitive to theatre's historical role in nation-building and political upheaval. Commemorations theatricalize and theatres commemorate. Bodies are choreographed and plotted, moved into positions, postures, geometries, attitudes and scenarios to fulfil various aims marked for memory – often with clearly demarcated celebrants and dissidents.[2] Depending on where one sits in relationship to the activity, a commemoration or commemorative theatre event might aim to give account of the past, create community through narrating the past, exclude outsiders by delimiting the past, inform outsiders of their exclusion, redefine inclusion by retelling the past, complicate a received narrative, simplify a received narrative, challenge power, solidify power, make restitution, demand restitution, call for restorative justice, debase or ignore calls for restorative justice, celebrate privilege, challenge privilege, counter dominance, maintain dominance, realize social change, uphold social norms and work for and/or against racial, gender, ethnic and/or class justice. Remember to remember or remember to forget. Time-based arts can sometimes make several of these aims appear at once, telling stories of competing orientation and effectively asking audiences or participants to watch themselves negotiate the political machinery of living historiography as it takes place. Under the auspices of commemoration, all history is theatrical, after all – at the very least because the telling of historical tales takes place in time out of joint (one time in another time, as mentioned earlier). And we can commemorate, here, Bertolt Brecht's argument that all theatre-making should explicitly engage historicization so that audiences might critically witness the ways deeply consequential choices are made not just in but across time. At any rate, acknowledging commemoration as a minefield of intention at a crossroad of times is a starting point. What 'we' do at the crossroads and how 'we' do what 'we' do, is the matter of performance studies.

We know that the past, as story, as affective residue and as ongoing event, is always a mix of fact and speculation. In fact, 'fabulation' as commemoration may be especially important to communities or groups whose histories and memories have withstood erasure or theft under colonialism, through the power jockeying of nation states, displacement of peoples and the extractive violence of the capitalist machine (Hartman 2008). If it is common to claim that 'history' has been written by those with the means to transmit knowledge across time, we also know that it is not only those with the power of the 'victors' who transmit memory, legacy and otherwise ways of knowing. Many colonized, harmed, destabilized, enslaved, refugee and removed peoples have nevertheless transmitted a 'past that is not past,' moving through, around and under time (Sharpe 2016: 13).[3] Where there has not been the means to inclusion in, say, national archives, there has been the means to flesh, in Hortense Spillers's sense, and the returns of flesh are many (Spillers 2003; Weheliye 2014). Flesh houses not only the commemorative potentials of what Michel Foucault called 'counter memory', but also ways of memory beyond the binarized dynamics of dialectical countering.[4] Flesh may be simultaneously fugitive, fungible, commemorative and speculative of otherwise futures (King 2016). Here I cite Indigenous knowledge-ways again: Leanne Betasamosake Simpson has written that 'resurgence' of the past moves body to body in ceremony – in dance and in gatherings of people outside the logics of colonial recognition (2011). As such, decolonial gesture rather than document – or *as* document – is a mode not only of survivance but also of resurgence for ways of living otherwise (Vizenor 2008).

It has been argued that performance is always already the stuff of crossing time – doubling, repeating and reiterating. Anything presented self-consciously as 'theatre' or 'performance' is already at least twice-behaved, argued Richard Schechner from the belly of the twentieth century. I, too, focused on repetition in a 2011 book I titled *Performing Remains,* hoping to unpack the ways that live performance and overtly theatrical photography cracked open and troubled the linearity of time and the reliability of so-called authenticity. I wanted to explore how 'we' may be invited to 'think again' about received narratives of history as it plays across bodies. For me, as a scholar indebted to Brecht's insistence on historicization, the energy in repetition could be harnessed for critical thinking, for social change and for reparation. More recently, however, some theatre and performance theorists have tired of the limits of repetition and smartly asked us to think against or to the side of repetition and towards restoration, attention and care in commemoration – especially commemorative acts bent on reparative justice in raced relations or decolonial memory practices (Colbert, Jones and Vogel 2020). I agree with this call. Repetition runs the risk of just that and only that: repetition. Similarly, Indigenous scholars have distanced Indigenous ceremony from colonial cultural practices of commemoration that aim at national 'recognition'. Such scholars have worked to distinguish Indigenous practices from national commemorative practices that would 'recognize' Indigenous sovereignty without fundamentally changing modes of interaction (Simpson 2011; Coulthard 2014).

Swirling around all the re- words like repetition and recognition, re-enactment and reiteration are the politics of againness and the purposes towards which againness (restoration, recouperation, restitution and ceremony) is engaged. Decolonial and restorative justice work on commemorative practices requires vigilance and care regarding the tracks of European capital-colonial ways of seeing and experiencing time and history – the habits of knowing Tiffany Lethabo King refers to as 'conquistador subjectivity' (2020: 83). For many familiar with precarity, sometimes daily living against the stream of capital-colonial erasure is itself a mode of commemorating ancestors. Sometimes surviving another day is, at its most profound level, an act of being in and with a past that is not past. As Christina Sharpe makes clear in *In the Wake: On Blackness and Being*, something as vast as the sea itself can be read as an elemental theatre of commemoration if we acknowledge that the molecules that roll up upon the shore contain ancestors, alive in the afterlives of the transnational flesh trade (2016). In Derek Walcott's words, distinguishing African diasporic memory to 'monumental' white history: 'The sea is history.' To go to sea could be, then, commemoration.

How far out is too far out in stretching the possibilities for resurgence, ceremony and restorative commemorative acts? At the end of this foreword, we stand with commemorative theatre at the edges of oceans, moving in. Afterall, we make worlds, submerged and resurged, afloat in the theatre or in the dancing round or in the spaces among fleshly gestures and songs. As Sylvia Wynter has written, alluding to the not-yet but becoming 'we' of restorative justice after humanism, 'the ceremony must be found' (1984).

Notes

1. I use the phrase 'genres of we' to recall Sylvia Wynter's analysis of the 'modes/genres of being human.' See Wynter (2003: 281). This foreword is broadly indebted to Wynter's thought.
2. In '1492: A New World View', Wynter makes clear the ways in which celebrants and dissidents in modern national commemoration activities are linked in a binary opposition that she historicizes as the product of a globalized modernity (1995).
3. See Macarena Gómez-Barris on the 'submerged' history commemorated in decolonial artistic acts that counter capitalism's extractive barbarisms (2017: 1–16).
4. As we might imagine moving beyond the limits of the celebrant/dissident dialectics (and related binaries such as human/animal, male/female in which an 'other' is seen as 'counter'), and as we aim to challenge the limits of the 'human' as imposed by the knowledge-ways of liberal white humanism, we should be careful that a means to 'beyond' should not become another means to erasure. What are ceremonies of commemoration that remember to remember even while fostering outer worlds – worlds outside the habits, rituals and deadly practices of *homo economicus*, or the genre of 'Man' of the racial capitalocene? (See Jackson 2015, 2020; Vergès 2017).

References

Colbert, S. D., D. A. Jones, Jr., and S. Vogel, eds (2020), *Race and Performance after Repetition*, Durham: Duke University Press.

Coulthard, G. (2014), *Red Skins, White Masks: Rejecting the Colonial Politics of Recognition*, Minneapolis: University of Minnesota Press.

Gómez-Barris, M. (2017), *The Extractive Zone: Social Ecologies and Decolonial Perspectives*, Durham: Duke University Press.

Hartman, S. (2008), 'Venus in Two Acts', *Small Axe* 12 (2): 1–14.

Jackson, Z. I. (2015), 'Outer Worlds: The Persistence of Race in Movement "Beyond the Human"', *GLQ: A Journal of Lesbian and Gay Studies* 21 (2–3): 215–18.

Jackson, Z. I. (2020), *Becoming Human: Matter and Meaning in an Antiblack World*, New York: New York University Press.

Kimmerer, R. W. (2013), *Braiding Sweetgrass: Indigenous Wisdom, Scientific Knowledge, and the Teachings of Plants*, Minneapolis: Milkweed Editions.

King, T. L. (2016), 'The Labor of (Re)reading Plantationscapes Fungible(ly)', *Antipode* 48 (4): 1022–39.

King, T. L. (2020), 'New World Grammars: The "Unthought" Black Discourses of Conquest', in T. L. King, J. Navarro and A. Smith (eds), *Otherwise Worlds: Against Settler Colonialism and Anti-Blackness*, Durham: Duke University Press: 77–93.

Sharpe, C. (2016), *In the Wake: On Blackness and Being*, Durham: Duke University Press.

Simpson, L. B. (2011), *Dancing on Our Turtle's Back: Stories of Nishnaabeg Re-creation, Resurgence, and a New Emergence*, Winnipeg: Arbeiter Ring Publishing.

Spillers, H. J. (2003), *Black, White, and in Color: Essays on American Literature and Culture*, Chicago: University of Chicago Press.

Vergès, F. (2017), 'Racial Capitalocene', in G. T. Johnson and A. Lubin (eds), *Futures of Black Radicalism*, London: Verso.

Vizenor, G., ed. (2008), *Survivance: Narratives of Native Presence*, Lincoln: University of Nebraska Press.

Walcott, D. (2007), 'The Sea is History', in E. Walcott, E. Bough (ed.), *Selected Poems*, New York: Farrar, Straus and Giroux.

Weheliye, A. (2014), *Habeas Viscus: Racializing Assemblages, Biopolitics, and Black Feminist Theories of the Human*, Durham: Duke University Press.

Wynter, S. (1984), 'The Ceremony Must Be Found: After Humanism', *Boundary 2*, 12–13 (2, 1): 19–70.

Wynter, S. (1995), '1492: A New World View', in V. L. Hyatt and R. Nettleford (eds), *Race, Discourse, and the Origin of the Americas: A New World View* Washington: Smithsonian Institution Press.

Wynter, S. (2003), 'Unsettling the Coloniality of Being/Power/Truth/Freedom: Towards the Human, After Man, Its Overrepresentation – An Argument', *CR: The New Centennial Review* 3 (3): 257–337.

Introduction: Theatre, performance and commemoration

Alinne Fernandes, Miriam Haughton and Pieter Verstraete

How is theatre, by its very nature, commemorative? How, and why, does theatre centralize commemoration as a performative, conceptual, historical and political site from which to interrogate the inherent utopia and dysfunction of nationhood? Throughout these intersecting lineages of theatrical process and cultural production, how does selfhood, in its personal and public adaptations, become so committedly embroiled in this gesture of creative articulation and reference? This volume addresses these questions, noting the connections that converge across distinct forms of knowledge and disciplinary structures but which remain invested in ties of ritual and relationality through the event of theatre, a public and communal spectacle of imagining.

Commemoration refers to the relationship between the past and the present, relying on symbols of ritual and relationality to reassert certain value systems within the social fabric. Nationhood, and the various crises it reflects and produces throughout the twentieth and twenty-first centuries in the main, constitutes the starting point of this volume's enquiry. The responses generated by this project traverse a broad spectrum of narratives pertaining to macro and micro histories and memories on the stage that span established knowledge, tacit and haptic interactions, myth and legend, as well as the lesser-known or marginalized experiences. As the contemporary moment increasingly foregrounds a certain performativity of nationhood dominated by crisis, spectacle and discrimination, the discourse of nationhood – politically and philosophically – becomes urgent and, at times, overwhelming, in everyday contexts.

On the world stage in the twenty-first century, the instability of the machinery of nation is indisputable. Political conflicts continually worsen the transnational humanitarian crises, while societies are fraught by economic and cultural divides. The growth of far-right politics, as well as the tone and tenor of its discourse, signals a near-climactic point of tension among the realms of governance and multilateral negotiation. At the same time, the digitization and mediatization of global societies have renegotiated traditional hierarchies of communication and dissemination, splintering master narratives of space, time and self. Postmodern conditions of contradiction, fragmentation, anxiety and disorientation prevail in competing ideologies and world systems. 'Imagined communities', as Benedict Anderson (1991: 6–7) coins them, as well as their resulting 'invented traditions', as Eric Hobsbawm (1992: 1) puts forth, are being challenged in terms of their modern historical validity, value systems, boundaries and endurance.

Amidst this testing of 'imagined communities' and 'invented traditions' is a renewed focus on the shaping of memory, and making memory performative, by multiple stakeholders supporting diverse and often oppositional agendas. The documentation and construction of national histories via commemorative activity, largely deployed through performance and as performance, are politically infused with the rationale to reify the status quo. The drive to remember potent moments of identity-formation, embedded with 'profound emotional legitimacy' (Anderson 1991: 4), is inextricably linked with agendas asserting the incontestability of such identities, extending to the national, regional and personal. Yet these histories are increasingly met by voices of protest, dissent and doubt.

Case studies in this volume draw together theatre and commemoration in intensely political and historical contexts, occurring throughout Europe, the Middle East, Asia, Africa and Latin America. According to anthropologist Victor Turner, these ties speak of 'the power of symbols in human communication' (1982: 9) and are relevant to communities throughout the world. Identifying the explicit and nuanced connections between theatre and ritual, he itemizes these specifically in verbal and non-verbal taxonomies. The former may refer to persuasive tropes such as 'metaphors, metonyms, oxymora, "wise words"' (9) whereas the latter may include cultural uses of

> the entire sensory repertoire to convey messages: manual gesticulations, facial expressions, bodily postures, rapid, heavy, or light breathing, tears, at the individual level; stylized gestures, dance patterns, prescribed silences, synchronized movements such as marching, the moves and 'plays' of games, sports, and rituals, at the cultural level. (9)

Turner's summary of the mechanics of community and cultural ritual pithily captures the mechanics of theatre and performance and is thus fitting to open this volume's enquiry. The function and impact of ritual and theatre become heightened when they produce commemorative theatre and performance, capturing the particular concern of this project.

The act of commemoration is complex, multi-layered and fluid in its intentions, scope and affect. That is to say, commemoration may not always achieve the ideals and ideologies informing its official agenda. Commemoration, as the intentional performance of remembering and rejuvenating historical pasts, is a central tool in both the propaganda and truth-seeking of the politicized present. The main concerns regarding this duality may differ in each critical context. In post-colonial contexts, for instance, commemoration's political force often bears a heightened critical purchase, as narratives regarding state-formation of the past and for the future become enmeshed in the same temporal moment in performance. In feminist contexts, the identity politics embedded in the commemorative act are scrutinized against the backdrop of male privilege and patriarchal value systems to question whether erasure of women from the historical narrative has occurred, and if so, how structural and cultural forms of discrimination have been addressed, if indeed at all. The politics of race, migration and citizenship also inform critical conversations regarding commemoration, memory and nationhood throughout the historical past as well as the recent past. In the politicized nationalist climate of the early decades of the twenty-first century, how does one address these histories and current tensions moving forward? As Christopher Balme asserts on the theatrical public sphere, 'By means of allusion, allegory and sometimes downright subterfuge theatre has often provided a collective echo chamber for social and political concerns' (2014: ix). Indeed this 'echo chamber' is creatively addressed throughout this volume, stimulating a broad critique of commemorative narratives that evidence the inherent politicization of the very acts of remembrance and nationhood.

This intersection of commemorative narrative and politics is grounded in the past. Marvin Carlson, in *The Haunted Stage*, reflects on how theatre from the Middle Ages to the present day has been regarded by 'governments and other organizations, with varying degrees of consciousness' as 'a valuable tool for inculcating, reinforcing, and celebrating particular social concerns' (2011: 32). For Carlson, theatre's commemorative nature is in the reshaping and retelling of 'familiar narrative material' (33). That was precisely the case of modern nationalism with the 'recirculation' of national legends and historical events, together, of course, with the inauguration of national theatres across Europe. The recycling of old, familiar, legendary and heroic narratives with a political agenda reinforced the building of nations and state-formation in the nineteenth century. Needless to say, the twentieth century continued to be shaped by such narratives across the globe with dichotomic discourse markers embedded with 'us' versus 'them' narratives. Here one could think of the rise of McCarthyism and the fight against 'un-Americanism' in the 1950s that not only created an atmosphere of fear in the United States (Arthur Miller 1996), but also served as a mechanism of political and economic control over several Latin American countries for decades ahead. This discussion proves urgent in times when those dichotomic discourses are being constantly retold, and, when the rise of far-right governments in the twenty-first century fuel the stigmatization of otherness and fear.

Besides the discursive realms of theatrical retellings, Rebecca Schneider in *Performing Remains* addresses the problem of artistic 're-enactments' of war. For Schneider, those re-enactments necessitate our urgent reflection on tangled temporalities at the moment of witnessing in an 'attempt to literally touch time through the residue of the gesture or the cross-temporality of the pose' (2011: 2). Theatrical reproducibility inevitably reminds us that 'the past is not (entirely) dead, that it can be accessed live' (17), be it deferred in time or space. At its core are live bodies engaged in repetition as 'boisterous articulants of a liveness that just won't quit', thereby producing physical acts on stage as means 'by which the past and the present negotiate disappearance (again)' (39). It is in this space of bodily negotiation across and between temporalities that commemorative practices of rituality and relationality on the stage are being discussed.

Crisis constitutes a key theme for this study as the political present is in turmoil. Democracy and diplomacy are in danger of losing public confidence. Despotic models of leadership dominate public forums of communication. In a post-truth society, cyberspace is as much a site for conflict as any military target, or indeed, centres for trade and exchange. Victims and perpetrators cannot be easily identified in interlinking spaces and may at times coexist within the same individual or institutional body. How stories are being told as well as the content of such narratives have become a source of pervasive hostility leading to the spectacle of political showmanship as well as humanitarian devastation. The current crises of nationhood are being explored and exploited through narratives of print, live and digital media.

Recent explosive national performances include the collapse of power sharing and devolved government in Northern Ireland (2017–20; 2022–ongoing), the 2016 US presidential election and former president Trump's impeachment trial, the Brexit Referendum and EU withdrawal process (2016–20), the Turkish 'coup' (2016), the Brazilian 'coup' (2016), the Scottish independence referendum (2014) and potentially a second one in the coming months and/or years, ongoing tensions throughout Palestine and Israel, Afghanistan and Iraq, and devastation in Syria and now, Ukraine, to name but a few. Amidst these heightened performances of nationalism, the Covid-19 pandemic mocks borders as inherently futile while far-right populist leaders, like Brazilian president Jair Bolsonaro or former American president Donald J. Trump exploit social media and discontent to render the pandemic as 'fake news'. At the same time, we have seen the quick re-emergence of borders in national responses to Covid-19 as well as in nationalist discourses. For example, the border on the island of Ireland that legally separates Ireland from Northern Ireland is once more the centre of dispute, co-opted as a political weapon in Brexit negotiations among the EU and the UK.

As the world recovers from imbalances of capital flow after the pandemic, we see how Russia and Ukraine, bound by a myth of being brother nations due to a common past, are pushed to war. This Russian invasion of Ukraine is framed by trumped-up performances of nationhood and fabrications of Nazism, traitorism or a 'fifth column' by Russian president Vladimir Putin, who also asserted in a television speech that 'Ukraine never had a tradition of genuine statehood' (Vorobjov 2022), in order to keep the myth-based information war machine and its spectacle going. Not a month after the beginning of the invasion, Ukrainian president Volodymyr Zelenskyy proclaimed in a YouTube government video titled *Great Ukraine*: 'those who were lost, will be remembered', which resonated with the global loss of lives by Covid-19. The first commemorative installation in Lviv, organized by Svitlana Blinova in the midst of war on 18 March 2022, showed 109 strollers lined up in militaristic rows and a little girl sitting on a bench holding the Ukrainian flag, commemorating the children killed so far by Russian attacks (Farrant 2022). In commemorating their dead, their performance not only shows their resilience and hope for a better humanity but it also strengthens national unity in times of calamity.

When politicians choose to deny or twist the facts at the expense of the most vulnerable, how can the arts, or the theatre more precisely, respond to such calamities? Balme argues that 'the public sphere is almost never a real space but rather a set of rules enabling debate and discussion to occur. The question to be investigated historically is then: under what conditions do such rules pertain to the theatre and with what results?' (2014: ix–x). In response to his provocation, this collection offers a critique of how theatre and performance interventions from the twentieth and twenty-first centuries' global stage capture the lineage of these crises in the public sphere, the stakes of the political present, and hypothesize their potential legacy for generations to come.

Throughout this volume, the breadth and complexity of these national, international and transnational contexts are captured in the distinct case studies under scrutiny from across Europe, Latin America, Asia and Africa.

Stages of remembrance in the twenty-first century

This collection keeps to the foreground of thought that commemoration is an act of memory as well as of history; as a result, it is inherently performative, creative and changeable. It is also contingent on the politics of past and present. The etymology of the verb 'to commemorate' boasts a long legacy of impact and meaning. One of the most interesting attributes of the activity of commemoration is the call to worthiness, 'to mention as worthy of remembrance' (*OED*), which immediately encapsulates the politics of theatre and commemoration: What is considered worthy of commemoration? Which histories and narratives will find a voice in theatre, and how do those narratives speak to nationhood, particularly at this time of crisis? At this juncture, the motivations for unlocking the structures and strategies of commemoration have never been so urgent or, indeed, so telling. The centenary of the First World War emerges at the beginning of the twenty-first century and anticipates the centenary of the Second World War. This moment has sparked commemorative theatre and performance worldwide alongside a rejuvenation of memory studies, particularly in relation to how concepts and histories of nationhood are central to contemporary theatrical, cultural and political sites of power. The performance of nationhood, as manifest through struggles for dominance and legitimacy, pervades the public space, and this performativity has become tensely foregrounded in theatrical activity.

This collection explores and critiques commemorative theatre in the twentieth and twenty-first centuries, emerging at a tense moment in global politics when heightened ideas and ideals of nationhood are gathering pace. They do so, most often, by reference to imagined pasts, relying on ritual and relationality to support the aesthetics and process of imagining. At times, this is intended to simultaneously safeguard the status quo while stimulating imagined futures. In many case studies under analysis here, there is a sustained provocation of value systems in the present, which underpin the inherent political leanings of theatre as a public medium. Established structures of power internationally seek to reassert their legitimacy and dominance on the global stage, alongside a notable increase in visibility and activity by more recently emergent political factions in mainstream political, social and cultural spaces. Identity politics is a central tool in harnessing ideas of nationhood with the capacity to stir passionate responses regarding the relationship between self, place and belonging. The theatre, with its multifaceted modes of storytelling, has long operated as a site from which to investigate the subject and subjectivity, desire and power. Storytelling constitutes one of the most powerful ways to examine relationships, and 'history' (not to be wholly conflated with 'the past') offers one of the most standardized methods of legitimizing them.

Within the theatre, the dialogical processes that occur as a result of the co-presence of performers and audiences further query these relations and philosophies that both inform and prescribe, to an extent, the performativity and construction of self, community and politics. Theatre, as a public medium and shared space, has always occupied a central role in the public and social navigation of national and personal politics. It is a public forum that, since classical Greece to the present day, has both instructed and explored the nuances informing identity politics, personhood, the state and ideas of nationhood to bolster, legitimize, reflect on and, at times, debunk the status quo. It does so through mimetic and non-mimetic narrative and staging strategies, occurring across live, recorded and digital platforms. In this respect, theatre harnesses what Erika Fisher-Lichte calls a 'paradigmatic' (2009: 400) role for society. By virtue of theatre's necessity to occur within and occupy public space, she argues, it creates an aesthetic and political situation, involving doers and onlookers. Fischer-Lichte speaks to this regarding the interweaving of diverse cultures specifically, but her fundamental point regarding the potential transformative affect of theatre and performance cross-pollinates this enquiry. She asserts, 'all that occurs publicly in them – both between the performers and between the performers and spectators – may reflect, condemn, or negate the surrounding social conditions or anticipate future ones. In performance, new forms of social co-existence are tried and tested' (ibid.). The act of theatrical commemoration, the central focus of this collection, concerns how a nation, region, institution, community and/or individuals see, question and construct themselves in theatre and performance, which may 'reflect, condemn, or negate the surrounding social conditions or anticipate future ones' (ibid.). Throughout this volume, these ideas will be explored and tested from multiple ideological and theatrical perspectives, which synthesize and scrutinize the critical purchase of commemorative theatre as it intersects with the philosophy and politics of performance, nationhood, memory, history and community.

Imagined pasts and performances of nationhood

Jane Taylor's thoughts in *The Performance of Secularity* (2017) explore how 'the self' (while making room for a post-Freudian interpretation of what/who that may be) navigates ideas of place and nationhood to construct a performance of sincerity and authenticity. Locating her study in the early modern era, Taylor notes of this time, 'There is, moreover, an emerging sense of "nation" as a geographical locus of a set of beliefs and practices' (26), as 'secularism is, in ways, an attempt to generate an authentic personhood that can reconcile questions of geography and conviction' (ibid.). From the early modern period on, the nation as a geographical locus, she argues, operates as a territorial site from which beliefs and politics regarding religion, secularism and the construction of the self become contested, converted and, indeed, indisputably performed. Taylor's study points to how ideas that became conceived of as natural were strategically embedded, embroiled in the politics and power dynamics of the day. In the modern era, the major commemorations that occur are led by secular and sacred traditions with roots planted from centuries previous, yet they remain tied to this geographical locus of the nation, where the self is constructed and informed by ideals of nationhood. Tolerance, Taylor claims, has then been negotiated historically, particularly in relation to the nation, considering the emergence of a 'toler(n)ation' (2017: 29). She writes, 'I suspect that we can assent to the melancholy notion that difference is more often tolerated than celebrated' (ibid.). Expanding on how the politics of difference and tolerance affects world politics in contemporary times, she questions:

> In light of the world-historical upheaval taking place, with mass migrations of refugees and migrants across the globe, it is an ever more pressing obligation on us to consider what toleration means. How does that idea come to us, freighted with so many predetermined and over-determined values, obligations, and ambitions? (ibid.)

Commemorative theatre and performance identify these 'values, obligations and ambitions', particularly regarding their current critical purchase nationally, by their very presence, or absence, on the stage.

In *Theatre and Nation*, Nadine Holdsworth details that 'theater, as a material, social and cultural practice, offers the chance to explore national histories, behaviours, events and preoccupations in a creative, communal realm that opens up potential for reflection and debate' (2010: 6). She also reminds us that theatre functions in the *construction* of the national through the imaginative realm, as well as providing a site for play and analysis. Through the theatre, a past, present and future can be imagined and shaped, interweaving unities (often from discontinuities) of time and history with priorities of the political present. In the twentieth and twenty-first centuries, the performance of nationhood as expressed through commemorative theatre has signalled a sense of looming crises and anxieties, played out in performance spaces globally.

In what ways can performances of nationhood take place? How do often distinct cultural groups of people become ideally, or theoretically, united under the label of 'nation'? In *Giving an Account of Oneself*, Judith Butler, expanding on Adorno's ideas on moral philosophy, speaks of the violence perpetrated by conservative forces in order to maintain a collective ethos when a community starts to question moral norms of behaviour that were once widely and blindly accepted:

> What is strange historically – and temporally – about this form of ethical violence is that although the collective ethos has become anachronistic, it has not become past; *it insists itself into the present* as an anachronism. The ethos refuses to become past, and violence is the way in which it imposes itself upon the present, but also seeks to eclipse the present – and this is precisely one of its violent effects. (2005: 5; emphasis added)

We see a similar mechanism in some of today's nationalist narratives extending the anachronism of an already imagined past, thereby imposing a collective ethos on a collective body of the nation. The construction of nationhood may go hand in hand with conservative approaches to politics and policymaking.

For the purposes of this collection, we do not perceive commemoration and theatre as events that are exclusively confined to traditional theatrical spaces. Commemorative theatre can often be located in civic buildings or landmark public spaces, providing fresh perspectives into forms of site-specific and site-responsive theatre and performance. The scope for attracting audiences to commemorative theatre is also heightened as it typically engages communities with a keen interest in historical or local events, educational institutions, public bodies as well as traditional theatre-going audiences. In these contexts, commemorative theatre has the potential to produce affordable new insights and knowledge regarding theatre and space, audience theory and the politics of reception. Furthermore, commemorative theatre may not only take the established dramaturgical form of the traditional well-made play on the naturalist stage but also make keen use of documentary theatre and strategies of a 'theatre of the real', as outlined by Carol Martin (2012). In this light, commemorative theatre operates as a flashpoint of approaches and methodologies in theatre and performance studies, as well as a point of intersection among the arts, culture, heritage and politics, examining the convergence of past and present in live space and time.

Nationhood can operate as a conceptual space, one that remains in constant flux, not unlike the theatre. It can also operate as a dialogue between people, creating the reality it speaks of through the very act of speaking. There are parallels in this regard with the act of theatre and performance. Fischer-Lichte summarizes this autopoietic process, noting that 'performances come into being through the bodily co-presence of actors/dancers/singers/performers on the one hand and spectators on the other .... It is out of their encounter and interaction that a performance comes into being' (2010: 293). The bodily co-presence of different types of cultural actors is also required for nationhood to occur – politicians, religious figures, business people, communities, families – engage in both legal and social duties for the premise/promise of nationhood to become grounded in material reality. Thus, the representational and practical apparatuses of theatre and performance can track insights into the relationship between commemoration and nationhood, revisiting historical data in theatrical contexts.

Major questions these case studies explore include: how does commemorative theatre lay the groundwork for the future, or potentially, propose the future? If commemorative activity can reinforce a representation of 'us/them', then, does theatre attempt to reproduce that lineage continually and consistently in the same shape and form? Or, by consequence of its creative ontological methodology, can it expand the parameters and plurality of nationhood and history? Again, we turn to Fischer-Lichte's argument regarding the transformative power of performance, in particular, its scope for both agency and responsibility for performers and spectators. As she theorizes this possibility, 'the individual participants – be they performers or spectators – experience themselves as subjects that are neither fully autonomous nor fully determined by others; subjects that accept responsibility for a situation which they have not created but which they participate in' (2009: 391).

This certainly chimes with the thinking in Polly Low, Graham Oliver and P. J. Rhodes's collection, *Cultures of Commemoration*, a vast study from which they concur that 'images and ideas can be transformed: the present produces new forms of viewing the past' (2012: 2). Once more, the fundamental creative and performative nature of commemoration is reinforced. They argue, 'for commemoration is crafted. There is intentionality, or there are intentionalities, about acts of commemoration that are undeniable. But unpacking the intent of commemorative acts or rituals, monuments, and spaces can be difficult' (ibid.). Unpacking the intent is indeed difficult as is unpacking the potential affect of the commemorative acts. The editors query how the impact on spectators and audiences can be measured. Are such rituals appropriated in ways not intended by those who conceived of them? Such leading and significant questions cannot provide a concise response or one of collective consensus. And yet, such depth of terrain is a telling response in other ways. While cultures of commemoration do not always emerge from a central authority, they can produce 'a centralizing power that can often have the most considerable impact on such cultures', and, therefore, 'emotion and politics go hand in hand, and commemoration can channel both' (3–4). In this era of crisis and heightened nationhood, centralizing power is at the centre of political agendas internationally, and commemorative theatre is one way to channel collective and public voices to reaffirm and reinscribe particular ideologies.

The previous decade alone has witnessed humanitarian devastation in the Middle East, Africa and parts of Asia alongside utter global paralysis regarding any form of meaningful international intervention. The movement of peoples in distress has led to tragedies on precarious journeys of escape and exile, at borders and at centres of asylum. Political leaders appear increasingly protagonistic in their staged interactions with the public, employing strategies of spectacle through physical and digital platforms. These instances imply narrow and cheap characterizations of villains and heroes in attempts to dominate social media presence through micro-targeting, rather than creating a legacy of leadership that instils conditions for positive interactions or negotiates material terms of diplomacy, peace and reconciliation. Treaties, alliances and unions amongst nations that took lifetimes to build are being eroded in minutes and hours, often via Twitter. In the midst of this political theatre, the questions provoked by the cultural force of commemorative theatre resonate with this climate of national tension and political instability, as the chapters in this volume elucidate.

Commemorative theatre and performance: Chapter overview

The present volume examines theatre and performance as a site from which to address commemoration as both conceptual and material practice. As such, it aims to demonstrate the wide range of approaches and critical perspectives that reveal the diversity and density of commemorative theatre today and around the globe.

Part 1 focuses on the production of clearly articulated commemorative theatre and performance practices, including play texts and dance theatre, whilst uncovering the paradoxes that underpin them. The essays in this section introduce foundational mechanisms in the commemorative performative that materialize inner tension, like the role of fiction versus 'real' memories, representation of the past versus futurity, contestation versus myth, fabricated traditions versus authenticity. One key discussion in this section is on the role of contemporary dramaturgy, scenography and choreography for curating memory in the present, while balancing on a tightrope the commercial as well as ideological strategies of the commemoration industry closely tied to the idea of the nation and imagined communities.

The part opens with Tom Maguire's essay, which considers the complex tapestry of national commemorations of the First World War that occur in Northern Ireland, as a point of political nexus across Britain, Ireland and its own contested territory. Maguire argues that within the Decade of Centenaries (2012–23), theatre plays a particular role in what he calls an 'ecology of commemoration', because of its potency of 'embodied staging' of (fictionalized) human beings in close physical relations to one another, in this case of soldiers that gave life to the fossilized images from war memorials. He demonstrates how theatre can create a sense of a nation unified through collective remembering as a form of reconciliation with the past. Yet he also shows how two plays, the 2016 revival of Frank McGuinness's *Observe the Sons of Ulster Marching towards the Somme* (originally from 1985) and Martin Lynch's *Holding Hands at Paschendale* (2006) trouble the construction of white, masculine, heterosexual heroism and self-sacrifice of British soldiers from the island of Ireland as they are rather portrayed as 'unruly' and, as such, unable to be accommodated easily within heroic nationalist paradigms.

The following chapter by Jorge Palinhos and Karel Vanhaesebrouck takes us to the fiftieth anniversary of the May 68 protests in Paris, France, and how a sustained dramaturgical thinking around a theatre production can lay bare the ambivalences and relevancy of May 68 today as a temporal moment that marked a shift in political emancipation of many nation states around the globe. By examining the rehearsal process of Sanja Mitrović's *My Revolution Is Better Than Yours* (Les Amandiers, Nanterre, 2018), the authors who also served as dramaturges argue for theatre's significant potential to articulate a counter-hegemonic perspective on the nostalgic and largely reductive memorial industry around this significant 'lieu de memoire' in President Emmanuel Macron's future vision of France and the French identity. Against the general neglect in the commemorations of the global scale of May 68 (one could think of post-colonial struggle for emancipation on the African continent, for example, or the post-communist upheavals in Eastern Europe), Mitrović's play opens a potential for deconstructing ongoing cultural myths, including non-Western voices (thereby reconnecting the idea of civil disobedience to Europe's current migration crisis) as well as revealing 'the revolution' as a re-enactment experience rather than a reality.

Migration politics in Europe run also in the backdrop of Christel Stalpaert's study of Les Slovaks Dance Collective in Belgium, focusing on their production *Journey Home* (2009). Les Slovaks perform embodied memories of Slovak folk-dance traditions from their home in Slovakia to reminisce on personal and national heritage (Lepecki's 'bodies-as-archives') as well as to cultivate a new sense of hybrid belonging through a choreographic practice she calls *métissage*, an open or unbound mode of dancing, thereby mediating collective memory and identity. However, this choreographic approach is not unproblematic, as Stalpaert convincingly argues. Drawing from dance scholar Judith Hamera, she details how collective dance performance can also operate as manipulation and limitation in the production of imagined communities, including supra-ethnic, pan-Slavic national identities that level out differences through spectacles of mass configurations but also folk festivals like Východná. Stalpaert carries the discussion further by pointing to the pitfalls of a false authenticity in feeling united as a nation through the celebration of a gendered heroism or, as Palinhos and Vanhaesebrouck pointed out, of a deliberately reductive (re)constructed memory of a political event; Les Slovaks *métissage* technique seems then to challenge the boundaries of what is considered as the 'correct' script of executing folk dance, thereby unfolding an untenable myth of 'pure' or 'authentic' traditions. Fundamentally, she posits that *Journey Home* testifies of a hybrid emigratory condition, similar to the post-migrant identity, in order to move beyond the paradigm of belonging to one place or culture.

The section concludes by considering the politics of theatre and commemoration in Latin America with Sophie Stevens's insightful textual analysis of *Punto y Coma*, a play written by Uruguayan playwright Estela Golovchenko in 2003. The play deals with the fragmented lives of a father and daughter in a post-civic-military dictatorship society in Uruguay. Stevens demonstrates how Golovchenko, in her writing, makes use of the dramatic space to present powerful discourses about the past, which challenge those established by the state that facilitated a transition to democracy, yet told through the experiences of common people that reflect the ambivalences in the society. The vehicle for these discursive tensions to unleash is the disappearance of a mother during the Uruguayan civic-military dictatorship in 1985. None of the three characters has a name, which enables the interpretation that the play's story may refer to the stories of a number of victims of the regime. Stevens's textual analysis fosters a discussion on how the depiction of personal memories helps fill in the gaps and silences left by state narratives, thus creating more space in the society for further interrogation as it commemorates its absentees.

Part 2 of this volume examines how commemorative theatre and performance productions investigate memory in individual and collective contexts. By doing so, it seeks to identify how commemoration is reliant on memory, and how memory functions performatively and politically depending on various agendas and power regimes. This section opens with Yana Meerzon's critical account of intergenerational identities in contexts of migration, whose analysis reveals contested territories, physically, historically and metaphorically. Her object of study is Lebanese-Quebecois writer and director Wajdi Mouawad's *Tous des oiseaux* (*Birds of a Kind*). In Mouawad's play, and through his work as artistic director of La Colline in Paris, the politics of nationality, migration and intergenerationality are confronted on and off stage. Meerzon characterizes his play as 'a story of today's Romeo and Juliet' that portrays the conflicts of a Jewish family unfolding across generations and different geographies. Thus, the play not only seeks to stage a dialogue regarding the ongoing Israeli-Palestinian war, but also to question to what extent national identities are performative concepts, realized only through ongoing iterative encounters.

Meerzon's concerns are followed by Vicky Angelaki's critique of Vienna's Josefstadt Theatre founded in 1788, considering its very status as an institution both as a monument and register of history told through drama. Angelaki's enquiry is led by the affect of images of two young girls displayed on a banner at the theatre with opposing expressions of joy and sadness. The accompanying text, translated into English, reads: 'Whoever does not face up to their history, defaces history.' Angelaki argues that theatre, and henceforth performance, reiterates and retells discourses by means of the choices it makes, but programming also plays an important role in the representation of those histories. By doing so, the theatre can be a site for commemoration and reflection.

This period of potential change, in which storytelling becomes both method and material, is expanded further on in Aoife McGrath's exciting work on how dance and performance are foregrounding histories 'shadowed by political priorities', as Miriam Haughton (2018: 5) proposes. McGrath addresses the marginalized histories of women and children during Ireland's Decade of Centenaries by examining two Irish performances, both of which centralize women's experience of the historical past that is not fully accounted for in official national commemorative activity and state-led narratives. *Medicated Milk*, by dance artist Áine Stapleton, attempts to bring centre stage the voice and experience of Lucia Joyce, daughter of acclaimed Irish writer James Joyce. *Falling Out of Standing*, by choreographer David Bolger, speaks directly to Ireland's Decade of Centenaries and foregrounds violence against women. Like *Medicated Milk*, it speaks to the unique experiences of civilian individuals, rather than public figures and national leaders. This type of commemorative theatre and performance strays away from the established territory of militant, nationalist and hierarchical value systems, and instead foregrounds the significance of a plurality of experience and history, which may indeed impact audiences in the political present.

In Part 3, the authors examine how commemorative theatre and performance can remember and rejuvenate historical pasts as a central tool in both the propaganda and truth-seeking of the politicized present. In the politicized nationalist climate of the early decades of the twenty-first century, they ask: how does one address these histories and current tensions moving forward? Miki Flockemann's essay situates us on the African continent. Her analysis critiques the Marikana Massacre in 2012, exploring how it exposed South Africa as a nation in crisis. In her analysis, she considers how the reverberations of this crisis are manifest on a spectrum of events, including the site-specific production *Mari and Kana* (2015). This was staged three years after the massacre in close proximity to the Houses of Parliament. Flockemann notes that the intention of the playmaker was to initiate healing; however, questions are asked as to whether it may in fact enact a reiteration of trauma rather than a process of healing. The repetition central to the act of performance is also central to legacies of trauma, and the replaying of scenes in this context may not have the desired outcome. Thus, this play speaks to some of the problems of commemorative theatre, in particular the disjuncture between intention and consequence.

This haunting of the past underscores the crucial subject of Pieter Verstraete's close reading of the ongoing political crisis in Turkey, in particular the Kurdish Question, in which the stage's storytelling space can be a pivotal source of articulation of implied criticisms and what he calls, with Eviatar Zerubavel, mnemonic socialization. Verstraete considers how music theatre can play an essential role in commemorative practices, reasserting this significance through Aristotle's *Poetics*, which avow theatre's capacity for learning through repetition, as with the reliving of past events that theatre produces. Through the first Kurdish opera adaptation of *Tosca* (2019) by Amsterdam-based Theater RAST, he analyzes how a symbolic scenography and a new musical score interpellate diverse audiences while *unmaking* them as a temporary community, or as Jean-Luc Nancy (1991) has suggested, an 'inoperative community'. By discussing the influence of 'musicking' as a shared, social experience, Verstraete explains how commemorative music theatre practices can help to express underrepresented Kurdish identities while commemorating the Kurdish liberation movement in spite of decades of censorship of the Kurmanji language and its musical heritage in Turkey. However, he also points out the risk of falling into the trap of producing new myths by means of covert political symbols, musical motifs, traditional ways of singing from different parts of Anatolia and the re-enactment of the Kurdish dengbêj tradition.

This collection concludes with Bishnupriya Dutt's analysis of the politics of commemorative performance in India through a close reading of a political event reliant on commemorative performances to undertake varied strategic functions. Dutt's critical examination of how modern Indian nationhood is reasserted in problematic ways, particularly in relation to transnational politics, is acutely deconstructed in her essay. Her essay argues that the apparent celebrations worked to camouflage the present redundancy of cultural politics, focusing her analysis at the Third India–Africa Forum Summit in 2015. This resulted in a theatrical and cultural programme intended to rewrite the narrative of India as part of the state-led proceedings. Alongside the change in government leadership from the Nehruvian era to the rise of the right-wing Bhartiya Janta Party, Dutt reflects that what was once viewed as cosmopolitanism amongst the post-colonial nations was losing its appeal, and instead, a promotion of indigenous culture bordering on Xenophobic populism could be detected. Dutt argues for the significance of foregrounding Hobsbawm's classic work on invented traditions to analyse these events, particularly to discern when the past is manipulated in the interests of present-day political agendas.

Post-memory, crisis and change

No study of theatre, performance, and the past can be concluded without reference to Marianne Hirsch's seminal insights in *The Generation of Postmemory*. Hirsch's study opens with the question regarding how to keep certain memories of the Holocaust alive as the generation who survived it slowly begin to 'leave our midst' (2012: 1–2). Hirsch summarizes the significance of this moment in time, not only for Holocaust studies but also for remembrance culture more broadly:

> at stake is precisely the 'guardianship' of a traumatic personal and generational past with which some of us have a 'living connection', and that past's passing into history or myth. At stake is not only a personal/familial/generational sense of ownership and protectiveness, but an evolving ethical and theoretical discussion about the workings of trauma, memory, and intergenerational acts of transfer. (Ibid.)

Referring to Susan Sontag's 'pain of others', Hirsch asks how traumas of the past can be presented both respectfully and representationally in culture and the arts. Indeed, theatre's particular foregrounding of the embodied form and plural perspectives of the traumatic past make it specifically adept for examining such material. Hirsch maintains that 'the bodily, psychic, and affective impact of trauma and its aftermath, the ways in which one trauma can recall, or reactivate, the effects of another, exceed the bounds of traditional historical archives and methodologies' (2012: 2). Traditional historical archives and methodologies delineate fixed limitations on understanding and representing the past. Theatre and performance, however, as this collection shows, can navigate temporality and non-linear forms, utilize historical spaces and landmarks for performance and, most significantly, use mimetic and non-mimetic staging and performance strategies to create doubt as well as certainty.

For any study of commemorative activity, Hirsch's theorization of post-memory plays a vital role in considering the stakes at play for staging the past, particularly in terms of histories deemed nationally important, and/or, in crisis. She defines postmemory as 'the relationship that the "generation after" bears to the personal, collective and cultural trauma of those who came before – to experiences they "remember" only by means of the stories, images, and behaviours among which they grew up' (2012: 5). This is clearly problematic for the generation she identifies. How does one keep faith with the past of their ancestors, while acknowledging that it is past (in varying degrees), and yet constitutes a deeply personal relation? As she explains, 'these experiences were transmitted to them so deeply and affectively as to *seem* to constitute memories in their own right' (ibid.). Thus, there is the risk that one's own memories and life stories may become 'displaced, even evacuated, by our ancestors' (ibid.).

What Hirsch is considering is how the ties of commonality may inform the ways in which communities survive, in their own contexts, in the modernity of which we are a part. Change is inevitable, and communities will adapt to reflect this. Throughout the last century, history is frequently spoken of in terms of *histories* as a plurality of perspectives, informed by cultural politics, offering a multiplicity of voices: diverse, complimentary, oppositional at times but ultimately, interconnected. The political is acknowledged as personal, and the intersectional politics of identity are increasingly foregrounded in both academic and cultural discourse. Commemorative theatre and performance have played a major role in navigating and narrating these ties of kinship and relationality in global modern politics, as the very role and purpose of nationhood is represented and remembered, explored and questioned and indeed, celebrated and critiqued. The editors of this volume take these concerns seriously not only as researchers but also as citizens from countries, and connected to countries, in regular political crisis. Revolution dominates the past and is constantly on the precipice of the present. One must respect the past but not be imprisoned by it; the future can be a new space.

References

Anderson, B. (1991), *Imagined Communities: Reflections on the Origin and Spread of Nationalism*, second edition, London: Verso.
Balme, C. (2014), *The Theatrical Public Sphere*, Cambridge: Cambridge University Press.

Butler, J. (2005), *Giving an Account of Oneself*, New York: Fordham University Press.
Carlson, M. (2011), *The Haunted Stage: Theatre as Memory Machine*, fifth edition, Ann Arbor: University of Michigan Press.
Farrant, T. (2022), 'Lviv Square Displays 109 Empty Baby Strollers to Mark Each Child Killed by Putin's Forces', *euronews.culture*, 21 March. Available online: https://www.euronews.com/culture/2022/03/21/lviv-displays-109-empty-baby-strollers-to-mark-each-child-killed-by-putin-s-forces (accessed 29 March 2022).
Fischer-Lichte, E. (2009), 'Interweaving Cultures in Performance: Different States of Being In-Between', *New Theatre Quarterly*, 25 (4): 391–401.
Fischer-Lichte, E. (2010), 'Interweaving Cultures in Performance: Theatre in a Globalizing World', *Theatre Research International*, 35 (3): 293–4.
Haughton, M. (2018), *Staging Trauma: Bodies in Shadow*, Basingstoke: Palgrave.
Hirsch, M. (2012), *The Generation of Postmemory: Writing and Visual Culture after the Holocaust*, New York: Columbia University Press.
Hobsbawm, E. (1992), 'Introduction: Inventing Traditions', in E. Hobsbawm and T. Ranger (eds), *The Invention of Tradition*, 1–14, Cambridge: Cambridge University Press.
Holdsworth, N. (2010), *Theatre and Nation*, Basingstoke: Palgrave.
Low, P., O. Graham and P. Rhodes, (eds). (2012), *Cultures of Commemoration: War Memorials, Ancient and Modern*, New York: Oxford University Press.
Martin, C. (2012), *Theatre of the Real*, Basingstoke: Palgrave.
Miller, A. (1996), 'Why I Wrote "The Crucible" – An Artist's Answer to Politics', *The New Yorker*, 14 October 1996. Available online: https://www.newyorker.com/magazine/1996/10/21/why-i-wrote-the-crucible (accessed 23 March 2020).
Nancy, J.-L. (1991), *The Inoperative Community*, Minneapolis, MN: Minnesota University Press.
Oxford English Dictionary. Available online: http://www.oed.com.
Philips, T. (2020), 'Brazil's Jair Bolsonaro Says Coronavirus Crisis Is a Media Trick', *The Guardian*, 23 March. Available online: https://www.theguardian.com/world/2020/mar/23/brazils-jair-bolsonaro-says-coronavirus-crisis-is-a-media-trick (accessed 24 March 2020).
Schneider, R. (2011), *Performing Remains: Art and War in Times of Theatrical Reenactment*, London: Routledge.
Taylor, J. (2017), 'Of Hypocrisy: "Wherein the Action and Utterance of the Stage, Bar, and Pulpit Are Distinctly Consider'd" ', in M. Gluhovic and J. Menon (eds), *Performing Secularity*, 25–53, London: Palgrave.
Turner, V. (1982), *From Ritual to Theatre: The Human Seriousness of Play*, New York: PAJ.
Vorobjov, N. (2022), 'Putin Says Russia, Ukraine Share Historical "Unity". Is He Right?', *Aljazeera*, 25 February. Available online: https://www.aljazeera.com/news/2022/2/25/history-of-ties-between-ukraine-and-russia (accessed 29 March 2022).

Part 1

Commemorative Practices: Performing the Contradictions of Our Present

1

Unruly remembering: Great War anti-heroes and national narratives in Northern Ireland

Tom Maguire

Processes of historical revisionism within the commemoration of the Decade of Centenaries[1] have led to an extension of narratives of masculine heroic self-sacrifice on the part of those who served in the First World War beyond the idealized white, heterosexual male English private soldier, the 'Tommy'. Across the island of Ireland as part of the ongoing peace processes since the 1990s, this has included formal acknowledgement by both the British and Irish states and leading political actors of the role of soldiers who identified (or have been identified) as Irish nationalist (Graff-McRae 2010). Yet that extension has been less able to take account of the kinds of experience that resist or confound this heroic paradigm.

This essay argues that within a wider ecology of commemoration, theatre has had a particular role in the embodied staging of fictionalized experiences of British soldiers from the island of Ireland that are unruly, and as such, unable to be accommodated easily within heroic nationalist paradigms. Comparing two plays, Martin Lynch's *Holding Hands at Paschendale* (2006)[2] and the 2016 revival of Frank McGuinness's *Observe the Sons of Ulster Marching towards the Somme* (1985), this chapter traces how these make-believe accounts confound both dominant nationalist mythologies and historical concerns with 'the real' and authenticity (Hynes 1995).

These plays have been chosen because each exemplifies typical strategies in the representation of the experience of the war across a range of media and on the British and Irish stage:[3] the emphasis on the ordinary soldier within a realist setting, the drawing together of characters both highly individuated and in some way representative and the dramaturgy organized around the inevitability of their death. Nonetheless, each also resists the recuperation of that experience within national grand narratives, either British or Irish, and avoids the 'battlefield gothic' of first-hand accounts (Hynes 1995: 403). Within the context of a Northern Ireland culture learning how to remember its past, yet bridging its divisions in the unfolding peace since the Good Friday Agreement of 1998, the production of these plays resonates in ways that few others share in their invitation to remember differently. While outlining this iconoclastic potency, the essay argues that their efficacy in bridging the gap between the represented past and the experience of the present is situationally dependent, rather than a formal property. Their staging in Northern Ireland is crucial.

Commemoration

In *Theatres of Memory*, Ralph Samuel argued that memory 'is an active, shaping force; that it is dynamic – what it contrives systematically to forget is as important as what it remembers – and that it is dialectically related to historical thought, rather than being some kind of negative other to it' (1994: 10). Thus, commemoration must be considered not as some kind of neutral act bridging from the present moment to an absent past. Instead, public commemoration is an act of construction or projection. Its motor is the political imagination and its purpose the settling of present anxieties, not the restitution of past events. Accepting this, one can see then that the act of remembering together, through 'collective recollection and repetition' (Mitchell 2003: 443), has a significant potency to unite individuals in the present by constructing a shared sense of the past and through the repeated enactment of the shared remembering of that past. As the editors of this volume argue in the Introduction, collective commemoration has a significant role to play in legitimizing group identity; it is routinely mobilized to consolidate the political power of states and to validate nationalist claims over territory and peoples (Evershed 2018; Graff-McRae 2010; Mitchell 2003).

The identification of the ways in which remembering and forgetting are intertwined draws out the ways in which public commemoration involves acts of erasure (Connerton 2008; Ricoeur 2004; Samuel 1994): both a selectivity in what is remembered and how even this selection is reduced and homogenized. Mitchell points to the ways in which commemorative events and rituals are crucial in 'blurring the differences between individual interpretations of events, and creating single, highly idealized composite images' (2003: 443). The disciplining of multifarious experiences within processes of state-led commemoration suppresses differences and contradictions, smoothing out distinctions, forgetting some aspects and remembering others, substituting the latter as metonyms for the totality. The interplay between remembering and forgetting is such that the slogan of the British Remembrance Day, 'Lest We Forget', might more properly be rephrased, 'Lest We Remember'. Paul Connerton draws attention to this process in the ways in which the commemoration of the First World War 'gave rise to an orgy of monumentalization; memorials to commemorate the fallen went up all over Europe' (2008: 69); while ten million war-wounded were disremembered, their being forgotten a kind of humiliated silence. The nation state then has to conceal its own role in the political trauma of the war it has inflicted on its citizens, while at the same time rewriting such traumas into 'a linear narrative of national heroism' (Edkins 2003: xv).

As the Introduction to this volume also suggests, theatre and performance have the potential to play a significant role in such public commemoration, providing a place that is both public and replete with symbolism and ritual (Evershed 2018; Gleitman 2004; Westerside and Pinchbeck 2018). Hastings Donnan has proposed that 'effective memorials are synoptic in that they collapse the local and the national, the individual and collective, the past, the present and the future, not in the sense that they mean the same things to all people at all times but insofar as their interpretive flexibility and adaptability are responsive to context and change' (2016: xviii). Theatre in its function as a public space and with its capacity to both reproduce and represent the past in response to the concerns of the present has precisely this interpretive flexibility.

Moreover, as a live and embodied art form, performance can provide the capacity identified by Schneider 'to resituate the site of any knowing of history as body-to-body transmission' (2011: 104).

An ecology of commemoration

These general features of the ways in which states mobilize commemoration of traumatic events in the service of the construction of national identities (and other discursive power structures) are evident in the specific ways in which the First World War has been commemorated in the service of the UK. Although there is not enough space here to trace the history of such commemoration, it suffices to say that all commemorative acts exist within a complex ecology that stretches over time and synchronically across different forms and media, and varies according to the asymmetrical relationships between discursive formations across each of these axes (Evershed 2018). As Guy Beiner has argued, citing Maurice Halbwachs, 'remembrance is not an autonomous activity of an individual, but is dependent on the social contexts in which it takes place' (2016 14). In the following section, I draw out some of the key features of this ecology of commemoration to situate the two productions under discussion.

The first important aspect to note is that the commemoration of the First World War has been an arena contested between and within the competing nationalisms of British unionism and Irish republicanism, which has continued to play out to this day. This has been particularly the case in Northern Ireland, the partitioned unionist state created in the aftermath of the war (Evershed 2018; Graff-McRae 2010; Grayson and McGarry 2016). The newly formed Northern Irish state would follow the dominant British discourse that was largely uninterrupted over the remainder of the twentieth century. It was strengthened and specifically inflected by recourse to the sacrifice of the 36th (Ulster) Division at the Battle of the Somme within unionist discourses and commemorative activities, such that the Somme sits as part of the foundational mythology of Ulster loyalism (Bowman 1996; Graff-McRae 2010; Grayson 2010; Mulhall 2016).

The division, comprising three regiments, the Royal Inniskilling Fusiliers, the Royal Irish Fusiliers and the Royal Irish Rifles, had been formed in September 1914 and was sent to France the following year. Many of its volunteer units were based on the pre-war Ulster Volunteer Force (UVF), with former UVF officers commissioned directly within the division. By mid-March 1916, it had been deployed on the front line at the Somme. Following a week-long bombardment of German defences, on 1 July 1916, twelve battalions of the Ulster Division took part in a frontal attack on heavily fortified enemy lines (Bowman 1996). On that first day, of the almost 20,000 British soldiers killed, 2,000 came from the Ulster Division. Their sacrifice would become a foundational and totalizing identity narrative for the nascent Northern Irish state, a demonstration of the loyalty of Ulster Protestants to Britain, only months after the ill-fated insurrection of Irish republicans. The promotion of that narrative quickly elided the role of the four battalions of Tyneside Irish (the 103rd brigade of the 34th Division) and seven regular Irish battalions (Bowman 1996) and the joint deployment with the

16th (Irish) Division along the Messines Ridge later that year. A significant number of the Ulstermen who fought side by side in the British army in these different divisions included Catholic nationalists from West Belfast who came from streets within a short distance of the loyalist Shankill (Grayson 2010).

Irish republicanism colluded in this wilful forgetting (Beiner 2016: 22–3) of the role of members of the Irish Volunteers from across the island in the First World War and the longer history of Irishmen within the British Army (Bowen 2005; Denman 1991). Donal Fallon (2018) has identified the marking of Remembrance Day within the newly founded Free State, as well as the selling of poppies and the opening of the War Memorial Garden at Islandbridge in 1939, funded in part by the Fianna Fáil government of the day. However, he draws attention also to the ways in which by the 1930s commemoration of the participation of Irishmen in the British Army had become hotly (and sometimes violently) contested. Ronan McGreevy (2018) similarly notes that while the population of the new state had a significant minority of former servicemen and their families (some drawing a disability pension from the British state until the 1960s), many were treated with disdain and contempt. Seeking to identify its foundational identity in the Easter Rising and the War of Independence, the Free State and later the Republic were complicit in ceding the official commemoration of the First World War to the northern state and Ulster loyalism for much of the succeeding century.

As part of the war effort during the First World War, a homogenized heroic ideal of the ordinary soldier had already been deployed in the figure of the British Tommy, an ideal to which soldiers from Ireland north and south were to be trained to fit (Denman 1991: 354). This nickname was derived in the previous century from the advice of a War Office publication that showed how *The Soldier's Pocket Book* would be filled out, using an imagined soldier, Thomas Atkins. It was in wide circulation prior to the outbreak of the war (Holmes 2011), such that Rudyard Kipling was able to rely on its ubiquity in his eponymous poem of 1890. The fictional profile of Tommy subjugated regional and national differences to the service of empire within a discourse of English identity. During and after the First World War, as public commemoration and memorialization gathered pace, it was the Tommy who was most frequently invoked as the symbol of heroic masculinity in the service of an imagined British nation (Anderson 1983; Moriarty 1995; Winter 1998).

The representation of the serving soldiers had to be undertaken in such a way to preserve confidence in the war effort at home and the morale of those fighting, who, like McGuinness's character Millen, had to retain confidence in the officers leading the campaign. Though this followed earlier traditions, it was given added impetus as dissent and outright resistance and resentment began to emerge amongst the troops: memorialization was deployed to rally repeatedly the nation's resources in support of the war. As Winter writes, the erection of such memorials was 'an act of citizenship. To remember was to affirm community, to assert its moral character, and to exclude from it those values, groups, or individuals that placed it under threat' (1998: 80). Thus, even while representations of human figures appeared to avoid abstraction, the anonymized and idealized hero depicted had also to be rendered aesthetically, as racially pure, shorn of the markers of the war on his body, muscular, healthy and well-fed, fully equipped and clean (Moriarty 1995). Within Ulster loyalism, the Tommy was localized within the narrative of the Ulster Division as a 'Pals Regiment' of volunteers (Graff-McRae 2010; Grayson 2010; Grayson and McGarry 2016; Orr 2014). The figure of 'an Ulsterman in British army uniform, clad in khaki and clutching his Lee-Enfield rifle as he awaits orders to "go over the top" and face the German machine guns' recurs within loyalist iconography (Orr 2014). The Tommy would sit alongside William of Orange as the emblem of Ulster Protestant or Orange identity.[4]

For the 2016 centenary of the Somme, Jeremy Deller in collaboration with Rufus Norris, Director of the National Theatre, was commissioned to produce a live performance event as an act of national commemoration (Higgins 2016). *We're Here Because We're Here* was produced by Birmingham Repertory Theatre and the National Theatre, in collaboration with twenty-six organizations across the UK, with the Lyric in Belfast and The Playhouse in Derry coordinating activities in Northern Ireland. On 1 July, around one thousand, four hundred volunteers, dressed in First-World-War uniform, appeared unexpectedly in locations across the UK. Each participant represented an individual soldier who had been killed on that day one hundred years before. The volunteers remained silent or sang wartime songs, the only clue to their role cards handed out to members of the public, featuring information about the soldier they represented. While the event ran from 7.00 am until 7.00 pm, it was only after it had ended that the explanation of what had taken place was provided.

The performance appeared to offer the potential to retrieve the humanity of the ordinary soldier, and social media responses recorded spectators who were deeply moved by the encounter with this living memorial. It demonstrated Schneider's proposition that 'the past can simultaneously be past – genuinely pastness – and on the move, co-present, not "left behind"' (2011: 15), invoking an experience of the uncanniness of the way in which re-enactment disrupts linear time. It was startling in its animation of those fossilized images from the war memorials into living embodied human beings. Rufus Norris suggested that 'it is a political work – with a small p. That day is generally remembered as being the greatest disaster in British military history. It's not heroic. There was heroism all around, but it was a disaster, one that was neither necessary nor positive in its outcome' (cited in Higgins 2016).

Yet the riposte to sentimentality that he suggests the event makes was not apparent in the event or its reception. The event repeated the tropes of the figures from the war memorials, smartly dressed in their recreated uniforms, hale and healthy, unmarked by conflict, both embodied and ghostly abstracts. It absented the horrors of war and their impact on individuals, families and communities, disciplining the past within the conventions of the event. In this, it too was a form of forgetting: focusing on the silenced bodies that would go out to the war, the ideal that the war would destroy, rather than on the abject bodies of the dead and the wounded that would return, manifesting the destruction. The appearance of the soldiers simultaneously across the UK created a sense of a nation unified in its remembering, a national pageant, staged in person and in the coverage within newspapers and via online media tagged as #Wearehere. Its impact was what Barthes describes as the effect of a pageant: 'to abolish all motives and consequences: what matters is not what the audience thinks but what it sees'

(1972: 15). A mythological function is enacted in which historical details are taken to rise beyond their historical contexts in the service of functions of communal narrative. The persistence of such mythologization of the heroic and a-historical Tommy is the critical context for the reception of each of the productions under discussion here. While many of the interventions in the ecology of commemoration of the Decade of Centenaries did much to reinstate the humanity of those that served, few troubled the dominant discourses that what was to be remembered was what was lost, stripped of the political, economic or social factors that had caused such losses; and denuded of portrayals of the impact of those who came back, wounded and disturbed.[5] Thus, they emphasized and beckoned a response to the individual and human, without attending to the violence of the system or its dominant modes of representation (Žižek 2008).

Observe the Sons of Ulster Marching towards the Somme

Observe the Sons of Ulster of Ulster Marching towards the Somme was first staged in 1985, under the direction of Patrick Mason on the Peacock stage of the Abbey Theatre.[6] It opened in the following year at London's Hampstead Theatre under the direction of Michael Attenborough. The 1985 production was staged in the context of the negotiations that would lead to a formalized role for the involvement of the Republic in the affairs of Northern Ireland through The Anglo-Irish Agreement. By the time of its first major revival at the Abbey in 1994, the first Provisional IRA[7] ceasefire had been declared, seven years after the Remembrance Day bombing in Enniskillen in November 1987, 'an atrocity that deliberately attacked the significance of The First World War remembrance for the Ulster Protestant tradition' (Mulhall 2016).

The 2016 production was directed by Jeremy Herrin in a touring co-production between the Abbey Theatre, Dublin, Glasgow's Citizens Theatre, Headlong and Liverpool Everyman & Playhouse. The Northern Ireland tour was co-presented by the Lyric Theatre. Its revival was an intentional marking of the centenary year of the battle, its tour clearly an attempt at engaging it as a national British narrative. While its original 1985 production made for a unique contribution to the ways in which the First World War might be remembered, by 2016 the play had long since entered the canons of Irish drama. Its restaging for the centenary took place in the context of the well-established contours of the Decade of Centenaries (Evershed 2018) in which processes for the restitution of forgotten groups to the historical record of the First World War locally, nationally and internationally had been underway for some time. In Northern Ireland a joint conference held in 2011 between the Heritage Lottery Fund and the Community Relations Council had initiated discussions as to what kinds of commemoration might properly receive public funding and, more importantly, how could the past of one hundred years previously be remembered in a principled way (Mullan 2019). The 2016 production can be seen as engaging the theatre in the processes of collective remembrance as a form of reconciliation that had both preceded and become a hallmark of the Decade of Centenaries (Graff-McCrae 2010: 101–21). Even this short production history foregrounds the ways in which the situation of remembering that the performance of a play enacts is conditioned both by the play's own history as well as the previous productions that haunt it. As Helen Lojek comments, 'if *Sons of Ulster* began in part as a response to iconography, the play itself has assumed iconographic importance as an indication of increased understanding by Irish Catholics that Irish Protestantism is also part of the island's culture and heritage' (2004: 77).

McGuinness's script explores the ways in which the mythology of the Somme had come to dominate Unionist identity, serving too as a means through which the playwright might 'introject his unionist Other' (Kiberd 2005: 279). It is constituted through the remembering of Kenneth Pyper, asking the spectator to witness how he remembers and with what impact. Pyper is the only survivor from a group of eight young Ulstermen who fought together at the Somme. These are the ordinary soldiers – the Tommies – of the Ulster Division and no officers appear in the play, referenced only sporadically as an offstage presence, and Pyper's play acting the part. All have enlisted voluntarily. The group is drawn from the six counties that will become Northern Ireland: Pyper from Armagh's landed class; Anderson and McIlwain from East Belfast (Down); Craig from Enniskillen (Fermanagh); Millen and Moore from near Coleraine (Antrim); the Derry man, Crawford, and Roulston born in Sion Mills in Tyrone. While this may seem schematic, the individuality and humanity of the characters is predicated on their ordinariness, their lack of importance beyond themselves (Lojek 1988: 52).

The play is divided into four parts: Remembrance, Initiation, Pairing and Bonding that cover the men's first encounter in a barracks in France; a period of home leave and the preparations for the attack at the Somme, framed by two monologues by the elder Pyper in the present day. The elder Pyper's memory is far from reliable and the recollection of experience reveals how its rendering in language (Heininge 2002) has a potency in the present that simultaneously confirms and threatens his personal and group identity. He begins by refusing to remember, goaded into it by ghosts or gods, it is not clear which. His recall is contradictory, stilted and episodic in both his monologues and in the action that his remembering begets. He is trapped within a narrative, where the individuals he had come to know will merge into an abstracted collective myth of blood sacrifice. His remembering is determined by his present moment in an Ulster under threat – 'a cold house' – to serve as a bulwark against contemporary Fenianism, embracing death and the dead, yet firmly grasping onto life.

It is through the contradictions the play stages that it refutes the homogenized abstraction of the heroic Tommy. The elder Pyper proposes in his opening monologue that his comrades were heroes because they died without complaint for what they believed in: the play re-enacts the experiences that provide a counter-narrative to the fiction that he has concocted by way of consolation. His memories are unruly, refusing and disrupting the violence of their representation within the narratives of loyalism to which he has become so committed. McGuinness's inquiry into the Somme myth reveals the very different characters who will be unified within the collective imaginary. In many instances, however, the very things that might serve to bind them are the source of division and conflict between them. Under the pressure of life at the front, the certainties with which they enter in 'Initiation' fall away and their invocation in 'Bonding' is rendered useless by what they anticipate and what the spectator knows of the fate that will befall them.

Principal amongst these is their confidence in their own masculinity, a feature more generally of Ulster loyalist culture and its commemorative forms (Evershed 2018). Pyper's remembering is embodied and what is remembered is that very physicality and sensuality that is so evidently absent in his crumbling body now. The men are not seen performing heroic acts, the spectator sees them at play together: mock fighting and bickering, indulging in horse-play, having and playing sport, performing. Their presence is muscular and physical.[8] Craig has worked at his father's blacksmith's forge since he was a child; Millen is a baker; Moore a dyer in a textile factory; Anderson and McIlwain shipyard workers. Crawford is an aspirant footballer. Even Pyper has a deftness and speed that will make him a good, if dirty, fighter. Only Roulston seems unwilling to acknowledge his own physicality until Crawford goads him into attacking him in the church while they are on home leave. Many of the details of the performance focus on the ways in which the men's relationships are embodied in their physical relationships with each other, the enforced intimacy of living in such close proximity. It is this experience of intimacy that brings them together to see in each other the projection of an abstract Ulster. While they are initially wary in having to undress in front of each other and of making their beds side by side and sleeping together, by the final scene Roulston is able to put his hand down Crawford's shirt to scratch at the lice without comment from the others.

Much of their male identity is defined in a simplistic heteronormative binary opposition to the female. They refer to each other as 'boys', 'lad', 'man' and 'men'. Moore and Millen first enter mid-dispute about Moore's sexual experiences with an unnamed woman. The men put each other down by identifying womanly characteristics in each other or addressing each other as female. Anderson and McIlwain assert their superiority over the others when they arrive by calling the others 'ladies'. Millen's prowess as a baker can be undercut by suggesting he might be put in a skirt, yet he complains that he didn't join the army to do 'woman's work'. It is Pyper who for much of the play disrupts this binary and who presses on all the boundaries that hold their collective identity together. Craig's question about whether he is a fit *man* for army life resonates throughout the play. Pyper exploits the group's bigotry in enthralling them with his tale of marrying a Papish whore who turns out to be a cross-dressing man whom he ends up killing.[9] He watches Craig intently as he undresses at their first meeting and invites Millen and Moore to admire his remarkably fine skin. Such camp flirtation disturbs the other men's understanding of their own sexual identity. Later an incident is recalled when Craig saves Pyper's life in battle. Moore remarks not only on Craig's courage but also how he recognized how Craig resuscitated Pyper as a kiss. McIlwain can commend Pyper as a good fighter, but Anderson is troubled by the look on Pyper and Craig's faces. None of the others is witness to the consummation of the relationship with Craig when he and Pyper are on leave in 'Pairing'. Even here, Pyper refuses to have his – or anyone else's – sexual identity fixed.

Craig   They don't look like men or women.
Pyper   Depends on the man or woman.
Craig   They could be either.
Pyper   They could be both. (McGuinness 1996: 149)

The second bond the men appear to share is their religion. While they are all at least nominally Protestant, their attitudes to religion vary enormously. Roulston, a former lay preacher, has abandoned that mission by the point he joins the group, though he still has recourse to scripture. The most overtly committed to his religion, he appears to seek in it a transcendence of his brute human nature. Pyper hints that this is in reaction to the unhealthy interest in younger boys at school. On first meeting, Moore thumbs through Roulston's bible looking for dirty pictures; and while prayer and hymn-singing recur, there is no strong sense of the consolation of faith shared by the men. The prayers they make cannot mitigate the reality of their situation and the subjunctive 'If' leaves their petitions conditional on the vindication of a Protestant god who never delivers (Heininge 2002: 38). Millen declares in 'Bonding', 'He deserted us when he led us here' (McGuinness 1996: 177). For the group, the appearance of a shared religious affiliation seems to be at best a reflex response to what they are not, Catholic and Irish; at worst a proud and naked sectarianism. It is this that causes Crawford to conceal that his mother was Catholic and that he might himself have been baptized in that faith. Even here, the group separates. While Millen and Moore are staunch Orangemen, they cannot be persuaded to march with Anderson and McIlwain to The Field to commemorate the Twelfth of July.

Finally, even the sense of place that will give rise to the construct of Ulster is shown to be unstable. There is rivalry between, for example, Anderson and McIlwain from Belfast and the others from rural areas and Crawford from Derry when they first come into the barracks. Anyone attuned to the varieties of Ulster speech will quickly pick up the different cadences of their local accents that mark out their spatial segregation. When the pairings return home on leave, McGuinness locates the scenes in sites that similarly accentuate that for each of them the imagined 'Ulster' has a very different local habitation and name. This sense of their geographical separateness is reinforced in the final moments before they go over the top. Recalling the Bann, the Foyle, the Erne and the Lagan becomes the occasion for a dispute about their relative merits. Pyper attempts through a rousing speech to superimpose the rivers of each of these home landscapes onto the muddied fields around the upper reaches of the Somme river. Craig reprimands him, however. The others have already committed to their self-sacrifice in service of an imagined homeland, he has just been slow to catch up with them: 'You're trying too hard, Pyper. It's too late to tell us what we're fighting for. We know where we are. We know what we've to do. And we know what we're doing it for. We knew before we enlisted. We joined up willingly for that reason' (McGuinness 1996: 188).

These are three of the axes along which the collective identity of the group might be mobilized, and yet each also differentiates the individuals from each other. As they prepare to advance on German lines, their putting on of Orange sashes is the fulfilment of the promise that such difference can be subsumed into a single Ulster identity of national we-feeling. Yet McGuinness, himself from Donegal – one of the traditional nine counties of Ulster that would be excluded from the Northern Ireland, but borders it – would also have been keenly aware that these men in 1916 could not even envisage such a state. He would know that the Boundary Commission would not eventually fix the borders of the partitioned state until 1925. The attempt by

Pyper to talk them into a cohesive unit by recourse to the tropes of a single identity palls when confronted with the shared knowledge that they will face death; it rings even more hollow in the Elder Pyper's final commitment to the abstraction that is Ulster.

By contrasting the distinctions between the enacted and embodied relationships between the men with their recuperation within the rhetorical formation of Ulster loyalism, McGuinness invites his audience to undertake a double manoeuvre. On the one hand, by allowing the differences between them to act as a strength in their characterization, he encourages the spectator to appreciate their individual humanity in the round. The loss of each, then, can be felt as a metonym for all of the losses suffered at the Somme and the war more generally. On the other hand, this very emphasis on their individual ordinariness creates a resistance to their idealization within a heroic and totalizing mythology upon which the foundational origins of the Northern Irish state and territorial claims of Ulster loyalism might be based. In the second production that I explore, one can see a similar intent to disrupt the certainties of the war memorial by focusing on a different aspect of the experiences of the ordinary Tommy.

Holding Hands at Paschendale

Martin Lynch's *Holding Hands at Paschendale* was produced by Lynch's Green Shoot production company, and opened at the Lyric Theatre on 13 October 2006 as part of the Belfast Festival, before touring across Northern Ireland. It was revived by Cerberus Theatre at the White Bear Theatre, London, in March 2011. Its original staging predated the Decade of Centenaries which began in 2012, and opened up issues of commemoration ahead of the discussions of how the decade would be marked. This was particularly focused through collaboration with and the support of organizations representing the families of those who were shot for desertion, including the Shot at Dawn campaign, which worked to have those who were shot for cowardice to be pardoned (Maguire 2010b). The play is based on the real-life experiences of Martin Lynch's grandfather during the third battle of Passchendaele in 1917. Lynch's grandfather had been serving as a gunner in the Royal Field Artillery.[10] On the tenth day of a non-stop bombardment of the German lines, the infantry moved in beside the guns and a young soldier from London broke down and refused to go over the top. The soldier was arrested and ended up being handcuffed to Lynch's grandfather for four days and four nights, before he was shot by a firing squad for refusing to fight in the face of the enemy (Coyle 2006).

The play is not, however, a historically accurate retelling of this family lore: it is an entirely fictional account of two ordinary Tommies; one from London, Maurice Boris (Mo) Coutts, the other from Greencastle, County Antrim, Willie Harvey. In the original production Mo was played by Freddie White, and Willie by Ciaran McMenamin, under the direction of Hannah Eidinow. Mo is an ex-vaudeville entertainer who became a Kitchener volunteer. Having lost his brother to the war a few weeks prior to this, he has been arrested for throwing away his rifle prior to an attack on the German lines. Willie, serving with the Royal Artillery and standing close by Mo at the time, has been designated as his arresting officer, having to guard him until his regiment can move him back down the reserve lines to face court martial.

The two are confined for four days in a farm outbuilding since Mo's regiment is engaged in the attack. Responsible for Mo, Willie too is trapped by his adherence to army rules since he actually has the key to open the handcuffs that lock them together. Their enforced physical proximity is the source of both antagonism and, eventually, mutual understanding. The play traces the impact on both men of their experiences that had led them to this point. As in *Observe the Sons of Ulster Marching towards the Somme*, the army hierarchy is a constant if distant offstage presence, frequently invoked in the conversations between the two men. Initially, each man demonstrates a trust in military process: Willie's is a resigned conformity to the army and its rules; Mo's is a hope in his immediate superior Major Vaughan, who he expects to speak up for him. Here, the unfolding intersubjective relationship of Mo and Willie is juxtaposed with the systemic violence (Žižek 2008) that the military code demands as Mo's punishment.[11]

In the opening scene, Mo declares that he is allowed to talk, to which Willie responds, 'Nobody's listening.'[12] This is the challenge that the production stages to its audience: to listen to experiences that cannot be accommodated neatly within the discourses of heroic sacrifice promoted by different forms of nationalism, both British and Irish. It provides a corrective to each, demonstrating their inadequacy in the face of human experience and the cruelty of their outworking on individuals like Mo. Such unruly anti-heroism is a recurrent feature of Lynch's work. In the second act, Mo and Willie drunkenly discuss the merits of soldiers from each of the home nations, slagging[13] each in turn according to well-worn stereotypes, yet demonstrating demarcations that undercut any sense of a single British identity. Mo is well aware of his own mongrel ancestry, including his Russian grandfather. Willie too has something of the mongrel about him: his father is Catholic, his mother Protestant, although he identifies himself as Catholic. In childhood he was just as likely to be attacked for being a 'Prod' as a 'Fenian' (respectively, colloquialism for 'Protestant' and 'Catholic', often negatively intended in the Irish and Northern Irish contexts). Each man's sense of self is also shaped by their experience of other cultures: Mo refers to the diversity of immigrants that inhabited the East End in which he had been brought up and his repertoire of songs references American popular culture, including Al Jolson and Charlie Chaplin. Both men have planned to get to America to start a new life there. Willie has encountered other places through his work as a gardener following his own migration, working in England, Scotland and Wales. They do not conform neatly to any national stereotype.

The play is organized under two acts within the single setting of a farm shed in Flanders, rendered naturalistically in the original design by Mike Lees and in the modes of characterization of Mo and Willie. It begins in the early morning of the first day and proceeds through a series of episodes, until 4.05 pm of the fourth day. The opening scenes delineate the men's mutual antipathy, with Willie, the dominant figure, who does nothing to hide his resentment at being forced to guard a whining deserter. As a two-hander, the dialogue carries much of the weight of the exposition and in the revelation of the back stories of each character, each is allowed to construct his own identity through the stories they tell about themselves. Just as in *Observe the Sons of Ulster Marching towards the Somme*, these identities collapse under the pressures exerted by each man on the other, pressures are further compressed by their spatial confinement and the passage of time that intensifies the anticipation of the fate awaiting Mo stressed by Willy in the opening scene.

This is not to say that the action is carried only by dialogue. The physicality of their experience is expressed in references to their bodily needs for food and drink; defecating; and at one point Mo discloses that he has an erection. In the first two days, there is a constant threat of physical violence between them that erupts into sporadic attacks on each other. By the evening of the third day, the two men have started drinking the supplies of rum stored in the outbuilding, and it is through this that they discover their shared humanity. Their physical interaction shifts from aggression and attack, replaced by playful performance, singing and dancing together.

Earlier in Act Two, Mo had confessed that he joined up to impress his girlfriend, Veronica Cordell, not for love of country. In this scene, Willie reveals that his reason for joining up was not the nagging of his Protestant mother but to escape the violence of his abusive Catholic nationalist father. They have this in common: each abused by their father, each committed to a memory of a loving mother who begged them not to join up. They complete the process of stripping away the myths and lies, both public and personal, that they have observed to justify their role in the war:

> **Willie** What a life? Here we are two latches from the back streets, one waiting to have his heart shot out by the English and the other waiting to have his head blown off by the Germans – and we're both pissed. (Lynch *Act Two*, Draft 3: 22)

The realization of each man of their shared backgrounds and values leads Willie to unlock the handcuffs and encourage Mo to escape. However, Mo recognizes the futility of this and, guilty over his part in the death of his brother, accepts his fate. Now it is Willie who rails against the officer class. He divulges how lots of soldiers find ways to hide in the midst of the battle and, in the most overt attack on the values of heroism, rejects the war effort:

> **Willie** If only we had all done what you did. If everybody had refused to fight at the very start? Now, we're all human wrecks, nerve ends forever blunted, the people we used to be left back at the spot we killed our first German. (Lynch *Act Two*, Draft 3: 28)

The expression of the interpersonal reconciliation of the two men is expressed in their joining of hands, instigated by Willie who had previously refused to hold Mo's hand in the first act. It is a poignant moment:

> *Willie snatches Mo's hand. He pulls Mo towards him and clasps Mo's tightened fist up to his chest, below his neck. Willie clasps both his hands around Mo's fist. He passionately kisses the back of Mo's hand. He does it again and again and again. Mo stares emotionlessly at Willie's face.* (Lynch *Act Two*, Draft 3: 32)

A final coda is provided by a monologue from the ghost of Willie that explains that he survived the war and had tried and failed to visit Mo's family. He had eventually settled back in Greencastle, got married and started a small greengrocer's business, raising his family. He died in a house fire in 1961.

Concluding remarks

Each of these two plays confounds the simplistic rendering of their characters as uncomplicated and heroic Tommies. The emphasis in each on the physicality of the men contrasts with the rhetorical formations that seek to recuperate them within heroic narratives. Their physical presence proffers a site through which the spectator experiences a body-to-body memorialization, not the cold granite or bronze of a statue. Each play, then, achieves the restoration of the humanity of the serving soldier delivered by *We're Here Because We're Here*. The dialogue in each, however, goes beyond this to vocalize powerfully a critique from within of the experiences that the soldiers are forced to endure and the systemic violence of the nationalisms that had caused them. In their talking together, under the pressure of the experience of the war and their close proximity to each other, the stories that had lured them to join up –both public mythologies and personal creeds – disintegrate. They feel not bravery but fear expressed in ways that resists the heroification of the war memorial.

The potential for the plays to act as a corrective to dominant mythologies, however, was limited by the situation of their performance. By 2016, *Observe the Sons of Ulster Marching towards the Somme* had become such a key element in the theatrical canon of the First World War that the very ways in which its original production had opened up discussion of the war had been accommodated into the mainstream. While *Holding Hands at Paschendale* was able to collaborate with the Shot at Dawn campaign, the decision to pardon all of the 306 men who were shot for cowardice had already been taken in August 2006. I have suggested elsewhere that the play offered some opportunity for a revision to patterns of remembrance that allowed for processes of reconciliation to take place (Maguire 2010b). Yet, for both plays, in the face of the mobilization of nationalist discourses directed by the British state, their resistance to their dominance could only be limited at best. The commissioning of art works such as *We're Here Because We're Here* by 14–18 NOW was only part of the UK's arts programme for the First World War centenary. This organization commissioned new artworks from 420 contemporary artists, musicians, film-makers, designers and performers, inspired by the period 1914–18. The sheer scale of these activities and audiences reached far outstripped what either of these productions might manage: *We're Here Because We're Here* was witnessed live in fifty-two locations across the UK, attracting an audience of two million live and a further twenty-eight million through print, broadcast and social media (Burns 2019: 6). Unruly performances such as those presented here can be so easily swamped by the disciplined narratives of the state, especially when it uses art to 'complement ceremonies of the church, state and military' (Burns 2019: 6).

Notes

1. The Decade of Centenaries programmes in Ireland and Northern Ireland focused on the commemoration of significant centenaries occurring over the period 2012–22 (Department of Culture, Heritage and the Gaeltacht [online]; PRONI [online]). Primarily, these were concerned with the build-up to the First World War and the Irish War of Independence that would eventually lead to the partition of the island of Ireland into two separate jurisdictions: the independent Free State and Northern Ireland, which remained part of the UK though with its own devolved government.
2. The play opened as part of the Belfast Festival at Queen's, before touring, directed by Hannah Eidinow, with Ciaran McMenamim as Willie and Freddy White as Mo.
3. Heinz Kosok (1996) provides an appendix of plays written by authors from Ireland about the First World War that begins in 1916 and stretches across the twentieth century.
4. The Loyal Orange Institution, commonly known as the Orange Order, is a Protestant fraternal order, founded in County Armagh in 1795 and dedicated to the defence of the Protestant Ascendancy following the victory of William of Orange over the Catholic King James II in the early 1690s. Wearing their Orange sashes, its members celebrate that victory through marches to commemorate key victories in the Williamite War, with the Twelfth of July the high point of the marching season commemorating the defeat of the Jacobite forces at the Battle of the Boyne in 1690.
5. See Culture Northern Ireland's *Decade of Centenaries* webpages for examples of such interventions.
6. The premiere was directed by Patrick Mason, with Ian McElhinney as Nat McIlwaine, Michael James Ford as Martin Crawford, Tom Hickey as Christopher Roulston, Mark Lambert as William Moore, Niall O'Brien as John Millen, Lorcan Cranitch as David Craig, Bosco Hogan as the young Kenneth Pyper, Oliver Maguire as George Anderson and Geoff Golden as the old Kenneth Pyper. Notably it had been turned down by Field Day (Maguire 2006).
7. The Provisional IRA had been engaged in an armed campaign to secure the reunification of Ireland since its formation in 1969, following a split within the Irish republican movement. Its political wing, Sinn Féin, would eventually enter into coalition government in the devolved assembly for Northern Ireland after the Belfast Agreement in 1998.
8. This is notwithstanding the emphasis they each place on the performative power of talking (Heininge 2002).
9. McGuinness here echoes both J. M. Synge's Christy Mahon in *The Playboy of the Western World* (1907) (who similarly garners respect by claiming to be a murderer) and widespread sectarian mythology.
10. Liam Harte notes this as the first of a series of plays manifesting Lynch's 'increasing preoccupation with drawing on his own and others' memories of conflict and war' (2018: 126).
11. Žižek identifies forms of 'subjective' violence (such as violent criminal activity or terrorist attacks) where attention is drawn to the actions of recognizable human actors. By contrast, systemic violence is characterized as a form of 'objective' violence, perpetrated through economic structures, political systems and institutional practices. Its structural nature is articulated in rules and procedures that appear natural or

inevitable, even as they directly and negatively impact on individuals and sub-groups. Conformity with these structures is often enforced by the threat or actualization of violence.
12. References here are to the unpublished third draft of the script provided to the author by Martin Lynch.
13. The function of slagging, or name-calling, is discussed further in Maguire (2010a).

References

Anderson, B. (1983), *Imagined Communities: Reflections on the Origin and Spread of Nationalism*, London: Verso.

Barthes, R. (1972), *Mythologies*, London: Paladin.

Beiner, G. (2016), 'Making Sense of Memory: Coming to Terms with Conceptualisations of Historical Remembrance', in R. Grayson and F. McGarry (eds), *Remembering 1916: The Easter Rising, the Somme and the Politics of Memory in Ireland*, 13–23, Cambridge: Cambridge University Press.

Bowen, J. (2005), *Heroic Option: The Irish in the British Army*, Barnsley: Pen and Sword Books.

Bowman, T. (1996), 'The Irish at the Somme', *History Ireland* 4(4). Available online: https://www.historyireland.com/20th-century-contemporary-history/the-irish-at-the-somme/ (accessed 20 June 2019).

Burns, J. (2019), *14–18 NOW Overall Summary of Evaluation*, London: Morris Hargreaves McIntyre. Available online: https://issuu.com/1418now/docs/03560_1418now_jo_burns_report_v4_wr (accessed 29 May 2019).

Connerton, P. (2008), 'Seven Types of Gorgetting', *Memory Studies* 1(1): 59–71.

Coyle, J. (2006), 'In History's Shackles', *Irish Times*, 9 October. Available online: https://www.irishtimes.com/culture/in-history-s-shackles-1.1013137 (accessed 29 May 2019).

Culture Northern Ireland [n.d.], *Decade of Centenaries*, Derry/Londonderry: Nerve Centre. Available online: https://www.culturenorthernireland.org/tags/decade-centenaries (accessed 17 September 2019).

Denman, T. (1991), 'The Catholic Irish Soldier in the First World War: The "Racial Environment"', *Irish Historical Studies* 27(108): 352–65.

Department of Culture, Heritage and the Gaeltacht [n.d.], *The Decade of Centenaries*. Available online: https://www.decadeofcentenaries.com (accessed 17 September 2019).

Donnan, H. (2016), 'Foreword', in R. Viggiani (ed.), *Talking Stones: The Politics of Memorialization in Post-Conflict Northern Ireland*, xi–xv, Oxford: Berghan Books.

Edkins, J. (2003), *Trauma and the Memory of Politics*, Cambridge: Cambridge University Press.

Evershed, J. (2018), *Ghosts of the Somme: Commemoration and Culture War in Northern Ireland*, Notre Dame: University of Notre Dame Press.

Fallon, D. (2018), 'Forgotten by Whom? The Memory of The First World War in Ireland', *The Journal.ie*, 10 November. Available online: https://www.thejournal.ie/readme/forgotten-by-whom-the-memory-of-world-war-i-in-ireland-4333128-Nov2018/ (accessed 18 June 2019).

Gleitman, C. (2004), 'Reconstructing History in the Irish History Play', in S. Richards (ed.), *The Cambridge Companion to Twentieth-Century Irish Drama*, 218–30, Cambridge: Cambridge University Press.

Graff-McRae, R. (2010), *Remembering and Forgetting 1916: Commemoration and Conflict in Post-Peace Process Ireland*, Newbridge: Irish Academic Press.

Grayson, R. (2010), *Belfast Boys: How Unionists and Nationalists Fought and Died Together in the First World War*, London: Bloomsbury.

Grayson, R., and F. McGarry (eds) (2016), *Remembering 1916: The Easter Rising, the Somme and the Politics of Memory in Ireland*, Cambridge: Cambridge University Press.

Harte, L. (2018), 'Conversations on a Collaboration: An Interview with Martin Lynch,' *Irish Studies Review*, 26(1): 124–34.

Heininge, K. (2002), 'Observe the Sons of Ulster Talking Themselves to Death', in H. Lojek (ed.), *The Theatre of Frank McGuinness. Stages of Mutability*, 25–40, Dublin: Carysfort Press.

Higgins, C. (2016), '#Wearehere: Somme Tribute Revealed as Jeremy Deller Work', *The Guardian*, 1 July 2016. Available online: https://www.theguardian.com/stage/2016/jul/01/wearehere-battle-somme-tribute-acted-out-across-britain (accessed 20 June 2019).

Holmes, R. (2011), *Tommy. The British Soldier on the Western Front 1914–1918*, London: Harper Collins.

Hynes, S. (1995), 'The Man Who Was There', *The Sewanee Review*, 103(3): 394–413.

Kiberd, D. (2005), 'Frank McGuinness and the Sons of Ulster', *The Yearbook of English Studies*, Vol. 35, Irish Writing since 1950, Modern Humanities Research Association: 279–97.

Kosok, H. (1996), 'Two Irish Perspectives on World War I: Bernard Shaw and Sean O'Casey', *Hungarian Journal of English and American Studies* (HJEAS), 2(2): 17–29.

Lojek, H. (1988), 'Myth and Bonding in Frank McGuinness's *Observe the Sons of Ulster Marching towards the Somme*', *The Canadian Journal of Irish Studies*, 14(1): 45–53.

Lojek, H. (2004), *Contexts for Frank McGuinness's Drama*, Washington, DC: Catholic University of America Press.

Lynch, M. (2006), *Holding Hands at Paschendale*. 19 October–24 November 2006 Lyric Theatre, Belfast.

Maguire, T. (2006), *Making Theatre in Northern Ireland: Through and beyond the Troubles*, Exeter: University of Exeter Press.

Maguire, T. (2010a), 'Martin Lynch', in M. Middeke and P. P. Schnierer (eds), *Methuen Guide to Contemporary Irish Drama*, 178–93, London: Methuen.

Maguire, T. (2010b), 'Radical Remembering: Contaminating Memory in the Works of Martin Lynch', *Kritika Kultura* 15: 77–92. Available online: http://kritikakultura.ateneo.net/issue/no-15 (accessed 15 June 2019).

McGreevy, R. (2018), 'Ireland's First World War Veterans: Shunned, Ostracised, Murdered', *Irish Times*, 10 November 2018. Available online: https://www.irishtimes.com/culture/heritage/ireland-s-first-world-war-veterans-shunned-ostracised-murdered-1.3691036 (accessed 27 June 2019).

McGuinness, F. (1985), *Observe the Sons of Ulster Marching Towards the Somme*. 18 February–30 March 1985, Peacock stage, Abbey Theatre.

McGuinness, F. (1996), *Frank McGuinness: Plays 1 – The Factory Girls, Observe the Sons of Ulster Marching Towards the Somme, Innocence, Carthaginians, Baglady*, London: Faber & Faber.

Mitchell, K. (2003), 'Monuments, Memorials, and the Politics of Memory', *Urban Geography*, 24(5): 442–59.

Moriarty, C. (1995), 'The Absent Dead and Figurative First World War Memorials', *Transactions of Ancient Monuments Society*, 39: 7–40.

Mulhall, E. (2016), 'Somme Voices: The Sons of Ulster', *Centenary Ireland*, RTE/Boston College. Available online: https://www.rte.ie/centuryireland/index.php/articles/somme-voices-the-sons-of-ulster (accessed 19 November 2022).

Mullan, P. (2019), 'The Decade of Centenaries and a Methodology for Engaging with "Difficult Heritage"', in E. Crooke and T. Maguire (eds), *Heritage after Conflict: Northern Ireland*, 34–48, Abingdon: Routledge.

Orr, P. (2014), 'For God and Ulster … No Surrender', *Irish Times* 22 October. Available online: https://www.irishtimes.com/culture/heritage/for-god-and-ulster-no-surrender-1.1950967 (accessed 2 June 2019).

PRONI [n.d.], *Decade of Centenaries*, Belfast: Public Records Office of Northern Ireland. Available online: https://www.nidirect.gov.uk/articles/decade-centenaries (accessed 17 September 2019).

Ricoeur, P. (2004), *Memory, History, Forgetting*, trans. K. Blaney and F. Pellauer, Chicago: University of Chicago Press.

Samuel, R. (1994), *Theatres of Memory*, London: Verso.

Schneider, R. (2011), *Performing Remains. Art and war in times of theatrical reenactment*, London: Routledge.

Synge, J.M. (1997) *The Playboy of the Western World*, London: Nick Hern Books.

Westerside, A., and M. Pinchbeck. (2018), *Staging Loss: Performance as Commemoration*, London: Palgrave Macmillan.

Winter, J. (1998), *Sites of Memory, Sites of Mourning, The Great War in European Cultural History*, Cambridge: Cambridge University Press.

Žižek, S. (2008), *Violence*, London: Picador.

2

My Revolution Is Better Than Yours: Remembrance, commemoration and counter-memory of May 1968

Jorge Palinhos and Karel Vanhaesebrouck

On 6 May 2018, the performance *My Revolution Is Better Than Yours* premiered at the Theatre of Nanterre-Amandiers in France. Directed by the Serbian artist Sanja Mitrović, the performance showcased an international cast that ranged from Spain to Russia, including an immigrant from Libya. The premiere took place almost fifty years after the protests of May 1968 in Paris at the Theatre of Nanterre-Amandiers, not far away from the University of Nanterre, where the first demonstrations happened. The purpose of the performance was to celebrate that historical event and to reflect upon its heritage, contradictions and present-day relevance. However, both the rehearsal process and the final result of the piece raised a number of interesting questions regarding the complex connections between memory, celebration and contemporary documentary performance. We, authors of this chapter, both intensively participated in the rehearsal process as dramaturges.

The dramaturgy of memory and commemoration

Recently, a vast field of what Carol Martin (2012) named 'theatre of the real' appeared on stages everywhere. The phrase encompasses directors, playwrights and companies as diverse as Tricycle Theatre, Rabih Mroué, DV8, Rimini Protokoll, David Hare, Lucy Prebble, Milo Rau, Hans-Werner Kroesinger and many others. In Belgium, directors like Raven Ruell, Sanja Mitrović and collectives like the Nimis Group and Cie Art & tça have developed specific theatrical methods to question the representational strategies of mainstream media in their coverage of 'the real'.

Traditionally, the most natural and recurring strategy of theatre to engage reality is through memory. This goes back to the ritual origins of theatre, as an enactment of a collective memory, and memory itself is a mental image of an embodied experience, which draws from the same tools of dramaturgy. Thus, commemoration has an organic theatrical motivation in this regard, as the very iterative process that constitutes theatre as collective memory is reaffirmed by the occurrence of commemorative contexts, but with a designated focus on 'history'.

In *How Societies Remember*, Connerton considers 'the pervasive importance in many cultures of actions which are explicitly represented as re-enactments of prior, prototypical actions' (1989: 61). He describes this feature as 'that of ritual re-enactment' and considers it to be of 'cardinal importance in the shaping of communal memory' (ibid.). Contemporary theatre tries to question and explore the constructed nature of this communal memory.

Sanja Mitrović's *My Revolution Is Better Than Yours* offers a case in point to explore this ambiguous nature of documentary theatre and memorial culture. Mitrović was born in Zrenjanin, in the former Federal Republic of Yugoslavia, and witnessed that country being torn apart by various nationalisms. Her experiences have made her a significant witness in terms of not only how collective memory could be shaped according to political needs, but also how memory can both exist socially as well as in tension with individual memories, which in their turn can many times reflect and contradict that socially accepted memory.

The work of Mitrović can be defined by the confrontation between the individual and the cultural, the personal and the social. This confrontation in Mitrović's performances usually takes as its starting point memorial artifacts: either individual memory, through oral narrative or body memory; or registered memory, through photographs, videos and memorabilia; or even official memory, through documents, news clips, political speeches, historical and sociological tracts. Usually, the exploration of these social and individual memories aims to question specific cultural or social practices or to investigate the roots of social issues.

The performance *My Revolution Is Better Than Yours* (2018) was supposed to rely on the memory of the May 1968 troubles, with the aim of celebrating the fiftieth anniversary of those historical series of events (that was at least the official, institutional commission), but it faced a particular set of problems that single it out from the rest of Mitrović's work. First of all, the subject of the protests of May 1968 is one of the most memorialized events of recent history, with countless books, articles, studies, official statements, political evaluations, personal memoirs and film re-enactments commemorating its occurrence, as well as its continued significance. This fact alone immediately raises the problem of handling such an immense corpus of memory not only for research, but also for the performance. Additionally, it raises the question of what kind of counter-memory could be used against such a serially memorialized event. Most of the key witnesses were quite aged, and had left an abundant memorial legacy, now part of the official memory of the event. Rather than paying 'homage' to this legacy, Mitrović wanted to explore what new elements could be found that, in their turn, may provide a new framework for such a familiar event.

The memorial industry of May 1968

The events of May 1968 constitute one of the great mythical events of the twentieth century in Europe. They occupy a central place in European memorial culture, its trail of subsequent commemorations being produced by a 'mini-industry in itself that perpetuates the myths and the monuments' (Scott-Smith 2008: 1). In France, May 1968 is a true 'mythomoteur', a constitutive myth that seems to define the very quintessence of Frenchness, a discursive formation that is being eagerly reproduced through all kinds of memorial discourses: the French 'esprit' as freethinking, argumentative, liberal, passionate, open and profoundly progressive.

The year 2018 was that of the 1968 memorial boom. The commemorative events served a clear goal for President Macron, visible in an official Elysée press statement referenced by different media, for example, *Europe 1*:

> to think through this moment and to take lessons from it that are neither 'anti' nor 'pro' but that take into account these events in the light of present-day mentalities, because 68 was both a time of utopias and a time of disappointment and we no longer have any utopias left and have lived way too many disappointments. (Rédaction Europe 1.fr.; our translation)

Macron here instrumentalizes the events of 1968 to perform his role of a national 'réconciliateur', reuniting the different political factions in a shared identity of dialogue and exchange and hence, reaffirming the possibility to identify with a shared history of emancipation and individual liberation. His ambition to reunite the French nation around the memory of 1968 is all but a coincidence. As a former student of Paul Ricoeur, he has examined the performative potential of memorial discourse and how history can be politically mobilized.

Of course, Macron's memorial discourse is not an exception: it is a standard strategy of any nation state trying to stabilize its own identity through a unifying discourse that pretends bringing together people of all backgrounds. However, this very same discourse fits Macron, the self-proclaimed challenger of traditional party politics. Through his political party La République en Marche, he aspired to bring together the French under one and the same banner of economic and cultural positivism. The momentum of the May 1968 celebrations fits this agenda, as it allows him to combine a literally progressive aiming at a new future – in other words, his vision of the nation's future – with a sense of cultural and nationalist nostalgia, that is, France as the cradle of intellectual and political emancipation. May 1968 thus functioned as the centrifugal point of different ideological dynamics and Macron arguably understood that a president, as a symbol of the nation, embodies these seemingly contradictory dynamics.

The memorial culture of May 1968 rose surprisingly quickly. In a commented bibliography of 1969, only one year after the event, Michel de Certeau identified seventy publications about it in the French language alone, excluding photographic albums. Contrary to what is often repeated in memorial discourse, May 1968 did not start in Paris. Warsaw, Rome, Rio, New York, Tokyo and Leuven – each has its own history of 1968. Furthermore, it did not involve only students, but also workers, farmers, artists, high-school students (*lycéens*) and many other demographic groups. In her historical study, *1968: De grands soirs et petits matins* (2018), which is largely based on primary archival research, Ludivine Bantigny deconstructs what she calls the 'canevas simplificateur' (a simplifying canvas). Both historians and the media have systematically reproduced the same, simplifying narrative: first there was the student strike in Nanterre, then there were the events at Quartier Latin, which led in their turn to the general strike on 13 May. Bantigny meticulously reconstructs how workers all over France (e.g. in Besançon) prepared the strikes by occupying their factories. Yet she also insists on the fact that, from the point of view of contemporary France, May 1968 was a point of no return, a landmark of creativity, which stimulated political imagination as the sole option for the future, a moment when people realized that they had an actual legitimacy to speak up.

In her book, *May 68 and Its Afterlives*, Kristin Ross shows how memorial discourse in France tended to reduce the events of 1968 to a cultural and sexual revolution rather than a major political event. May 1968 was a clash of generations, a perspective reaffirmed by the title of the TV series and subsequent book publication, *Génération*, by Hervé Hamon and Patrick Rotman. But it was not a systemic crisis of the actual political system as Ross elucidates

> The official history which has been written down, then publicly celebrated in a number of commemorative spectacles produced by mass media and finally transferred to us, is that of a family drama, a generational drama, totally devoid of violence, of its edginess and of its political dimension. May 68 was a benign transformation of the mores and lifestyles intrinsically linked to the modernization of France and its passage from an authoritarian bourgeois society to a new, modern bourgeois cherishing the values of economic liberalism. (Ross 2002: 12; our translation)

More specifically from the 1980s onwards, May 1968 seems to have been revised under the light of the (neo)liberal ideology of individualism and competitiveness. Through an intricate process of social amnesia, May 1968 was subject to a clear teleological historiography, in which each period evaluated to what extent these events had influenced the then present. Ross details that 'a discourse was produced, for sure, but it also had as an effect that seems to erase, or better, to blur the history of May 68' (Ross 2002: 12). Strangely enough, little attention was paid, up to now, to what actually happened (hence the importance of Bantigny's book). The official history of May 1968, certainly in France, as related by official discourse in mainstream media and official memorial discourse, has been reduced all too easily to the role of the 'leaders', while it was in reality a collective revolt of about nine million people.

Finally, the dominant discourse on May 1968 is largely Eurocentric and centred on Western European countries. In confronting the dominant discourse, Klimke and Scharloth, in *1968 in Europe* (2008), argue for a transnational perspective on the history of 1968, bringing together the histories of Western and Eastern Europe. The first student uprising occurred in Poland in March 1968, so not in Paris. It was less a generational conflict than a fight for freedom of expression and democracy. The Prague Spring, during which communist reformist Dubcek, elected in January 1968 as first secretary of the Communist Party of Czechoslovakia, tried to give a human face to communism, promised to be a true turning point for Eastern Europe, but was brutally ended by the Soviet March in August 1968. In Eastern Europe, people fought to free themselves from the Soviet-type totalitarian socialism. In the West a reverse dynamic took place: young communists tried to 'unblock' the democratic system through collective dynamics and egalitarian principles while, at the same time, ironically enough, idealizing the more totalitarian variant of official Soviet communism during that specific era, the same communism that put an end to the reforms of Dubcek.

When announcing the celebrations for May 1968, in mid-2017, Macron seemed to immediately regret his proposal. His entourage thought of it as a rather risky idea (Chrisafis 2018; Maniglier 2017; Riché 2017), as he was to implement quite harsh education reforms and to change important aspects of labour legislation. Why stimulate one's nation to commemorate its mythical revolutionary moment of post-war France, if he risked causing a new one as a reaction to his reform measures? Elysée officials placed increasing emphasis on other commemorative moments (see for example *L'Express*, 5 November 2017). The year 2018 would also be the sixtieth anniversary of the constitution of the Fifth Republic (4 October) and, of course, the last year of the First World War celebrations. When Macron passed his education reform bill, which imposed a competitive process of selection and early specialization on the students, to counter high dropout rates and overcrowding of courses, his commemorative enthusiasm backfired. Instead of celebrations and speeches, France got student strikes, campus occupations, general outrage and social unrest. The students were quickly joined by other fractions, such as railway workers, Air France workers and immigrants, who either went on strike or occupied public infrastructure in order to fight what they described as Macron's elitism and social injustice. Fifty years after 1968, the year 2018 got its own 'convergence des luttes' (convergence of social struggles).

Celebrating revolution?

The idea for *My Revolution Is Better Than Yours* started in 2016 following an invitation from Philippe Quesne, then director of the Nanterre-Amandiers Theatre in Paris, to present a performance related to May 1968 during the festival Mondes Possibles in May 2018. At the time of the invitation, Sanja Mitrović was rehearsing and presenting her performance, *I Am Not Ashamed of My Communist Past*, which used Yugoslav cinema and personal memory to confront the social support that communist systems gave to their citizens, in comparison with the current neoliberal system.

The invitation opened the possibility of addressing one of the main myths of the West: the idea of revolution. However, there was also a clear conscience that 1968 was an over-discussed and overrepresented historical event, for which it would be difficult to bring fresh ideas and perspectives. Additionally, the performance would coincide with the fiftieth anniversary of the event, and it could fall into the celebratory trap of joining the memorial industry of nostalgia, instead of confronting any current real issue.

At the time Mitrović was reading the diaries of the Yugoslav director and Black Wave pioneer, Živojin Pavlović, where he described his feelings after a student protest in Belgrade against the rule of Tito was squashed in June 1968. This led to the story of Stevo Zigon, a famous Yugoslav actor, who, at the climax of the protests, addressed the students with part of the speech of Robespierre from *The Death of Danton*, by Georg Büchner. The artistic team found this overlapping of revolutions and its theatricalization intriguing. It was as if protest, or revolution, was feeding upon its own representation.

This discovery also led us to explore other protests happening at the same time. We were aware of the protests of the Prague Spring in Czechoslovakia; the Students' March in Warsaw, Poland; the protests against the Vietnam War in the United States; or the ones against the Nazi legacy in West Germany. Gradually, we discovered more and more protests happening at that time in many other countries, like Mexico, Japan and China. We came across a book by Rolf Werenskjold, *A Chronology of the Global 1968 Protest*, which lists 382 pages of international student and worker protests in that year, giving substance to the argument that the protests of 1968 were a global phenomenon. We found not only about the strong exchange of experiences and influences among students, but also how the effects of the protests in Western and Eastern Europe had differing impacts on the lives of activists. So, our first focus was on exploring these different international experiences with a special interest in the dichotomy between East and West.

With that in mind, a casting call was made looking for performers from different countries with a personal engagement with protest and activism that could confer a modern perspective on the subject. We settled on four performers: Vladimir Aleksić, who had been engaged in the successful protests which overthrew Slobodan Milošević, and who had a personal connection with Stevo Žigon; Jonathan Drillet, whose family history was related with the political transformations of France in the last fifty years; Maria Stamenković-Herranz, of Serbian and Spanish ascendancy, who had a unique perspective on the difference between Western Europe and Eastern Europe, and Olga Tsvetkova, who knew first-hand the danger of protesting the autocracy of Russia.

With them, the artistic team hoped to develop not only an international, but also a personal perspective on the protests in the world of 1968, while connecting them with present-day issues. Later, during the rehearsal process, we realized the importance of third-world struggles for 1968 activists and understood that we needed to find a contemporary connection that could also question those Eurocentric protests with fresh eyes. Thanks to the dramaturge of Nanterre-Amandiers, Camille Louis, we managed to meet Mohammed Nour Wanz, whose personal testimony would prove to be an important challenge to the European perspective of ourselves and also of our future spectators.

Unweaving memories

After the casting, there was approximately a year of research, which included examining books, studies, essays, testimonials and CIA reports, watching films and documentaries on 1968, and trying to understand the multiple strands and perspectives on 1968.

We learned about sexual liberation, both from heterosexual and LGBT+ perspectives, the evolution of riot police after the protests, the evolution of some of the more radical movements towards the terrorist groups of the 1970s, like the Red Army Faction or the Red Brigades; the connection between the student movements and the movements of liberation in colonized countries, or the authoritarian violence in Latin America. It was especially enlightening to understand how the youth of the 1960s had strong international connections – through television, frequent travel, the youth camps, conferences and meetings that took place – especially in Eastern communist countries. In a way, they were anticipating the globalization of the present times through political means. We came across the stories of many activists, which we collected as testimonials to be used as a counter-memorial strategy – activists from Poland, Czechoslovakia, Hungary, Yugoslavia, who often faced prison, torture, poverty and exile, giving a face and a personal memory to lesser-known versions of the events.

Another relevant strand took shape while watching multiple videos and films. These taught us that revolution is most of all a representation of something, a ritual, that when used in the present sends us to mythical times of the past and of the future. But, at the same time, the time of the revolution exists by itself, as its own mythical time. And this time is defined by rituals of protest, like throwing stones, building barricades, facing the police and displaying heroism and suffering while (re)connecting one with the revolutionaries of the past, and hopefully with the revolutionaries of the future. That is, the concept of 'revolution', independently of its political aims and contexts, is most of all a myth working within its own codes, representations and connections, a celebration of human agency against any given political *status quo*. By enacting symbolic gestures of past revolutions, each revolutionary generation is celebrating and finding comfort in a traditional narrative of struggle against oppression, celebrating a past revolution by enacting another one. Presenting that enactment as representation could be a way of questioning that memory of revolution. This strategy sheds light on individual motivations and political forces involved in the unrest and, with the distance enabled through theatrical representation, other narratives can emerge from the past – more complex and less heroic, challenging tropes of individualized anti-establishment heroism.

During the rehearsal process the artistic team made numerous attempts at re-enacting some scenes, like the famous speech of Stevo Žigon or the debates at French universities. This led us to the main dramaturgical device of the performance: re-enactment of the past as a tool of transformation – the idea of actors re-enacting the past as a way of changing the future and, thus, inspiring a new revolution. Hence, commemorative re-enactment became a central dramaturgical strategy.

Dramaturgical framework

An important part of the discussions in the artistic team concerned the search for a suitable dramaturgical framework that would allow us to bring the material together and provide a reason to edit and present the results of our historical research. What could be the initial situation, the state of being that could function as a lever to experiment with different representational strategies? Two movies played an important role in this quest. The first one, Peter Watkins's film on the Paris Commune, was on the table from the very beginning; Louis Malle's *Viva Maria!* (1965) was an accidental but crucial discovery.

La Commune (Paris 1871) is a 2000 historical drama film about the Paris Commune. Shot in thirteen days in an abandoned factory, the movie takes the form of a historical re-enactment in the style of a documentary. This is a counter-memorial film: it critiques the generally accepted French historiography for consciously obliterating specific moments in its own history. Through the re-enactment of these often overlooked historical events, Watkins criticizes the predominant position of bourgeois historiography, which systematically takes the French Revolution as its pivotal moment. However, from the perspective of working-class history, the Paris Commune might be considered at least an equally important historical moment. Watkins proposes an alternative perspective on the historiographic hegemony as it is reproduced through the French educational system and its national culture of commemorations. Re-enacting this particular episode of French history becomes a strategy to rewrite that very same history. *La Commune* is also a movie about film-making itself as it proposes a critical reflection on the process as well as the crew as a real-life community. Watkins actively implied his actors in the research preceding the shooting of the movie, inviting them to conduct their own historical research. So, *La Commune* is not only a movie about a specific historical event, it is also the result of the group's discussion on that same event and its present-day ramifications. This double status, as both process and end result, would prove to be a crucial insight for *My Revolution Is Better Than Yours*, in which the act of conducting research would become the heart of the final performance.

Viva Maria! is a 1965 adventure comedy by Louis Malle. Brigitte Bardot and Jeanne Moreau play two revolutionary women fighting for a fair world (Buelens 2019: 686). The movie depicts the revolution as both fun and sexy, as a festive act, even a grotesque vaudeville. With its burlesque take on the revolution, *Viva Maria!* became a true box office success fuelled by an elaborate marketing campaign. At the same time the movie also proved to be able to trigger actual revolutionaries. One of them was Rudi Dutschke, who got so excited after seeing the movie that he founded the Viva Maria Group. The movie, he explained, taught him two things: firstly, that revolution is not solely about intellectual discourse, but that it fuels on pleasure and energy, and, secondly, that the problems of the first world cannot be disconnected from the third world problems and vice versa. Malle's movie incarnates the quintessential paradox of the 1960s: the systematic alliance between marketing and revolution.

Viva Maria! provided the framework we were looking for. The four actors would represent four young people re-enacting scenes from that film in a low-budget film studio, attempting to get a better grasp of what revolution might mean and what the heritage of 1968 would be. These attempts to re-enact Malle's movie were subsequently intercut with documentary material resulting from our historical research, mostly speeches and testimonies of different historical figures from both Eastern and Western Europe, intertwined with testimonies in which the actors recounted their own particular links with revolution. Mitrović also developed a number of visual performance scenes in which the actors choreographically evoked the idea of revolution, while at the same time commenting upon its media representations and as some sort of ritual in which the re-enactment attempts to merge the mythical memory of May 1968 with the 2018 social protests. Juxtaposing different historical discourses, *My Revolution* thus tried to show how memorial culture is multifaceted and often contradictory and how this same culture is streamlined through complex processes of commemoration, mythologization and instrumentalization.

The different dramaturgical layers in *My Revolution* constituted a considerable challenge for the four performers, as they had to shift from one representational system to the other, from simply being on stage as themselves to character impersonation. From the very beginning, narrator Mohammed introduces them as actors:

> The people you see here, on this stage, are Europeans.
> They are artists, just like me.
> …
> Vladimir – I always call him Vladimir Putin.
> He's Serbian, but he really, really likes French cheese, and he can't stop talking.
> Olga actually comes from the land of Vladimir Putin.
> Maria is more quiet, she's a bit like me.
> She travelled across different countries and doesn't feel she really belongs to any place. Jonathan is French.
> French from head to toe. (Mitrović, Palinhos and Vanhaesebrouck 2018: 3–4)

Subsequently, they announce whom they will be playing, not only within the *Viva Maria!* re-enactment scenes, but also as go-betweens for the different historical discourses: Rudi Dutchke, Peter Uhl (Maria); Stevo Žigon, Jan Palach (Vladimir); Gyorgy Pör, Ulrike Meinhof, Natalya Gorbanevskaya (Olga); Tiennot Grumbach and Michèle Firk (Jonathan). They also announce that they will be playing themselves. The performers had to shift between different levels of presence: they are on stage as themselves while role-playing in *Viva Maria!*, they step forward to give voice to voices from the past and they perform metaphorical images of revolution. The performers had to manage this complex representational system by constantly stepping in and out of the theatrical frame, shifting between being and playing, between performance and representation, between acting and non-acting.

This multi-layered complexity of *My Revolution* requires the four performers to swiftly move along the continuum of theatrical representation: mimesis, simulation, doubling, imitating, copying, just being there, back and forth between all these layers. The set design supported this complexity, as the spatial design of the stage helped both performers and spectators to navigate between the different layers. The stage is not only a film studio for *Viva Maria!*, but also just a stage, literally a platform on which four people now and then step forward to testify of their research by just saying or rather reiterating the words of a historical character. At the same time, it is also a clear theatrical frame of which Mohammed, who introduces the four persons present on stage as 'actors', is not a part – he is the link between the material present onstage and the social world of the spectators. Through him we recognize the theatrical nature of the facts presented on stage; it is also his presence that forces us to de-fictionalize and, most importantly, to de-melodramatize the words and actions performed by the actors. He forces us to understand that these ghosts from the past are not just memorial fragments but that they can help us to situate ourselves in our present-day world.

Revolution as ritual

Throughout the rehearsals, we kept on being confronted with two insistent questions: What defines a revolution? Were the international protests of 1968 a revolution? We concluded that there are several kinds of revolutions. There is historical revolution, which is a gradual process of social and political transformation, usually only recognizable much later. There is political revolution, which consists in the violent attempt to remake a political system. But probably the most relevant one is ritual revolution, as a sort of counter-memory of society, where social forces and agents enact an appearance of revolution, not only as a commemoration of some past revolution, but also as a demonstration of strength and dissatisfaction with the status quo.

This idea of revolution as ritual seems to be related to the teleological and linear evolution of the Western framework. As the Western conception of time is based on the Judeo-Christian idea of linear time, revolution appears as the resetting of that time, by going back to a mythical time of change and creation. This myth seems to be especially relevant in the modern age, where the attempt to overthrow or remake political and social systems is regarded as vital, at least since the time of the Protestant Revolution, in the sixteenth century. This ritualistic practice seems to have a conservative side, of re-enacting and remembering previous revolutions or attempts at revolution: the protests of June 1968 in Belgrade attempted to continue the protests of May 1968 in Paris, which were themselves the continuation of the protests of April 1968 in West Berlin, which were the continuation of March 1968 in Warsaw, which was the continuation of the protests of January 1968 in Prague. They all were not only continuing the protests against the Vietnam War, but also trying to re-enact the Paris Commune, which was trying to proceed with the French Revolution, which was trying to repeat in France the Glorious Revolution of England, which, for itself, was an attempt at re-enacting the Protestant Revolution of Martin Luther. This ritualistic re-enactment of the past is usually led by the youngest, against consolidated power, and aims at improving the lot of the poor, the weak, the disenfranchised, the foreigners and the refugees.

As for the second question, it became clear to us that, although the immediate result of the protests was a failure, in almost every country, 1968 surely reshaped the West, Europe, France and other countries. The social rigidity and sexual conformism slowly eroded, LGBT+ rights gradually took their place on the political stage, societies became much more diverse and multicultural. Many of the leaders of 1968, like Daniel Cohn-Bendit, Joschka Fischer, Petr Uhl and others became political leaders and figureheads of their countries and even of the European Union. At the same time, the political aims of 1968 were largely a fiasco, with its social policies of defending workers and promoting social equality seeming more and more a mirage. Yet it is quite clear that our world would not be the same without the significant year of 1968.

The research during the rehearsal led us to more questions, which became central to the performance: are the revolutions of the past still an inspiration for today? In which way? Would such a revolution still be a real possibility today? Those were the questions that troubled much of the rehearsals, the dramaturgy and the final performance. The performance was largely defined as a re-enactment of revolution that exposed the myth of revolution as not only a representation by itself, but also a representation that ritualistically attempts to address the future, by evoking the past. Therefore, the performance was composed in several layers, with historical documents (videos), personal testimonies of protagonists of 1968, re-enactments of revolutionary rituals (specially protest) and re-enactments of mythical representations of revolution (*Viva Maria!*), with present-day questionings on the nature of revolution, of society, of personal engagement with protest and of the (im)possibility of real revolution today. That is why, after remembering, telling, re-enacting, near the end of the show, the performers remain alone on stage, without anything else but their own words, trying to figure out what kind of revolution they still could personally believe in. The penultimate scene takes the form of a full re-enactment of a protest, exploring its theatrical and emotional power that is gradually replaced by actor Mohammed filming the protest. This underlines the scene's mimetic nature, before the performer gives his sober but brutely honest account of a personal experience of political turmoil and a subjective balance of the 1968 myth, pondering on what the future may hold:

> My revolution is not the one of 1968, but the one of 2011.
> Even though my life was defined by revolution
> I was always only a witness.
> …
> There are no heroes in my story.
> In Viva Maria all the heroes were mostly Westerners.
> The locals, who they wanted to liberate,
>   seemed to be there just to play dead. (Mitrović, Palinhos and Vanhaesebrouck 2018: 63–4)

The ritual of re-enactment

At first sight, *My Revolution* would be a very poignant example of one of the key research themes in present-day academia: the re-enactment of historical events or artworks. In *Performance Remains* (2011), Rebecca Schneider describes the re-enactment as 'the practice-based wing of what has been called the twentieth-century academic "memory industry"' (2). The popularity of re-enactments, both as a practice and as a research theme, is an integral part of our present-day memorial culture that seems to be so obsessed 'to bring that time – that prior moment – to the fingertips of the present' (ibid.). However, the category of re-enactment is a description that only partly fits *My Revolution*. The performance is in the first place a research presentation: it presents the results of a very sustained research into a particular historical period, while at the same time confronting this primary research material with present-day concerns, not by explicitly actualizing it, but by simply juxtaposing it.

In this intricate construction, the link or tension between the performers/actors and the historical material is crucial. The four performers step forward not to impersonate historical characters but to give their voice a place in history, because for one reason or another they personally feel linked to their stories (for this reason, Sanja Mitrović asked each of the performers to choose the characters they felt closer to). They strongly believe that these voices have something to tell us. The performers testify, as it were, within the shared space time of the performance, of their research and of the ways their research impacted them, not by explaining this impact, but literally by giving a voice to this historical discourse, while at the same time making it resonate with the present. In that sense, the testimony has also a memorial side: it gives a voice from the past a place in the present. *My Revolution,* however, is not a re-enactment; it is a re-presentation in the most literal sense of the word: it makes present again in order to uncover the different layers of hegemonic historical narratives and to reveal mechanisms of historiographic exclusion. *My Revolution* is rather a 'spectral' performance: raising the overheard voices from the death, to haunt our present, rather than to comfort our past.

Connerton (1989) notes that the present and the past are indeed closely intertwined, that the past always haunts the present, and our present informs the ways we make the past exist. Although this can work on multiple levels, memory is an especially relevant tool for that, as a way of legitimizing the current social order, or questioning it (Connerton 1989: 3).

Such confrontation of past and present through memory was especially significant for France in 2018, in its complex relationship with the French May 1968, and played a major role in the rehearsal process of *My Revolution,* throughout the whole process and also in the final result.

As we explained before, an important trigger for Mitrović and her team were the general strikes and protests happening in Paris at the time of the rehearsals of *My Revolution*, and specially the protests and blockades happening at French universities. The creative team visited the university of Nanterre and came across slogans and meetings and an overall procedure that, consciously or not, was ritually replicating the modus operandi of May 1968. This was especially interesting as the events of May 1968 were, by themselves, a ritual replication of previous Parisian insurgencies, like the Commune of 1830, and an imitation of other protests happening in other countries in Europe and the United States. This was embodied in the slogan that was also used deliberately in the performance: 'On ne celebre pas, on continue' (We don't celebrate, we fight on; Mitrović, Palinhos and Vanhaesebrouck 2018: 29). In other words, the protests happening in Paris and France in 2018 were consciously replicating and continuing the memory of the protests of 1968, as a memory that still existed in the present, and shaped the present.

This ritual re-enactment was happening outside of the theatre, and on stage, and both attempted to explore a common memory. The protests of 1968 are still a personal memory to many of its participants and witnesses, but mostly they entered the realm of myth for the younger population, through images, films, studies and stories told. In fact, May 1968 is to the French probably the most mythical of all the protests happening around the world in that year, mostly due to the multiplicity of its images and because the generation of 1968 took care in creating an image of those events that could express a set of cultural values of youth, of freedom, of hope, of change and of hedonism, which helped turning it into a myth, and also a ritual, that found echo in the French society of 2018.

My Revolution Is Better Than Yours, therefore, was facing an event that was already mythical and ritualistic in itself, but whose symbolic power was still strong enough to be happening around us. The performance had to handle the fact that this was not only a personal memory, but also a mythical and ritual memory that was being celebrated on stage, not only in Nanterre but also in many other theatres in France. It was also being re-enacted in the streets and universities of Paris and France. The performance gave us the opportunity to explore the mythical and ritualistic aspects of memory, by only using personal memory as an element of myth, as a way of disrupting the univocal, curated, clean, memory of May 1968. We did that by complicating that memory with contradictory experiences of the time and with the still raw conflicts of 2018.

Rather than commemorating May 1968, which would be the more common thing to do, as the whole French nation seemed to be celebrating its self-proclaimed historic courage, Mitrović questioned the status quo of the present. The memorial May 1968 boom clearly had other goals: it had to unify the divided French nation around a shared heritage of liberation, freedom and creativity, and to mask the huge socio-economic inequalities defining twenty-first-century France. The presence of Mohammed was crucial from that perspective, even though he was a mute presence for most of the performance. Mohammed makes commemoration impossible, as he reminds us of the world out there. Through his presence the whole enterprise to re-enact *Viva Maria!* becomes a vain, almost obsolete and certainly failed attempt of cultural nostalgia. At the same time the different historical voices we hear resonate with another context, not that of May 1968, but that of the present-day world. This includes the world of refugees occupying universities and other official buildings in order not to be expelled but to be treated as human beings; or the world of citizens resisting the neoliberal fiction of austerity and efficiency for which they consider the May 1968 baby boomers to be responsible. Additionally, there is the world of ecological activists resisting the mantra of growth (Macron's start-up nation which is hollowing out labourers' rights), the world of the ZAD ('Zone à Défendre' or Zone to Defend) at Notre Dame des Landes occupying the lands threatened by the construction of yet another airport, and indeed, the world of young women defying the paternalism of the so-called heirs of the sexual revolution.

Therefore, *My Revolution Is Better Than Yours* presented a counter-hegemonic perspective on the commemoration surrounding May 1968, willingly disconnecting it from national discourses and laying bare the many interferences between different times and places. It did that through three counter-memorial strategies: it displayed the different voices of the past and their existence as dramaturgical research, it showed the myth of 1968 to be a Eurocentric, Western and capitalistic memory that survived by excluding the voices of other, non-Western experiences and it revealed the revolution as a re-enactment experience and not an experience of reality or even memory.

References

Bantigny, L. (2018), *1968, de grands soirs en petits matins*, Paris: Seuil.
Buelens, G. (2019), *De jaren zestig. Een cultuurgeschiedenis*, Amsterdam: Ambo.
Certeau, M. de (1969), Une littérature inquiète: mai 1968. Pour un mode d'emploi. *Etudes*, May: 751–63.
Connerton, P. (1989), *How Societies Remember*, Cambridge: Cambridge University Press.
Chrisafis, A. (2018), 'Macron Faces National Debate over Anniversary of May 1968 Protests', *The Guardian*, 15 January. Available online: https://www.theguardian.com/world/2018/jan/15/macron-faces-national-debate-over-anniversary-of-may-1968-protests (accessed 9 February 2020).
Hamon, H., and P. Rotman (1988), *Génération*, 2 volumes, Paris: Seuil.
Klimke, M., and J. Scharloth (2008), *1968 in Europe: A History of Protest and Activism, 1956–1977*, Basingstoke: Palgrave Macmillan.
La Commune (Paris, 1871) (2000), [film], Dir. Peter Watkins, France: La Sept ARTE et Musée d'Orsay, INA.
L'Express. (2017), 'Finalement, pas de Mai 68 pour Emmanuel Macron?', *L'Express*, 5 November. Available online: https://www.lexpress.fr/actualite/politique/finalement-pas-de-mai-68-pour-emmanuel-macron_1957826.html (accessed 9 February 2020).
Maniglier, P. (2017), 'Mai-68: Macron face au "spectre qui rode"', *Nouvel Observateur*, 27 December. Available online: https://bibliobs.nouvelobs.com/idees/20171227.OBS9820/mai-68-macron-face-au-spectre-qui-rode.html (accessed 9 February 2020).
Martin, C. (2012), *Theatre of the Real*, Basingstoke: Palgrave Macmillan.
Mitrović, S., J. Palinhos and K. Vanhaesebrouck (2018), *My Revolution Is Better Than Yours*, unpublished script, Nanterre: digital copy.
Rédaction Europe 1.fr. (2017), 'Mai 68 Macron envisage de commémorer les 50 ans des événements', 20 October. Available online: https://www.europe1.fr/societe/mai-68-macron-envisage-de-commemorer-les-50-ans-des-evenements-3469841 (accessed 9 February 2020).
Riché, P. (2017), 'Commémorer Mai-68: le prix de consolation de Macron pour la gauche?', *Nouvel Observateur*, 19 October. Available online: https://www.nouvelobs.com/politique/20171019.OBS6220/commemorer-mai-68-le-prix-de-consolation-de-macron-pour-la-gauche.html (accessed 9 February 2020).
Ross, K. (2002), *May 68 and Its Afterlives*, Chicago: Chicago University Press.
Schneider, R. (2011), *Performing Remains: Art and War in Times of Theatrical Reenactment*, London: Routledge.
Scott-Smith, G. (2008), 'We Are All Undesirables: May 68 and Its Legacy', *European Journal of American studies*, 3 (2), 8 September 2008. Available online: http://journals.openedition.org/ejas/2802 (accessed 9 February 2020).
Viva Maria! (1965), [film], Dir. Louis Malle, France, Italy: Metro-Goldwyn-Mayer, United Artists.
Werenskjold, R. (2011), 'A Chronology of the Global 1968 Protest', in M. Klimke, J. Pekelder and J. Scharloth (eds), *Between Prague Spring and French May*, 283–307, New York: Berghahn Books.

3

Dancing the emigratory experience: Challenging the boundaries of (imagined) communities and (invented) traditions

Christel Stalpaert

In this chapter, I investigate notions of identity, memory, history and nationhood to analyse how dancers of the Brussels-based dance collective Les SlovaKs perform their emigratory lived experience through performance. As (self-)exiled artists with a migratory background, and with lived experience of traditional Slovak folk dance, these dancers explore the commemorative potential of Slovakian folk culture, dance, music and polyphonic singing as a source of inspiration. Having been trained partly at the Slovakian J. L. Bella Dance Conservatory in Banská Bystrica, at the Comenius University of Bratislava, School of Music and Dramatic Arts, and the Torzo Ballet Company in Bratislava, the members of this dance company find themselves in their subsequent dance training at P.A.R.T.S. (Performing Arts Research and Training Studios), the Brussels-based modern dance school by Anne Teresa de Keersmaeker, after which they individually join diverse Belgian dance companies, like those by Wim Vandekeybus, Sidi Larbi Cherkaoui, Rosas by De Keersmaeker and the Akram Khan Company. Yet, it was when they became residents of the Dans Centrum Jette Workspace in 2006 that Les SlovaKs Dance Collective was formed, with which they created (and tour worldwide) *Opening Night* (2007), *Journey Home* (2009) and *Fragments* (2012).

Based on the second production, my departure point will be a discussion of the commemorative practice of dancing Slovak folk dance in light of a disruptive emigratory experience. In *Journey Home*, les SlovaKs create short dance scenes in which one of the five dancers alternatingly becomes a lead character: 'the folk dancer', 'the tough rock guy', 'the inseparable brothers' and so on. These dance vignettes present individual particularities of the performers in combination with social dance practices. The performers impress with virtuosic Slovak folk dance and polyphonic singing, but the performance also playfully refers to Eastern and Western European traditions and shared histories, always with a touch of humour. I will observe, from a dance and theatre studies perspective, how the demonstrated technique of Slovak folk dance in *Journey Home* serves as 'a useful synecdoche for the complex web of relations that link performers to particular subjectivities, histories, practices, and to each other' (Hamera 2007: 5).

I argue that the dancers of Les Slovaks Dance Collective reveal to us the constitutive powers at work in the commemorative practices of dance communities. In *Journey Home*, they perform the commemoration script of 'traditional' Slovak folk dance while at the same time challenging the boundaries of (imagined) communities (Anderson 1983) and (invented) traditions (Hobsbawm 1983). Instead of cultivating an 'authentic' Slovak dance style, they explore a dance technique of what I call 'embodied acculturation'. In accumulating their Slovakian traditional dance training with their diverse contemporary dance training, they unfold the hybrid, complex network of their bodies-as-archives (Lepecki 2010). This network cannot be squeezed in one homogeneous commemoration script. The choreographic practices of unbound dancing and *métissage* support this observation.

The recognition of the overall plurality of life stories demands a mutual dialogue between performers and spectators. Therefore, I shift to the level of (audience) perception and the binary logic of integration at work in nationalist politics and 'Flemish' communities. After a (critical) discussion of the 'postmigrant aesthetic' (Geiser 2015), I propose an ethical perspective.

Identity, memory and melancholy

As Polish philosopher Zofia Rosińska observed, three concepts form the structural basis of the emigratory experience: 'identity, memory and melancholy' (2011: 31). As a result of the inevitable loss of a physical habitat as 'object of identification', feelings of melancholy and displacement lie at the heart of the emigratory experience. In dealing with these disrupting feelings, memory plays a triple role; it is identity-forming, therapeutic and community-forming (39). Drawing on the connection between landscape and memory (Schama 1995), I first discuss in detail the feelings of displacement and melancholy in the emigratory experience. Second, I observe how the commemoration practice of dancing Slovak folk dance together serves an imaginary restoration of that physical habitat. When the dancers of Les Slovaks Dance Collective share their embodied memories of dance traditions of their home country, Slovakia, with the audience, they cultivate a sense of belonging to a group.

Art historian Simon Schama observed the connections between place, space, identity, nationalism, history and memory in *Landscape and Memory* (1995). Individual and cultural memory is embodied in the environing landscape from ancient times to the present:

> For although we are accustomed to separate nature and human perception into two realms, they are, in fact, indivisible. Before it can ever be a repose for the senses, landscape is the work of the mind. Its scenery is built up as much from strata of memory as from layers of rock. (6–7)

People derive a significant part of their individual and collective identity from the landscape (or cityscape) in which they are raised, or live for a substantial part of their lives. Through interaction with a physical environment, people develop associations and attach memories and symbolic meaning to it. Their sense of belonging to a place is hence deeply rooted in (embodied) memories of a landscape's features, the objects in it, its smells, colours and sounds.

Following these insights, it should be no surprise that the effects of displacement, forced migration, expulsion, exile, banishment and war on individual and collective memory have received increased attention in memory and trauma studies. Inhabiting physical places is crucial to the development of memory, identity and subjectivity. A sudden and drastic change in the inhabited place hence entails a sense of displacement with regard to individual and cultural identity. A 'fundamental interruption' of subjectivity is at stake 'when discontinuous bits of experience remain dissociated from one another by virtue of traumatic conditions' (Butler 2001: 32). These traumatic conditions are the experienced distance from the home(land), the falling away of security, wholeness of home and one's own language.

Following Rosińska, the 'emigratory experience' is constitutive of a 'sense of estrangement, want of meaning in life, and, most significantly, a loss of identity' (2011: 36). Memory scholar Julia Creet similarly observes in *Memory and Migration* how the emigratory experience particularly entails 'the dislocation of memory from space' or 'the break of *locus* and topography' (2011: 13). Displacement for that matter has not so much to do with moving to another location, or with leaving a particular geographical region or physical setting. It rather involves the loss of a physical habitat as an 'object of identification'. Rosińska explains how nomadic tribes, for example, move from one settlement to another without experiencing a loss of identity. They constantly relocate themselves and physically change their surroundings, but they 'do not change that which they identify with most: their group and their customs' (31). The physical habitat is hence more than an actual place, a geographical setting or owned property. It entails the physical habitat of 'home' that is connected with 'lifestyle, value system, language, faith, or ideals' that constitute an identity (ibid.). It is the varied experiences and impressions of 'belonging to a group' (33), to a 'homeland' or a '"home" in the broad sense of the word' (31).

The loss of the physical habitat and the resulting loss of identity encompasses diverse corporeal intensities. The embodied sens(ing) of the world is disrupted. As Rosińska observes: 'it is the smells, the views, the sounds, the intonations, warmth and cold, desires, hopes, disappointments, and finally, safety' (ibid.). It is, for example, not only a matter of language as mother tongue that falls apart in expressing oneself in the 'new' world. The new language, as opposed to the native language of the migrant, is experienced as 'disembodied signs pointing to objects' (Eva Hoffman in Rosińska 2011: 32). The embodied relation to language is disrupted. Similarly, Vladimir Nabokov, in his several years as a man without identity before finally becoming a US citizen, described the loss of his 'natural language' as 'his private tragedy' (ibid.).

A loss of the physical habitat as the object of identification always generates a sense of displacement. People may decide to leave their homeland in the hope of finding better living conditions, or they are compelled to do so because of political repressions, but feelings of displacement will always occur, as one cannot carry along the group or physical habitat which one identifies with. As such, the self-exiled dancers of Les SlovaKs Dance Company experienced a similar sense of displacement. By enrolling in the programme of the Brussels-based dance school P.A.R.T.S., they sensed an estrangement not only in language, but also in habitual ways of moving and dancing, and in the value that was attributed to certain types of dances. Slovak folk dance in Belgium, indeed, did not enjoy the same status as in their home country.

The difficulty of returning home inevitably feeds these estrangements that manifest in the everyday. 'Nothing remains the same, including ourselves', observes Rosińska (34). What Rosińska coined as 'the melancholy of no return' expresses a longing for a lost home, a longing for 'memory's point of origin' (40). Even if the migrants do have the chance to return, the place they used to call 'home' has become irrevocably different, it is in any case altered by their experience of exile itself. Julia Creet (2011) stresses the emotional relation we have with places, and the idea of return to them, in memory: 'If value is a measure of what causes us to fix a particular memory in place (a return of *loci*), melancholy is what constitutes to draw us back to it' (10). The sharing of memories is an expression of a melancholic state of mind. *Journey Home* is then not a dance performance about the personal emigratory history of each of the six performers, but about their memory of it, trying to offer the spectators a vision of their lost world. In this sharing of memories, Rosińska adds: 'memory aids in holding to identity, but most of all it has a therapeutic effect, soothing the suffering caused by this sense of loss' (34). When Les SlovaKs Dance Collective share their embodied memories of traditional Slovac folk dance with one another, they create a sense of belonging to a (lost) national and cultural group. The collective creates a community amongst fellow dancers who have left their homeland. In what follows, I draw on performance and dance studies to investigate how Les SlovaKs translate their feelings of displacement and melancholy through dance. I discuss the commemorative practice of dancing Slovak folk dance together in light of their disruptive emigratory experience.

(Folk) dance as commemorative practice

In examining dance performances as part of the construction of culturally diverse communities, dance scholar Judith Hamera considers dance as a powerful 'social force, as cultural poesis, as communication infrastructure that makes identity, solidarity and memory sharable' (Hamera 2007: 1). From a dance studies perspective, the demonstrated technique of the Slovak folk dance in *Journey Home* serves as 'a useful synecdoche for the complex web of relations that link performers to particular subjectivities, histories, practices, and to each other' (5). Moreover, the celebration of traditional Slovak folklore in festivals such as the Východná folk festival facilitates an intensified, collective act of public remembrance on stages, mediating collective memory and identity.[1]

Nevertheless, the commemorative strategies of theatre and dance differ significantly. Performance scholar Richard Schechner would say that the form of their scripts differs. Scripts 'act as a blueprint for the enactment, and ... persist from enactment to enactment' (Schechner 1973: 6). Dancing can take the form of a script in the sense that it can take 'a "persistent" (or "traditional") shape' (6). In folk dance, particular dance patterns and dance techniques pre-exist any enactment and are transmitted from enactment to enactment by dancers who have been taught how to move in a correct way. While drama is 'a pattern of doings ... encoded in a pattern of written words' (7), the dance script takes shape and is manifest in the dancers' moving bodies. The commemorative efficacy is, hence, contained in retrieving the script from the body-as-archive and in dancing the script correctly. The formal transmission is then corporeally geared and is inherently embodied. Les SlovaKs dancing folk dance together in *Journey Home* resembles an embodied 'identity-framing' memory practice (Rosińska 2011: 39), negotiating with the commemoration script of Slovak folk dance.

Journey Home premiered in Brussels in November 2009. When calling their dance collective 'Les SlovaKs' in 2006, the dancers did not conceal their ethnic and national background. On the contrary, they turned their shared yet very individual migratory past and memory into their trademark: all dancers in Les SlovaKs were born in Slovakia, and this heritage inevitably infiltrates in all of their productions. 'Of course, everyone's personal history is part of his dancing', explains Peter Jaško, dancer and co-founder of the collective, 'those tools are all we have, they are what we do. That exploration of using those memories and playing with the present moment is our work and it creates the pieces themselves' (Archatheatre 2011).

The five dancers – Milan Herich, Peter Jaško, Anton Lachký, Milan Tomášik and Martin Kilvády – were all acquainted with Slovak folk dance from a young age. Milan Herich and Peter Jaško learnt their first dance steps in the Slovak traditional children's dance company, Dumbier. Anton Lachký started to dance at the age of five at the folk-dance company, Maly Vtácnik. Given the dancers' familiarity with traditional folk dance, it is not impossible that as children, they shared the stage at the Východná folk festival, the biggest and oldest festival of folklore in Slovakia. Every year, during the first week of July, they gathered as young dancers for this nationwide folk festival in the village of Východná, at the foot of Kriváň mountain.[2]

The festival is a site of commemoration, bridging a distance in time, with five amphitheatres providing a physical place for retrieving the past, and with the traditional music, costumes and dance techniques functioning as vehicles for commemoration. During the folklore festival, 'the past is revised in terms of a collective memory' (Hobsbawm 1983: 103). The physical space of the amphitheatres differs from the original place where folk dances took place; the tourist setting of a competitive festival is remote from the rural settings of these primarily ritual dances, in which the main concern was to invoke rain, good hunting, health, fertility and success in battle.

The transfer from rural ritual to staged folklore performance serves the interests of nationalist identities. In 1973, the American anthropologist Dean MacCannell introduced the term 'staged authenticity' to point at the commemorative arrangement of social space in tourist settings like the Východná folk festival. Political anthropologist and cultural historian Eric Hobsbawm confirmed this and introduced the commonly used concept of 'invented tradition' to point at its possible fabrication in connection with ethnicity, nationalism and national identity. The performances by folk-dance groups at the Východná festival might thus be called 'theatres of history' (Bogataj in Istenič 2011: 58), yet meant for a tourist setting, where commemorative elements are used in an artificial, directed manner, as part of an 'imagined dramaturgy' (58).

Halbwachs pointed at the manipulative potential by social institutions in commemorative practices as vehicles for collective memory:

> When it comes to historical memory, the person does not remember events directly; it can only be stimulated in indirect ways through reading or listening or in commemoration and festive occasions when people gather together to remember in common the deeds and accomplishments of long-departed members of the group. In this case, the past is stored and interpreted by social institutions. (Coser in Halbwachs 1992: 24)

Since the mid-1990s, dance studies have revealed how folk dance served the modern state's bio-politics and developed a spectacle of nationhood. Folk dance and music regulate a disciplined body, assessing social, cultural and political developments within the nation. Andrew Hewitt similarly pointed out that choreography is the modality through which dance reflects 'a way of thinking about social order' (2005: 11). Hamera observed similar strategic and tactical operations in dance that 'limit' the constitution of communities (2007: 22), particularly through the manipulative potential of dance techniques and choreographies.

Levelling out differences through communal dance practices is most obvious in the mass spectacles of the Sokol movement, which have been performed throughout Eastern Europe. The manipulation of individual bodies through mass configurations disseminated spectacles of nationhood and the constitution of supra-ethnic identities. Mass-choreographed festivals, called *slets*, were performed to constitute a pan-Slavic identity, aiming at uniting all the Slavic people. Likewise, folk-dance motifs integrate themes from national folklore to perpetuate national groundings in the quest for identity. A supra-ethnic, national identity is performed beyond religious, ethnic, cultural or gender differences. This supra-ethnic, national and antagonist grounding of dance technique and choreography is repressive as it constitutes a community at the expense of one's individual (dance) potential and ideals, beliefs, burdens and dreams.

A similar levelling out of differences is at work in the Východná folk festival. Certain aspects of Slovakia's past and its heritage are selected, revived and presented as authentic. The festival prides itself that it works under the auspices of CIOFF-UNESCO, the International Council of Organisations of Folklore Festivals and Folklore Art, aiming to preserve authentic cultural heritage. In their definition of traditional programmes on stage, the CIOFF outlines its selection criteria. It claims that intangible cultural heritage should be 'transmitted from generation to generation' in order to provide 'a sense of identity and continuity' (CIOFF 2013). A programme is considered an authentic expression 'if the costumes are authentic or faithfully reconstructed' and 'if music and dance are presented without arrangement' (ibid.). In drawing visitors from near and far to the traditional folk festival, high value is attributed to authenticity: its commemoration script should follow the institutionalized practices commonly understood around traditional Slovak dance. The best dance company is the company who can dance to the commemoration script correctly. This claim for authenticity causes some travel agencies to promote the 'vintage' festival as a must-go for 'ethno-lovers' (ethno-tourism), thereby directly exposing the link of this 'invented' tradition with ethnicity, nationalism and national identity.

The commemoration script of Slovak folk dance was firmly inscribed in Les SlovaKs' bodies-as-archives.[3] Even when they had to leave behind their homes and their material belongings, their bodies-as-archives travelled with them. Digging into these corporeal archives is an act of remembrance. As such, it is not a surprise to detect many Slovak folk-dance motifs in *Journey Home*, negotiating with the commemoration script of Slovak folk dance that is ingrained in their dancing bodies.

A particular common motif is the structure of the dance. Choreographically, one performer acts as the leader, while the others line up and watch, waiting for their opportunity to show off their virtuosity. The leading performer makes vigorous jumps and agile squats, often raising one hand, as to make an even stronger and proud impression. Sometimes the performers dance together, raising their hands too, but making more simple, uniform stamping strides. The most obvious reference to the folk-dance motif lies in the footwork of the dancers with the occasional clicking of the feet together and the slapping of a leg. Other common motifs consist of the dancers' repeated and quick turning around their axes and the clapping of the hands in a syncopated rhythm.

The dancers do not conceal their ethnic or national background. On the contrary, they draw material from it as scripts deeply rooted in their bodies-as-archives, much like what Delgado and Muñosa describe as identification taking 'the form of histories written on the body throughout gesture', in this case, through dance movements (Hamera 2007: 22). This is supported by the presence of other commemorative vehicles, such as music and costumes. The collective boys' dance is accompanied by polyphonic singing and violin music, which is a dominant feature of Slovak folk dance. The clothes – wide-legged pairs of trousers and adjusted casual T-shirts resembling the typical Slovak blouses or *blúza* – are equally reminiscent of traditional Slovak clothing.

One could suspect that Les SlovaKs adopt a supra-ethnic, national grounding of dance technique and choreography. However, they do not retrieve the commemoration script from their bodies-as-archives in an 'efficient' way; they purposefully do not dance the script 'correctly'. Instead, they are remarkably creative with the traditional patterns of folk dancing. In the next section, I discuss how, in *Journey Home*, the dancers challenge the boundaries of (imagined) Slovak communities and (invented) folk dance traditions, and thereby, the social institutions that gear them. By retrieving material from their hybrid bodies-as-archives, they develop a dance technique of, what I call, 'corporeal acculturation' and a choreographic practice of *métissage* as an 'open' or 'unbound' mode of dancing.

Challenging the boundaries of (imagined) communities and (invented) traditions

Les SlovaKs do not perform 'authentic' Slovak folk dance; they produce what they themselves call 'new traditional dances' (programme brochure). Snaps and bits of folk-dance phrases are combined with other, more contemporary, dance techniques and motifs. A kick forward, typical of the folk-dance footwork, prolongs in a ballet pose, with the leg now stretched *en pointe* and the back bent backwards. The subsequent horizontal full twist in its turn gives way to a spinning dazzling turning around the ax. Virtuosity also links with humour, with some dance sequences having a stark 'Chaplinesque' quality. These dancing bodies testify to the complex interconnections of traditional Slovak dance motifs with several subsequent dance trainings and techniques. The result is a very diverse and personal encounter of 'traditional' folk-dance motifs, starting from an individual body-as-archive. The interconnections are often displayed in one and the same dance sequence, and in an accumulative way, as in a hybrid flow. This hybridity is more than a mixing of cultures, it is a hybrid associational arrangement, flowing with improvisation. Martin Kilvady explains: 'We use the Slovak traditional dance as a source of inspiration. Not to recreate or reconstruct, but to find and apply what is valuable and enriching for us and offer that generously to the spectators' ('Residencies 2010'). Folding back on their bodies-as-archives, they rebel and accept, they reject and confirm, they erase and repeat and they isolate and accumulate bits and pieces of their personal corporeal dance archives in astonishing virtuosity.

In this way, *Journey Home* questions (rather than confirms) national groundings of their dance moves in a continuous quest for identity. In displaying a corporeal acculturation of dance styles, the performance possesses 'the genuine capacity to be in potential "dissensus" with the social order' (Anzaldi 2012: 160) as it is generated by folk dance, flags and costumes. The dancing bodies here 'display the intrinsic diversity that composes each citizen-body' and, hence, surpasses the strictures of the dance technique that align bodies with authority (Martin 1998: 21). In 'playing' with traditional folk-dance motifs, Les SlovaKs point out that, however 'monumental' or rigorously drilled into generations, dance techniques are not 'static' and 'forever'. They depend on dancing bodies, which keep them in motion and play, and might re-fashion them along personal bodies, histories and desires (Hamera 2007: 4).

Instead of cultivating a 'pure' or 'authentic' Slovak dance style, *Journey Home* explores, what I call, a dance technique of 'embodied acculturation'. In the process of 'acculturation', a double identity is maintained, as in the 'existence of two selves' (Rosińska 2011: 32). In the context of *Journey Home*, I would consider this in light of an existence of many selves. Acculturation entails then the accumulation of different cultural identities. Rosińska describes the issue of acculturation as 'the acceptance of the foreign culture and being accepted by it' (41). As such, it is opposed to the logic of integration, which demands from the migrant subject to disappear as 'Other' and to become one with 'us'.

This means that the dance phrase is not as easily related to an old-time culture that has disappeared in the past. In fact, there is no past, present and future constantly overlapping. 'Mnemonic time is not linear', argues Rosińska, but rather 'a circular mixing and overlapping of the past, the present, and the future' (38); and further, 'if we don't want to be stuck in the sensation of 'not here', and 'not in this time', in the feeling of dichotomy and longing, then new identifications are necessary' (41). In a similar vein, Les SlovaKs are not stuck in the past, they do not dwell in a melancholic *impasse*.

From a choreographic perspective, Les SlovaKs develop an 'open' or 'unbound' mode of dancing, 'principally not excluding any aesthetic or movement possibilities' (website Les SlovaKs). In displaying a very diverse set of dance and performance skills in their work, they aim to move beyond any categorization in dance. Embracing all potential styles available in their dance-bodies-as-archives, they develop what they call an 'inclusive' choreographic mode, 'promoting an inclusive social program' (website Les SlovaKs). That is the reason Les SlovaKs gather themselves in a 'collective' rather than a company. A dance company would need one choreographer; a collective denotes a *collective* way of working and decision-making. In the beginning of the creation process, this demanded the care 'for common skill in composing while performing', while at the same time, 'accumulating the set of rules in relating to each other and to the public while performing' (Herich 2020). Les SlovaKs consider the choice for organizing themselves in a collective as a 'human statement':

> Regarding each member (of the collective) as an irreplaceable asset to the whole, Les SlovaKs create a polyphonic dance that brings each dancer to the fore as a soloist and an instrumental part of a dynamic and familial collective. (website les SlovaKs)

By breaking with choreographic and technical strictures, they allow for alienation, uncertainty anxiety and discomfort in the creation process, in order to proceed, to move forward, not despite but *because* of the feelings of displacement and the disequilibrium attained. As such, *Journey Home* cultivates a hybrid emigratory condition in order to move beyond a paradigm of belonging.

An ethical call for differential futures

As a final point, *Journey Home* invites us to look at its hybrid aesthetic form from an ethical perspective as a 'postmigrant' performance. The latter term has been principally developed in the German context by curator and artistic director Shermin Langhoff to inaugurate a particular category of performances by artists with a migration background, mostly from the second and third generations.[4] Langhoff's use of the term was a statement, giving voice to the refusal of artists of colour to be labelled migrants. To them, this labelling entailed a reduction of their identities, fitting the ongoing polarization discourse and serving a national integration politics. Migrant theatre was considered not to be part of a 'German theatre' or a 'German culture'. The appropriating, self-labelling gesture of 'postmigrant theatre' was an urge to move away from prejudices and assumptions about 'migrant theatre' and to unsettle 'the perpetual 'migrantization' of people of colour and of people with actual or ascribed migrant background' (Petersen, Schramm and Wiegand 2019: 4). As Naika Foroutan observes: 'The "post" has the intention to create irritation in order to break with the hegemonic way of speaking about migration' (Foroutan, Karakayali and Spielhaus 2018: 10; my translation). Without disregard of their particular emigratory experience, post-migrant performers wanted to move beyond their narrow designation as migrants.

They demand 'the acknowledgements of the overall plurality of life stories and the multiplicity of backgrounds as fundamental conditions of contemporary society and the social and cultural interaction among all its members' (Petersen, Schramm and Wiegand 2019: 3).

Journey Home does exactly this: in communicating the transformations that they experience from a post-migrant perspective, Les SlovaKs stretch the label and discourse of 'the migrant'. The journey home in the dance performance is not a nostalgic longing for their home country, but a blue print of their struggles and negotiations of finding a place in current and future societies. In that sense, they develop what Myriam Geiser called a 'postmigrant aesthetic', communicating their 'experiences of multiple belonging and the hybridizing processes of identity formation' (2015: 595, cited in Schramm et al. 2019: 13). I consider the post-migrant aesthetic to be at work not only on the level of aesthetic production, but also on the level of (audience) perception. After all, the recognition of the overall plurality of life stories demands a dialogue between performers and spectators. Challenging the boundaries of (imagined) communities and (invented) traditions, les SlovaKs not only point at the constitutive powers at work in the commemorative practices of dance communities. With their unbound dancing and their complex citing of dance styles, they also question the logic of integration itself. Their post-migrant aesthetic is then an urgent, ethical call to the audience to let go of their stereotypical thinking, of prejudice and preconceived ideas, challenging the logic of integration in nationalist politics. This heterogeneous aesthetic is not a mixture of different cultures, but a disturbance of cultural identity thinking itself, pointing at the impossibility of *any* clear-cut identity, including ours, as spectators.

Despite their loss of a homeland as a physical habitat and as an object of identification, the dancers of les SlovaKs are not grieving. The title of their performance obviously refers to the desire of migrants to belong somewhere. Moving from a 'past' home to a possible 'future' home, they move in between. Even when a better future is on the horizon, there is also displacement and disruption of subjectivity as necessary condition. *Journey Home* inaugurates an artistic dialogue with a 'new' home; with new sociopolitical realities. In other words, it is not only directed towards a traumatic past, it is also engaging in differential futures (Burns and Kaiser 2012). Corporeal acculturation does not bring back – be it imaginatively – a lost past, but it creates appeals to a new acculturated society. By dancing through complex time knots in their bodies-as-archives, Les SlovaKs co-create the past, the present and the future, with the spectator as their ethical witness.

Journey Home is not only the story of Slovakian migrants, it is also a story of us all, confronting ourselves *through* the migrant 'Other'. The emigratory experience thus performed calls for introspection on evolving interpersonal relations within a migrating Europe, or – as Creet describes it – for an encounter 'with one's self *through* the Other' (2011: 11). The performance confronts us with our own expectations around folk dance. In re-fashioning traditional Slavic folk-dance motifs, it presents 'ambiguous' identities and challenges our 'Western' stereotypes of what we believe are 'Eastern' European identities. Les SlovaKs do not perform the migrant as a mourning 'Other'. Rather, they travel in between identities, whilst revealing how folk dance is always by and of itself a hybrid, living archive. Because traditional folk dance and music are being passed down for centuries, they inevitably carry traces of the many cultural influences in Slovakia's heritage (Celtic, Roma, Hungarian, Slavic, German and others). It is particularly in the West that we tend to view Eastern European dance as having a similar technique and mass choreographic model. The new traditional dance style of Les SlovaKs deliberately calls for a re-evaluation of commonplace demarcations between tradition and modernity, between 'East' and 'West'. Their performances offer 'sites where participants actively confront and engage with different traditions, with corporeality and "irreducible difference"' (Hamera 2007: 1–2).

Hence, through its commemorative function, *Journey Home* reveals us a world-making potential for new relational identities (Mouffe 1988) and 'glocal subjectivities' (Trienekens 2006). Contemporary cultural identities are hybrid and can no longer be defined according to national origin or other types of inherent belonging, they are rather defined by 'the intricate and extensive web of relationships that different individuals and groups establish in their daily practice and in their imaginary enactments' (Olalquiaga 1999: xvi). Identity is a relational question, or, as Mouffe articulates, 'a subject constructed at the point of intersection of a multiplicity of subject-positions' (1988: 35). Trienekens adds to this that 'the creation of a sustainable relation between collective and individual identities … [is] the most challenging current sense-making project in multicultural cities' (2006: 133). In pleading for a glocal urban condition, she tries to overcome 'the unproductive binary perception of the global (universal) versus the local (particular)' as well as the unproductive notions of homogeneity (137). Difference is in this respect a *becoming*, 'based on *relation* rather than on affiliation, blood ancestry and land' (139).

With their open and unbound dancing, *Journey Home* invites the spectator to partake in this process of becoming, not as an act of integration, or as a skillful disappearing in the other, but as an encounter of the other in wonder in a Deleuzian sense, an opening up towards several possible meanings, relations and identities. This attitude no longer works with common sense to recognize otherness on the basis of easily recognizable external features, such as race, gender or age, but to encounter an *accord discordant*, a discordant harmony, according to an agreement to differ and disagree (Deleuze 2004: 183), to postpone interpretation and hence, judgement. The mirroring attitude of common sense is often enough reductive as far as 'mapping' the other is concerned. When we look for superficial characteristics of the other, such as form, function or kind, we annex the 'other' and capture them within language. We capture otherness within preconceived notions and identities, within representation, as a touchstone for our own so-called clear-cut, but reductive, identity. The swift citizen 'inflicted' with acculturation opens up to the other, without disappearing into the other.

This demands a certain willingness to encounter in wonder, without running the risk of losing oneself in the other. One approaches and is approached without dominating or being dominated. That is why we might regard the emigratory experience, as manifested through the commemorative dance of Les SlovaKs, simultaneously as a curse and as a promise. It holds a promise because it calls for a relational identity: as new opportunities emerge from the ruins of disrupted identities, from decaying national dreams, new life is emerging from the interstices of scattered subjects and identities.

Notes

1. In his canonical book *On Collective Memory*, sociologist Maurice Halbwachs investigates the social construction of memory. He outlines how memory functions in a collective context, constituting social groups 'through participation in commemorative meetings with group members' (Coser in Halbwachs 1992: 24).
2. This mountain plays an important symbolic role in the Slovak national identity. It appears on the Slovak flag since 1992 and on Slovakia's euro coin. In the last decades, it is increasingly being marketed as a symbol of Slovak pride, and claimed for Slovak ethnic and national activism.
3. In his influential article, dance scholar André Lepecki (2010) compares the dancing body with an archive: it constantly gathers techniques, movements, habits, bits and pieces of repertoire that are being stored for later use.
4. Already in 2004 Langhoff addressed migration issues. She invited Turkish-German artists at a film festival she curated at the Hebbel am Ufer, together with the then artistic director, Matthias Lilienthal. In 2006, she curated the *Beyond Belonging Festival*, in co-organization with Lilienthal. In 2008, she pushed her notion of post-migrant theatre to an institutional level, when she became artistic director of the Berlin Ballhaus Naunystrasse. For more detailed information, see Stewart 2017. The term 'post-migrant', however, has been used before. In 1995, editors Gerd Baumann and Thijl Sunier used the term in a collection of essays, titled *Post-Migrant Ethnicity: De-essentializing Cohesion, Commitments, and Comparison*.

References

Anderson, B. ([1983] 2006), *Imagined Communities. Reflections on the Origin and Spread of Nationalism*, London: Verso.

Anzaldi, F. B. (2012), 'Pitfalls of "the Political": Politization as an Alternative Tool for Dance Analysis?', in G. Brandstetter and G. Klein (eds), *Dance [and] Theory: Tanzscripte*, 159–66, Bielefeld: Transcript Verlag.

Archatheatre (2011), 'Les SlovaKs Dance Collective – Journey Home', archatheatre.cz, 11 October. Available online: http://2007.archatheatre.cz/en/menu/programme/11102011day.html (accessed 28 March 2022).

Baumann, G., and T. Sunier (eds) (1995), *Post-Migrant Ethnicity: De-essentializing Cohesion, Commitments, and Comparison*, Amsterdam: Het Spinhuis.

Burns, L., and B. M. Kaiser (eds) (2012), *Postcolonial Literatures and Deleuze. Colonial Pasts, Differential Futures*, New York: Palgrave Macmillan.

Butler, J. (2001), 'Giving an Account of Oneself', *Diacritics*, 31 (4): 22–40.

CIOFF (2013), 'Definition of Traditional Programs on the Stage', CIOFF.org. Available online: http://www.cioff.org/documentation/DefinitionTraditionalPrograms.pdf (accessed 28 March 2022).

Creet, J. (2011), 'Introduction: The Migration of Memory and Memories of Migration', in J. Creet and A. Kitzmann (eds), *Memory and Migration. Multidisciplinary Approaches to Memory Studies*, 3–26, Toronto: University of Toronto Press.

Creet, J., and A. Kitzmann (eds) (2011), *Memory and Migration. Multidisciplinary Approaches to Memory Studies*, Toronto: University of Toronto Press.

Deleuze, G. ([1994] 2004), *Difference and Repetition*, trans. P. Patton, New York: Columbia University Press.
Foroutan, N., J. Karakayali and R. Spielhaus (2018), 'Einleitung. Kritische Wissensproduktion zur postmigrantischen Gesellschaft', in N. Foroutan, J. Karakayali and R. Spielhaus (eds), *Postmigrantische Perspektiven Ordnungssysteme, Repräsentationen, Kritik*, 9–16, Frankfurt: Campus Verlag.
Geiser, M. (2015), *Der Ort Transkultureller Literatur in Deutschland und in Frankreich. Deutsch-türkische und frankomaghrebinische Literatur der Postmigration*, Würzburg: Königshausen & Neumann.
Halbwachs, M. (1992), *On Collective Memory*, trans. and ed. L. A. Coser, Chicago: University of Chicago Press.
Hamera, J. (2007), *Dancing Communities: Performance, Difference and Connection in the Global City*, London: Palgrave Macmillan.
Herich, M. (2020), 'Collaborations: Les Slovaks Dance Collective', milanherich.com. Available online: https://www.milanherich.com/data/collaborations-les-slovaks (accessed 28 March 2022).
Hewitt, A. (2005), *Social Choreography: Ideology as Performance in Dance and Everyday Movement*, Durham, NC: Duke University Press.
Hobsbawm, E. ([1983] 2000), 'Introduction: Inventing Traditions', in E. Hobsbawm and T. Ranger (eds), *The Invention of Tradition*, 1–14, Cambridge: Cambridge University Press.
Istenič, S. P. (2011), 'Texts and Contexts of Folklorism', *Traditiones*, 40 (3): 51–73.
Kilvady, M. 'Residencies 2010: Les SlovaKs', danscentrum.be. Available online: http://www.danscentrumjette.be/workspace/Files/index.php?year=2010&dates=&id=23 (accessed 28 March 2022).
Lepecki, A. (2010), 'The Body as Archive. Will to Re-enact and the Afterlives of Dance', *Dance Research Journal*, 42 (2): 28–48.
Les SlovaKs Dance Collective, https://documentacionescenica.com/peripecia/consultas/compania/compania_3720/les-slovaks-dance-collective (accessed 28 March 2022)
MacCannell, D. (1973), 'Staged Authenticity. Arrangements of Social Space in Tourist Settings', *American Journal of Sociology*, 79 (3): 589–603.
Martin, R. (1998), *Critical Moves: Dance Studies in Theory and Politics*, Durham, NC: Duke University Press.
Mouffe, C. (1988), 'Radical Democracy. Modern or Postmodern?', in A. Ross (ed.), *Universal Abandon? The Politics of Post-Modernism*, 31–45, Minneapolis, MN: University of Minnesota Press.
Olalquiaga, C. (1999), *Megalopolis: Contemporary Cultural Sensibilities*, Minneapolis, MN: University of Minnesota Press.
Petersen, A. R., M. Schramm and F. Wiegand (2019), 'Introduction: From Artistic Intervention to Academic Discussion', in M. Schramm, S. Pultz Moslund, A. Ring Petersen, M. Gebauer, H. C. Post, S. Vitting-Seerup and F. Wiegand (eds), *Reframing Migration, Diversity and the Arts. The Postmigrant Condition*, 3–10, London: Routledge.
Rosińska, Z. (2011), 'Emigratory Experience. The Melancholy of No Return', in J. Creet and A. Kitzmann (eds), *Memory and Migration. Multidisciplinary Approaches to Memory Studies*, 29–42, Toronto: University of Toronto Press.
Schama, S. (1995), *Landscape & Memory*, London: Fontana Press.
Schechner, R. (1973), 'Drama, Script, Theatre and Performance', *TDR*, 17 (3), September: 5–36.

Schramm, M., S. Pultz Moslund, A. Ring Petersen, M. Gebauer, H. C. Post, S. Vitting-Seerup and F. Wiegand (eds) (2019), *Reframing Migration, Diversity and the Arts. The Postmigrant Condition*, London: Routledge.

Stewart, L. (2017), 'Postmigrant Theatre. The Ballhaus Naunynstrasse Takes On Sexual Nationalism', *Journal of Aesthetics and Culture*, 9 (2), (Post)Migration in the Age of Globalisation. New Challenges to Imagination and Representation: 56–68.

Trienekens, S. (2006), 'Making Sense of Diverse Collectivities in Contemporary Cities: (Re)considering Cultural Identities, Citizenship and the Role of the Arts', *A Prior Magazine*, 13: 133–43.

4

Representations of transition, memory and crisis on stage in *Punto y coma* (Ready or Not) by Uruguayan dramatist Estela Golovchenko

Sophie Stevens

This chapter examines *Punto y coma* (Ready or Not, written in 2003) by Uruguayan dramatist Estela Golovchenko. The play depicts a meeting between a young woman and her father after many years of estrangement which began when he fled Uruguay during the dictatorship (Golovchenko 2003a).[1] Following the end of the Uruguayan civic-military dictatorship in 1985 and the subsequent transition to democracy, playwrights began to explore how the legislation and narratives created by the state in order to facilitate this transition affected the lives of individuals, their decisions and the opportunities open to them. In a 2009 study of theatre that emerged in the post-dictatorship period in Uruguay, Roger Mirza specifies techniques used by dramatists to approach the topic of the recent past. He identifies the depiction of two characters presenting opposing views as a recurring trope for the central dramatic conflict in a number of plays (2009: 46). *Punto y coma* therefore emerges in the context of new theatre productions in Uruguay which examine how the transition to democracy affects family relationships, particularly across generations, and seek to explore the repercussions of the dictatorship, including the crisis provoked by the attempt to silence narratives other than those perpetuated by the state.

The reunion depicted on stage is a moment of crisis in which father and daughter come into conflict as they seek to reconcile their personal memories of the past. Their contrasting ways of commemorating this past, both publicly and privately, demonstrate how it continues to have an impact upon them in the present. If, as the Introduction to this book posits, we think of theatre as inherently commemorative then *Punto y coma* is a theatre play which commemorates and captures some of the conflicts, tensions and crises arising from a period in history marked by transition. At the same time, through the characters' concerns, resistance to dominant discourses, and conflicting opinions, Golovchenko creates a dramatic language that powerfully conveys the complexity of any attempt to commemorate a period in history which is marked by a process of change. This is intensified by a portrayal of the impact of loss: the character of the mother was abducted during the dictatorship and the question of how she can and should be remembered sparks key aspects of the conflict within the play. The playwright uses the dramatic space to depict discourses on commemoration which challenge those established by the state. In this way, *Punto y coma* shows how a distance emerges between the official discourses surrounding the transition to democracy and the experiences, practices and needs of individuals in society.

Golovchenko works as a dramatist and a teacher, and between 2015 and 2020 she held the role of Director of Culture for the Department of Río Negro, Uruguay. *Punto y coma* was awarded the first prize in the Segundo Concurso de Obras de Teatro de la Comisión del Fondo Nacional de Teatro (COFONTE) in 2003 (Golovchenko 2003b). The play was performed at Teatro Sin Fogón in Fray Bentos, Uruguay, in 2004 and directed by Roberto Buschiazzo. The Teatro Sin Fogón company has played an important role in raising the profile of theatre created outside of the capital, Montevideo (Duffau and Gómez 2011: 13). I translated *Punto y coma* into English as *Ready or Not* and the translation is published in *Uruguayan Theatre in Translation: Theory and Practice* (Stevens 2022). All translations are my own; page numbers refer to the Spanish text and the quotations are included in Spanish in the notes. *Ready or Not* was performed as a rehearsed reading on 13 July 2017 at Cervantes Theatre, London, directed by Camila Ymay González as part of the Out of the Wings Festival of Play Readings from Spain, Portugal and Latin America (details of the festival and performance can be found at the Out of the Wings Festival website).

In the play there are four characters: Mother, Father, Daughter and Santiago. Santiago is the only character given a name. The first scene is a flashback to Daughter's childhood and the second scene takes place in the present day when Daughter meets her father as an adult. The character list indicates that the character of the daughter is played by the same actor in all scenes. The play begins as Mother and Father discuss how Father will soon leave to go into hiding and Mother and Daughter will join him later. There is a sense of urgency: 'You've got to go' (Golovchenko 2003a: 1), and the presence of an external threat: 'They know how to put themselves in our shoes and they move quickly' (2).[2] In the next scene, we see Daughter waiting for her father at his office. Their meeting takes place in the Palacio Legislativo, Uruguayan Parliament, because the character of the father holds the role of a senator. He is delayed at a meeting and so she talks to his young assistant, Santiago. There is tension between them and her anger at the setting of the meeting, a place where she feels she does not fit in, is blatant: 'I'm against all politicians' (4).[3] However, she takes the chance to tentatively ask questions about her father, which indicate the length of their estrangement and Daughter's underlying curiosity.

The dramatic structure of the play alternates scene by scene between flashbacks to the past, where Daughter is with her mother in the refuge or hiding place, and the present-day meeting in the senator's office. Through this back and forth and the discussions that take place, we learn that Father left Uruguay for Buenos Aires and made plans for his wife and daughter to join him, but these plans never came to fruition because Mother was abducted by soldiers during the repressive regime and she is presumed dead. Daughter remained behind, living with her grandmother, searching for her mother and maintaining the Communist political beliefs that her parents held. We learn that Father was confronted by the military and he was given a choice: 'They came for me at home. By that stage I had fought with everyone in the world. I didn't give it much thought. I needed to believe in something else' (Golovchenko 2003a: 22), and so he decided to stop actively fighting against the regime and accepted a political role.[4] We also learn that he has been diagnosed with lung cancer and he asked his daughter to come to his office in order to transfer the ownership of properties and a bank account to her.

One might infer that the pressure of ill health is the primary motivation for Father's request for a meeting with his daughter after their long separation, but it is Santiago, and not Father, who reveals that he is ill. Knowledge of her father's illness motivates Daughter to stay and talk to him because, as Santiago points out to her, she may not get another opportunity in the future (*Punto*, scene six). The analysis that follows demonstrates how the reunion depicted on stage reaches a crisis point as Daughter seems to seek out commemoration whereas her father seems to shun it. The play, the difficult reunion and the stark contrast in experiences of commemoration portrayed demonstrate the need for possibilities for commemoration to be negotiated between individuals and the state. *Punto y coma* interacts with the political context in Uruguay and is in dialogue with discourses on commemoration, the memory of the dictatorship and the transition to democracy.

The ongoing impact of the transition to democracy in Uruguay

In an interview with me, Golovchenko described how she wrote the play after hearing the story of a woman who was separated from her children when she went into exile in Spain (which many people were forced to do) during the civic-military dictatorship in Uruguay.[5] Following a military-backed presidential coup on 27 June 1973, Uruguay entered a period of severe political repression 'characterized by totalitarian control over the population, ensured by the widespread use of prolonged mass imprisonment and systematic torture' (Lessa 2013: 39). Those detained and tortured included political leaders, trade union members and student activists. Uruguay previously had a reputation for being a liberal, democratic and stable country but, as Lawrence Weschler, former political and cultural staff writer for the *New Yorker* (1981–2002), points out: 'From having been the freest nation in Latin America, Uruguay had transmogrified itself into the country with the highest per-capita rate of political incarceration anywhere on earth' (1991: 85). In her study on theatre and collective memory in Uruguay, Beatriz Walker points out that the onset of the dictatorship was so shocking for people in Uruguay precisely because it had a reputation of being a democratic, progressive and stable country (2007: 61).

After a long period of negotiations that culminated in the Pacto del Club Naval in 1984, the transition to democracy was agreed with elections scheduled for November that year. During these negotiations and in the democratic period that immediately followed, the military held 'residual power' (Lessa 2013: 133). The elected president, Julio María Sanguinetti from the centre-right Colorado party, sought to create a peaceful transition, which looked to a democratic future, rather than allowing for a reappraisal of the recent past. As a result, the scope for accountability for human rights violations, particularly relating to disappeared people, was extremely limited (134). This was the case both in formal judicial settings and in less formal ways in civil society discussions. However, social justice groups did begin to emerge and demand explanations and some of these are discussed later in this chapter.

The silence surrounding these cases was compounded and perpetuated by the Ley de Caducidad de la Pretensión Punitiva del Estado (1986) which was used to prohibit investigations into these crimes and 'articles one to four particularly ended the possibility of judicial proceedings for past human rights violations' (Lessa 2013: 137). However, the end of the twentieth and start of the twenty-first centuries saw increased demands from civil society for the prosecution of crimes committed during this period and for proper investigation into the cases of disappeared persons. This climate of change in relation to attitudes towards the human rights violations committed during the dictatorship, coupled with the idea of a family reconciliation and its possible unfolding, motivated Golovchenko to write the play (Golovchenko 2013).

Cara Levey examines how, towards the end of the twentieth century, there was increased awareness of the types of crimes committed during the dictatorship, particularly in neighbouring Argentina, where there were several high-profile public confessions from officials involved in the capture, torture and murder of people during the dictatorship (Levey 2014: 13). She states that 'this had notable repercussions in Uruguay – not least because the majority of disappearances of Uruguayans had taken place in Argentina' (ibid). In May 1996, there was a confession by former Uruguayan military officer Jorge Tróccoli that the armed forces had been responsible for the torture of civilians (ibid). Whilst this public articulation of the brutal acts committed by the armed forces was a significant step forward, as Francesca Lessa points out, it was not until much later in 2005, when Tabaré Vázquez entered office, that this paved the way for accountability (2013: 147–8). Tabaré Vázquez (2005–10) was the first president from the Frente Amplio, a left-wing coalition party that was rendered illegal during the dictatorship, and he was president of Uruguay again from 2015 to 2020. He enabled some investigations into human rights violations to occur and paved the way for people being brought to trial:

> The unprecedented stand on accountability adopted by left-wing presidents Vázquez and Mujica signaled [sic] a rupture with past governments' lack of interest in – if not a blatant obstruction of – accountability; the sustained activism of human rights groups who strategically tackled impunity from different angles, combined with international pressures regarding the Gelman case and the unprecedented discovery of the human remains of Uruguayans who had disappeared, forced the government to provide long-awaited answers regarding past crimes. (Lessa 2013: 147–8)

In the confrontation between Father and Daughter, *Punto y coma* explores the pernicious effect of the lack of dialogue about these cases, the lack of certainty about disappearances and the lack of public commemoration. By placing these conflicts centre stage, the play serves a commemorative function in enabling the two characters to tell their stories, which might link to the experiences of audience members.

Therefore, the dramatic space serves as a way to recognize those experiences whilst simultaneously inviting the audience to imagine if the seemingly opposing attitudes to commemoration embodied in Father and Daughter could be reconciled in the future.

The second aspect of this climate of change, which is inherently linked to the attempt to create a smooth transition to democracy, is that people had to work to find a new place within society, politically and professionally, and for many the transition was problematic, which is an idea explored in the play. Golovchenko (2013) explained in the same interview that it was a period when 'many people who were part of the resistance movement became part of the Establishment and there is a sort of contradiction in that'.[6] She linked this to the leader of the left-wing Frente Amplio government at the time, José Mujica. The former president of Uruguay (2010–15) is perhaps the most emblematic example of this process of transition; he was previously a member of the urban guerrilla movement Movimiento de Liberación Nacional – Tupamaros and was imprisoned during the military dictatorship. However, the memory of the past, the question of how it can be re-examined and commemorated, as well as the extent to which these transitions might still need to be negotiated all persist. Any act of commemoration of this period forces the Uruguayan society to acknowledge and confront difficult issues, such as the reintegration of people responsible for carrying out enforced imprisonments and disappearances, and the ongoing impact of these experiences on the victims of repression.[7]

Father and Daughter come into conflict with each other when discussing how they remember the past and what they choose to remember. Memory and forms of personal commemoration, particularly in relation to the disappearance of Mother, come to the forefront as central themes of the play as the characters are forced to acknowledge their shared past and to admit how they have dealt with their experiences of the loss of Mother. The use of flashbacks also means that memory constitutes an essential aspect of the dramatic form of the play and this challenges the audience to consider the ways in which the past shapes the present and the ways in which individuals construct the narrative of their family history within the context of a national narrative. Susana Kaiser, in her study of how young Argentineans of the post-dictatorship generation remember the period, points out that 'since we cannot remember everything, memory is highly selective' and an individual's memory is influenced by 'mechanisms of historical memory and amnesia' shaped by the state, official reports, historians, the media, community groups and local oral narratives (2005:10). She proposes that remembering and forgetting are both acts of creating memories about the dictatorship (ibid.). An individual decides how and what to remember within a complex framework of influences, pressures, political discourses and family histories. Daughter accuses her father of erasing their family history: 'You never bothered me. Fine. But for you to erase history, our history, you who were the protagonist. That I can't understand' (Golovchenko 2003a: 14).[8] Therefore, this is a criticism of his active choice about what to remember and how to do it, which is in conflict with her own choice and desire to actively keep the memory of her mother, and the injustice that she suffered, alive. It also raises the issue of how to commemorate a relative when there is a lack of certainty over what happened due to the absence of the dead body or indication of a grave; how can this absence be commemorated and shared with others through a commemorative practice? Their encounter in the senator's office creates a crisis point in which they are forced to discuss their choices and explore whether a reconciliation with each other and their ways of understanding the past is possible.

The crisis begins in scene four when Father enters his office and speaks to his daughter for the first time. Having already spoken to the assistant, Santiago, Daughter is angry that Santiago knows nothing about her father's past, which she interprets as an attempt to forget about it altogether: 'I never realized that silence could be such an anaesthetic. Obviously, I live in a different world to you. You close the door and you're on to the next thing' (Golovchenko 2003a: 13).[9] Her reference to living in a different world from her father implies both her criticism of the way he has distanced himself from his past, and her as the living memory of it, and the political sphere in which he now operates, which echoes her earlier criticism of politicians. This scene also reveals the pernicious effect of the separation and the lack of dialogue between the characters because Daughter blames her father for abandoning the family and accuses him of living a false existence:

> I'm the only one who knows what you're really like. I know your absence, your back, your silence. That's why it drives me mad when they speak so well of you. Nobody would ever imagine that behind your generous and kind appearance, there's a complete bastard. (Golovchenko 2003a: 13)[10]

The language employed shows the strength of Daughter's feeling of resentment, abandonment and anger towards her father. This tension and anger at the start of their encounter indicates the destructive impact of the lack of information and the silencing of past experiences. Furthermore, her father's ability to break with the past and his choice to forget about it are hurtful for Daughter because they undermine her experience, her existence and her efforts to keep the memory of her mother alive. The rift between them is, therefore, absolutely linked to the disappearance of Mother, which is revealed later in the play, but in this first encounter we witness the foregrounding of the rupture in the family, the complexity of reconciliation and the harm that a conscious effort to forget can have on others. The emphasis placed on the family, which could be read as a way for the audience to connect with the story, functions as a recognizable structure that criticizes the larger mechanisms of memory, silence and accountability on a national scale. Therefore, the play shows some of the characteristics of a 'state-of-the-nation play' as identified by Nadine Holdsworth in *Theatre and Nation* through the use of the family as a microcosm for a society as it 'wrestles with changing circumstances' (2010: 39).

Moments of crisis: The stage as a laboratory

Theorist and translator Antoine Vitez argues for the capacity of theatre to allow the audience to reach a point of crisis, which facilitates examination and questioning of accepted norms and discourses:

The stage is the laboratory of the language and actions of the nation. Society knows more or less clearly that in these edifices we call theatres people work for hours on end in order to increase, purify and transform the actions and intonations of everyday life, also to question them, bring them to crisis point. (qtd. in Pavis 1996: 127)

The play can be seen to operate as a laboratory in which the conflicting views of Father and Daughter are exposed and scrutinized so that the complexity of the issue of reconciliation with the past is paramount and a crisis point is reached through their confrontation.

Throughout the play, Mother's presence haunts their discussion and this adds to the sense of urgency in their meeting. Her presence also serves to intensify the feelings of loss: the flashbacks depict intimate family relationships, moments of fear and determination and so the audience is constantly reminded of what was at stake politically and personally in the past and what was then lost. Furthermore, her presence constantly brings the audience back to the question of memory: how does one commemorate those who are absent? This laboratory serves a dual function as the play questions both the narratives that Father and Daughter have created and accepted about the past and consequently provokes questions about the accepted national discourse surrounding the history of disappeared people and the transition to democracy. The crisis point is reached through the confrontation between Father and Daughter, who are challenged to understand another point of view and reflect upon their own and this, in turn, poses a challenge to the audience to examine their own stance.

Through a fictional encounter, rooted in a moment of political change and which draws on recognizable human concerns, Golovchenko proposes a re-examination of a period of recent Uruguayan history and offers the perspective of two people from different generations. Golovchenko emphasizes the ways in which this experience cuts across different generations by incorporating play and games into the fabric of the dramatic action. The latter root the scrutiny of the national narrative in the experience of the young woman. The author conveys the potency of the conflict between Father and Daughter by dramatizing a discussion on memory. In the next section, I demonstrate how the themes of memory and play intersect to provoke questions about commemoration.

In scene eight, Father reveals that he has physically, emotionally and politically distanced himself from everything that reminded him of his wife:

> I cut myself off completely. Even from you. I got rid of everything that belonged to your mother. Even my wedding ring. I distanced myself from everything that was a link to her. I rejected our friends, our comrades, the ideals we shared. I couldn't stand all those things that reminded me of her. (Golovchenko 2003a: 21)[11]

In contrast, Daughter has, along with her grandmother, dedicated her life to searching for her mother and to keeping her memory alive. She confesses that she has kept everything that belonged to her mother:

> I have all her things. Her clothes, her perfume, her photos cover the house. I have boxes, shoeboxes, drawers of keepsakes. I kept everything that you could possibly keep: newspaper cuttings, letters, censored books, postcards, bits of string, stones, beads, lip liner, brooches, records, everything. The house I live in is a museum to the memory of mum. (ibid.)[12]

This indicates a kind of personal commemorative practice provoked by the lack of the grave at which to mourn. Daughter instead focuses on objects associated with her mother by creating the museum in her mother's memory to capture elements of her life which would otherwise be forgotten. Daughter's museum indicates the difficulty of the lack of closure regarding what happened to her mother: could her determination to preserve these objects also be motivated by the hope and desire that her mother will one day be found alive and want to return to these things?

However, throughout scenes eight and nine, both of these ways of dealing with the past are shown to be incomplete as Daughter cannot move on and she states that she still detests anything to do with the military (Golovchenko 2003a: 23), whilst her father still sees Mother fleetingly in his everyday life and in his dreams (21). Daughter also refers to how Mother appears in her dreams but does not speak, and so the constant memory of her does not enable her to have any kind of intimacy or fulfilment when her mother appears to her (ibid.). In scene eight, Father and Daughter express the ways in which Mother continues to haunt their everyday life. The stage directions state that Mother can be in any part of the stage, and this is the only moment, apart from the very end of scene one, in which the three characters of the family appear together (20). Therefore, the way in which Mother remains a real yet incomplete presence in the daily lives of Father and Daughter is striking because Mother silently haunts them at this moment as they confess how they have sought to cope with this haunting.

In the rehearsed reading of *Ready or Not* (2017) directed by Chilean theatre practitioner and scholar, Camila Ymay González, the hiding place, located in the past, where the flashbacks occurred was located upstage whilst the present-day encounter took place downstage to create two different spaces without imposing a divide. The actor playing Mother remained on stage in the hiding place at all times and so from the point of view of the spectator, she was always present. This enhanced the commemorative function of the theatre space as her constant presence and significant role in the play demonstrated the impossibility of forgetting the past and the persistence of memories. Diana Taylor's (1997: 30) study of theatre in Argentina during and after the dictatorship identifies that the memory of this state-executed violence constantly haunts the nation thus seeping into everyday reality and artistic representation: the spectre of the past is constantly present. The mother's constant physical presence on stage therefore served to challenge the idea that she has disappeared as we witnessed her physical intervention, yet it also acted as a constant reminder of this enforced absence and the need for her family to conjure up her memory and find ways to commemorate her.

Neither one of the characters is fulfilled by or satisfied with the strategy that they have adopted to deal with their memories of Mother. The contrast in the strategies adopted by Father and Daughter is evident, and the sense of loss destabilizes their respective everyday lives. The audience is presented with a sense of incompleteness in their coping mechanisms. This points to an incompleteness in the narrative created by the state about the disappeared which has left many questions unanswered and prevented the development of discourses in society which would enable families affected to articulate their experiences and create ways to commemorate the past.

As the discussion progresses, both characters admit that they admire each other, that constant distancing and constant remembering are cumbersome tasks and that they see the advantages of the strategy adopted by the other person. The instability that results from their respective approaches to dealing with the memory of the past becomes evident and indicates the need for a more nuanced approach. Father states that 'forgetting is an exercise and after a while, you see the results' (Golovchenko 2003a: 23).[13] As discussed earlier, the emphasis on forgetting was implemented on a national scale through the continued application of the Ley de Caducidad (there were two failed referendums to revoke it in 1989 and 2009, the second one took place after this play was written). This provided the apparatus which enabled a national exercise of forgetting to occur. The play highlights that it is necessary to find a way to confront loss and to create a national context that allows for a dialogue about that loss. The climate of change in Uruguay in which members of the society increasingly demanded explanations and denounced the injustice provided an opportunity for Golovchenko to write about this issue as a way to encourage people to seek more complex strategies for dealing with the recent past.

Gabriela Fried Amilivia (2011) refers to the 'interesting irony' of the recurring 'waves' of memories of the disappeared given the official efforts to suppress them. She adds that this demonstrates

> the underlying conflicts of the unresolved past woven into the fabric of the contemporary culture and politics, the effects of unprocessed experience that slowly simmered in the undercurrents of collective memory, occupying subjective and intersubjective intimate spaces, surviving and being sustained in the secrecy of everyday relationships of individuals, families and communities touched by state repression. (161)

Given the emphasis that Fried Amilivia places on the importance of families in sustaining memory, it is significant that Golovchenko tells the story by depicting members of the family unit at a point of crisis as a way to provoke questions about the 'actions and intonations of everyday life' on a broader, national scale (Pavis 1996: 127).

As an audience member, one is able to gain a retrospective understanding of the devastating rupture that Daughter's separation from her parents causes. However, for the young girl seen in the flashbacks, when both Mother and Father leave, their separation is framed as a game of hide and seek. For example, in scene two, after Father has left, Mother says that Father is hiding and warns her daughter that if they go to hide with him then they risk giving him away, just as in the game. At the end of the play, the mother leaves and one infers from her urgency that she knows that she is about to be arrested because she says, 'but they're going to come and I don't want them to find me here' (Golovchenko 2003a: 30).[14] As she prepares to leave, the moment is also framed as part of the game of hide and seek: 'So you can start counting now. I'm going to hide. But don't look for me. I'm going to be hiding somewhere around here for a long time' (ibid.).[15] She reassures her daughter that she prefers the game when she can hide rather than count and seek out the other players and so her daughter must ensure that she never gives her mother away, just like with her father. The repetition of this game throughout the flashbacks demonstrates the important role that it served in enabling Daughter to gain some understanding of the political situation and the role that she had to play in it. The emphasis placed on the game in the final moments of the play, coupled with the way in which Daughter accepts her mother's explanation for leaving her in the care of her grandmother, suggests that by framing the political narrative as a game of hide and seek, the mother has been training and preparing her daughter for this moment of separation. This creates an incredibly poignant moment at the end of the play, as Daughter is completely alone on stage.

Daughter remains alone on stage, having completed her counting. The title of the play comes from this moment in which Daughter calls out: 'Punto y raya, el que se escondió se calla; punto y coma, el que no se escondió se embroma' (Golovchenko 2003a: 31). This is a warning that she is about to start searching for the other players: those who have hidden should remain quiet and those who have not found a place to hide are in trouble. It therefore captures the moment of the game encapsulated in the more succinct version used in British English: ready or not, here I come. For this reason, in my translation into English, I have entitled the play *Ready or Not* as a way to capture the importance of this game in constructing the childhood narrative of the separation of the family members. This playfulness is also present in the dramatic structure of the play as the dialogue links scenes, meaning that a question posed in a scene in the refuge is then answered in the present-day senator's office. Golovchenko weaves the scenes together so that, even though the dialogue occurs in two distinct places and times, the actors move between these zones through the lines that they speak and this enables the transitions between past and present to occur. For example, in the last line of scene two, Santiago asks, 'and why did you come now?'[16] and at the start of scene three, which is a flashback to her time in the refuge with Mother, Daughter says, 'I want to see him' (8).[17] Daughter's line serves as not only a response to Santiago's question in the present but also as the first line of a new discussion with Mother in the past. In this way, the dialogue evokes the interconnectedness of past and present and creates a dramatic dialogue between the two. This sense of continuity enables both the actor and the spectator to move between the two spaces and times. Another translation that I considered for the title of the play was a more literal one: *semicolon*. This solution loses the idea of play, which, as my analysis has demonstrated, is central to *Punto y coma*. However, it does conjure up the sense of these unfinished moments between past and present, during which there is no sense of closure on the past but more of a hiatus or a pause.

In scene ten, the audience witness another important game when Daughter teaches her mother to make a wish. Daughter says that she learnt it from her schoolfriend, Santiago. His name is the last word spoken in scene ten and the first word of scene eleven as Father says, 'Santiago, could you take these papers to Mr Ugalde?' (Golovchenko 2003a: 26).[18] This is the first mention of the young assistant's name and Father reveals that he was Daughter's childhood playmate. He qualifies it by adding, 'you see it's impossible to cut off everything?' (ibid.).[19] Santiago's presence in the play, and the fact that he says that his own father was a good friend of the senator's (5) provokes questions about other experiences of the dictatorship and the following years, and the possibilities open to those who lived through that time. It reinforces the idea that each person had to negotiate their way in the newly formed democratic society. Santiago's attitudes seem to be in conflict with Daughter's, both politically and personally, as he reveals that he has not kept anything from his childhood, whilst she states that she is 'a depository of keepsakes' (28).[20]

Santiago's character serves to remind the audience of the plurality of intertwined, disrupted narratives which is evidenced in the context of Uruguayan society as the post-dictatorship generations have sought ways to speak out about how their families were affected. Levey's (2014) study, titled 'Of HIJOS and Niños: Revisiting Postmemory in Post-Dictatorship Uruguay', details the emergence of different groups of young people who came together in the post-dictatorship generation to find a shared space to discuss their experiences. HIJOS (Sons and Daughters), formed in 1996, is made up of the children of people who were victims of the dictatorship (ibid.: 6). They actively seek more information about their parents if they disappeared and demand justice for their disappearance. Niños en Cautiverio Político (Children in Political Captivity) was formed in 2007 by young people imprisoned or born whilst their parents were incarcerated (ibid.). The formation of these groups underscores the repetitions of repressive acts of violence that disrupted and distorted family units and, at the same time, emphasizes the need to understand the distinct experiences and stories of individuals and families affected. They are another example of civil society seeking to carve out a space in which to ask questions, tackle the crisis of the absence of dialogue and understand more of their fragmented family narratives.

Towards the end of *Punto y coma*, Father says, 'if for a moment we forget our feelings of resentment, we seem so close' (Golovchenko 2003a: 23).[21] Daughter responds, 'we seem', but her sentence remains unfinished and this is indicative of her conflicting feelings as she seems drawn towards her father's exercise in forgetting yet she is unable to leave her past and the disappearance of Mother unresolved (ibid.).[22] Golovchenko indicates the national context in the positions adopted by Father and Daughter in the play as for many years the Ley de Caducidad facilitated this forgetting. In the play, there are two references to an upcoming vote on a new law: one at the beginning, and a second one near the end of the play (3 and 30). These can be seen to allude to the Ley de Caducidad but Father never explicitly states how he will vote and so it is left to the audience to decide if the conversation with his daughter and, through her, a reconnection to the past might have an influence upon his decision.

At the end of the play, Father gives Daughter contracts which transfer the ownership of properties to her, but the audience must decide if this is a moment of reconciliation or conflict. It provokes challenging questions about what is important to leave as an inheritance for the next generation. It serves to reinforce the centrality of family connections and the way in which a national context of change, combined with the pressure of ill health, could provoke the re-examination of relationships, feelings of guilt and ideas around legacy. The idea of legacy is present in a different way in the home-made museum that Daughter refers to, which commemorates her mother. It provokes us to question how individual stories, experiences of loss and memories of people might be told and commemorated in years to come. Through the conflict between Father and Daughter, the play itself draws attention to and critiques different practices of commemoration whilst placing emphasis primarily on the importance of dialogue and opening a space for discussion. This is something that the dramatic action of the play does and has the possibility to provoke in the audience thus enlivening and demonstrating both the storytelling power and political potential of theatre.

Concluding remarks

Punto y coma portrays two family members who have adopted contrasting strategies for dealing with the memory of the dictatorship and the disappearance of the mother; the play demonstrates how the 'actions and intonations' (Pavis 1996: 127) of their everyday lives reach a crisis point through their encounter. The play can be inserted into a narrative created by the state which silenced discussions around human rights violations and instead sought to focus on the future, and Father seems to adopt this approach. The conflict that arises indicates the harmful effects of the lack of dialogue about the past, which creates rifts and crises. *Punto y coma* serves a commemorative function by depicting characters who voice their experiences and so pose a challenge to the state's attempt to silence these discussions. The play enacts and indicates the need in Uruguayan society for a more nuanced discourse around the aftermath of the dictatorship and the transition to democracy, which takes into account different versions of the past. It underlines the importance of negotiating how these narratives can feed into ways of commemorating the recent past. The dramatic action reveals the need for spaces in which members of the Uruguayan society can discuss their memories, pose questions about the losses of the past and rediscover their own incomplete family narratives. Through the exploration of reconciliation with an estranged family member, Golovchenko's play draws into question the reconciliation of the multiplicity of personal narratives and advocates both for a broader discursive framework and more spaces in society in which they can be interrogated and commemorated.

Notes

1. All quotations are taken from this version of the text. Since completing the research and writing of this chapter, and my translation into English, *Punto y coma* has been published in an anthology of work by Golovchenko (2021). Some of the analysis published in this chapter is also published in Stevens (2022).
2. 'Tenés que irte'; 'Ellos saben ponerse en nuestro lugar y actúan rápidamente.'
3. 'Estoy en contra de la clase política.'
4. 'Me fueron a buscar a mi casa. A esa altura yo ya me había peleado con todo el mundo. No lo pensé mucho. Necesitaba creer en otra cosa.'
5. I conducted the interview with Estela Golovchenko on 17 October 2013 in Spanish.

6. Ibid.
7. During the process of editing this chapter, twenty-four ex-officials, including Jorge Tróccoli who went into exile in Italy, were sentenced by the Court of Appeal in Rome to life imprisonment for their role in the systematic repression carried out in Latin America. See 'Italy Court Sentences 24 behind Dictators' Murder Pact', BBC News, 2019.
8. 'Nunca me molestaste, todo bien. Pero que borres la historia, nuestra historia, vos que fuiste protagonista, eso sí que no lo puedo entender.'
9. 'Nunca me había dado cuenta hasta qué punto el silencio funciona como anestesia. Claro, me muevo en otro círculo. Se baja la barrera y a otra cosa mariposa.'
10. 'Soy la única que te conoce tal cual sos. Conozco tu ausencia, tu espalda, tu silencio. Por eso me revienta cuando hablan bien de vos. Nadie se imagina que detrás de esa apariencia amable y campechana que tenés, hay un hijo de puta.'
11. 'Me aislé totalmente. Hasta de vos … Me deshice de todo lo que tenía de tu madre. Hasta del anillo de casamiento. Me alejé de todo lo que me vinculara a ella. Sentía rechazo por nuestros amigos, los compañeros de lucha, los ideales que tuvimos. No pude soportar reencontrarme con todo lo que me hacía recordarla.'
12. 'Tengo todo lo que era suyo. Su ropa, su perfume, sus fotos están por toda la casa. Tengo cajas, cajitas, cajones de recuerdos. Guardé todo lo que se podía guardar: recortes de diarios, cartas, libros censurados, postales, cuerditas, piedras, collares de mostacillas, lápices de labios, prendedores, discos, todo. La casa donde vivo es el museo de la memoria de mamá.'
13. 'el olvido es un ejercicio y termina dando resultado'.
14. 'Pero van a venir y no quiero que me encuentren aquí.'
15. 'Entonces ponete a contar ahora. Yo me voy a esconder. Pero no me busques. Voy a estar mucho tiempo escondida por ahí.'
16. '¿Y ahora, ¿por qué viniste?'
17. 'Quiero verlo.'
18. '¿Santiago, ¿le llevás estos papeles a Ugalde?'
19. '¿Ves que es imposible cortar con todo?'
20. 'Soy un depósito de recuerdos.'
21. 'Si por un momento nos olvidamos de nuestros rencores, parece que estuviéramos tan cerca.'
22. 'Parece.'

References

Duffau, M., and G. Gómez (eds). (2011), *Premio Autor Nacional COFONTE: Dramaturgia 2002-2005-2006*, Montevideo: COFONTE.

Fried Amilivia, G. (2011), 'Private Transmission of the Traumatic Memories of the Disappeared in the Context of Transitional Politics of Oblivion in Uruguay (1973-2001): Pedagogies of Horror among Uruguayan Families', in F. Lessa and V. Druliolle (eds), *The Memory of State Terrorism in the Southern Cone: Argentina, Chile and Uruguay*, 157-77, New York: Palgrave Macmillan.

Golovchenko, E. (2003a), *Punto y coma*, 'Dramática Latinoamericana', CELCIT. Available online:www.celcit.org.ar/publicaciones/biblioteca-teatral-dla/?q=golovchenko&f=&m= (accessed 18 October 2020).

Golovchenko. E. (2003b), 'Punto y coma', *Dramaturgia Uruguaya*. Available online: https://dramaturgiauruguaya.uy/punto-y-coma (accessed 17 October 2020).
Golovchenko, E. (2013), Interview conducted in Spanish, Montevideo.
Golovchenko, E. (2021), *Estela Golovchenko: Teatro*, Montevideo: Editorial fin de Siglo.
Holdsworth, N. (2010), *Theatre & Nation*, Basingstoke: Palgrave Macmillan.
'Italy Court Sentences 24 behind Dictators' Murder Pact' (2019), *BBC News*, 9 July. Available online: www.bbc.co.uk/news/world-latin-america-48920905 (accessed 12 July 2019).
Kaiser, S. (2005), *Postmemories of Terror*, New York: Palgrave Macmillan.
Lessa, F. (2013), *Memory and Transitional Justice in Argentina and Uruguay: Against Impunity*, New York: Palgrave Macmillan.
Levey, C. (2014), 'Of HIJOS and Niños: Revisiting Postmemory in Post-Dictatorship Uruguay', *History & Memory*, 26 (2): 5–39.
Mirza, R. (2009), 'Escenificaciones de la memoria en el teatro de la postdictadura: *Pedro y el Capitán, Elena Quinteros. Presente* y *Las cartas que no llegaron*', in R. Mirza and G. Remedi (eds), *La dictadura contra las tablas: Teatro uruguayo e historia reciente*, 37–81, Montevideo: Biblioteca Nacional.
Out of the Wings Festival. Available online: www.ootwfestival.com/festival-2017 (accessed 19 December 2021).
Pavis, P. (1996), 'The Duty to Translate: An Interview with Antoine Vitez', in P. Pavis (ed.), *The Intercultural Performance Reader*, 121–30, London: Routledge.
Stevens, S. (2022), *Uruguayan Theatre in Translation: Theory and Practice*, Cambridge: Legenda.
Taylor, D. (1997), *Disappearing Acts: Spectacles of Gender and Nationalism in Argentina's 'Dirty War'*, Durham, NC: Duke University Press.
Walker, B. (2007), *Benedetti, Rosencof, Varela: El teatro como guardián de la memoria colectiva*, Buenos Aires: Ediciones Corregidor.
Weschler, L. (1991), *A Miracle, A Universe: Settling Accounts with Torturers*, New York: Penguin Books.

Part 2

Disruptive Lessons: Thinking through the Affects of Memory

5

Know thy enemy: Wajdi Mouawad on history, memory and reconciliation at *La Colline*

Yana Meerzon

Linda Gaboriau, the English-language translator of Wajdi Mouawad's theatre, once said that writers 'are the witnesses of our time. They're people who really take the time to look more deeply into what's going on in human nature or in the political [and] social world around us' (in Giammaria 2019). Wajdi Mouawad is one such writer. A Christian Maronite theatre artist, he was born in Lebanon in 1968. He experienced the plight of war and exile at a very early age, when his family flew to France in 1978 and then, after they were refused necessary papers, to Montréal in 1983. In his plays, productions and novels, Mouawad uses storytelling to create a trace of the present and to commemorate the past, so his theatre often stages the present of today as the past of tomorrow. But history, to echo the title of his 2017 play *Tous des oiseaux*[1] (Birds of a Kind), can be of many kinds. It can be 'monumental' (Foucault 1977), as that of states and their governments; and it can be personal, as that of people. To Mouawad, a private history of a single family can turn into a special set of echoings, memories and secrets, in which a monumental story of making or dismantling a nation is reflected and revealed. This premise made his tetralogy *Le Sang des promesses* (including *Littoral* (1997), *Incendies* (2003), *Forêts* (2006) and *Ciels* (2009)) famous. Recent history with its global wars, mass migration and hatred of the other deeply marks each of its conflicts. It makes protagonists of each play responsible for setting this history right against their will or knowledge. In Mouawad's new play, *Tous des oiseaux*, a convoluted history of one family unfolds through decades of hidden truths and errors as well. It turns into a troublesome inheritance, which the young generation is called to understand and commemorate. Unpacking layers of lies that make the story of their family allows Mouawad's protagonists challenge the idea of nationhood and national identity as something fixed and singular. Mouawad turns the commemorative site of a family history into a symbolic image of a nation as something fluid, constantly rediscovering its past and readjusting itself in the present. In these functions, Mouawad's theatre serves as a warning sign. It rises against commemoration as problematic propaganda used by the ideologists of nationalism, and it appears critically conscious.

To discuss how Mouawad participates in the documentation and construction of national histories by means of commemorative activity that is deployed through performance and as performance, as suggested by the current collection, I offer a two-part argument. First, I examine how Mouawad's work as an artistic director of *La Colline – théâtre national* (the National Theatre of La Colline) in Paris, exemplifies an act of 'national mimesis', a cultural activity of 'representing the nation as well as the result of it (an image of the nation)' (Hurley 2011: 24). Then, I study *Tous des oiseaux* as an example of a philosophical treatise of reconciliation, a theatre work in which the artist's personal agenda to 'know thy enemy' is imagined and re-enacted.

La Colline: staging thy enemy

Named an artistic director of La Colline on 6 April 2016, Mouawad began his term with a political manifesto symbolically named *Ode à l'ennemi*, in which he summarized the artistic and pedagogical programme of his five-year appointment. Asked to explain why he moved to France in 2012, Mouawad cited personal reasons, as his wife lived in France, but also professional and cultural. After his prolific work in Montreal, Mouawad acted as an artistic director of the French Theatre of the National Arts Centre in Ottawa (2007–12). Since 2011, he served as an associate artist of Grand T, *Théâtre de Loire-Atlantique de Nantes*, to later cite the liberating nature of the French theatrical milieu close to his own cultural sensibilities of a Mediterranean man (Salino 2016b: 14). Mouawad interpreted his role as an artistic director of La Colline theatre as an opportunity to use this public forum to share his personal experience of being the Other and to question the hostility toward this Other, the migrant and the foreigner, in Europe. Aiming to change this marginal position of a migrant artist in French theatre, Mouawad decided to stage today's France in the gesture of national mimesis, both as a nation of a colonial past and of a migratory present.

To Mouawad, re-enforcing, questioning and commemorating this complex and violent history of oppression is the primary responsibility that La Colline, a state-funded cultural institution, must assume. To be politically relevant, it must address questions of anti-globalization, xenophobia and racism, which feed the ideology of today's nationalistic movements. Mouawad's own plays warn their audiences of the new nationalists' aggression towards 'the current globalist world order' and denounce their wish 'to restore the integrity of ... national borders and sovereignty' (Tirley 2018: 160). He is cognizant of the dangers in seeking religious fundamentalism, which leads to rejecting the 'secular aristocracy' of the global order (160); and he is weary of the nationalists' reaffirmation of the shared language (161). Recognizing their drive to unite 'against *globalism*', to act as 'radically *populist*' (i.e. reject international elite for the sake of common people), and to seek re-traditionalization of everyday life, identified by new nationalists as 'the spiritual awakening of the nation under a *religious* sentiment, which can lead to economic, cultural, and eventually a demographic spurge' (162; emphasis in original), Mouawad is deeply conscious of the multiplicity of histories and experiences that make up today's world. In his work, he insists on the hegemony of the Other, be this Other a refugee or a second-generation immigrant, and seeks the truth of the past. He stands ready to accuse the present and to fight the political right to come. 'There is an undeniable generosity in this artist', one of Mouawad's critics wrote. His artful productions 'never stop moving on the roads of reconciliation – the

Christian child Maronite thrown out of his country, Mouawad keeps searching and discovering [this reconciliation] in his theatre, in the books he writes, and the films he makes' (Salino 2016a: 18).

To translate his personal political stand into the artistic programme of La Colline, Mouawad introduced radical changes in the company's repertoire. In his unpublished manifesto *Le Pacte* (2016), Mouawad put forward his political and artistic programme (Diaz 2018: 137–9), which included internationalization of La Colline's programming, creation of stronger ties with youth, bringing in new audiences, mostly first-generation immigrants and their families, and fostering new dramaturgy. This four-step strategy stipulated Mouawad's wish to stage an image of a new France of displacement and migration. He identified the concept of *rencontre* as the leading principle of his administration and the major dramaturgical device of his writing (138).

The first two seasons (and the subsequent ones) that Mouawad programmed clearly reflect these objectives. Questions of what makes European identity and how its new history is created and experienced through peoples' displacements characterize their thematic through-line. Working with youth, both as the protagonists of his own plays and as the focus groups of the company's outreach work, constitutes its pedagogy. Developing new dramatic work created by immigrants or the artists of colour presents a sum of Mouawad's personal project of 'national mimesis', in which he turns the stage of a French national theatre into a space where each of its nation's subjects can re-enact and commemorate their personal histories, as well as re-imagine and re-enact their nation.

National mimesis can be as much an ideological concept as it is artistic. It refers to the work of cultural production, which 'opens the national field to marginalized constituencies and cultural productions' (Hurley 2011: 24). It demonstrates that because these marginalized constituencies are not cultural dominants, they 'are not immediately recognizable as nationally "authentic"' (ibid.). In their themes, subject matter and stylistics, the works of national mimesis often reflect the governing philosophy of the state and rely on a normalization of the existing artistic structures, dedicated to constructing a national theatre canon and its commitment to 'building a sense of national destiny' (Salter 1991: 12). However, national mimesis does not need to be 'limited to a reproductive or imitative iconic mode' (Hurley 2011: 24). It can also mobilize 'metonymy and simulation' to indicate 'dissimilarity or usage instead of on resemblance' between the subject matter, the nation and its image (24).

In Mouawad's project of national mimesis, La Colline must address the vital questions of today's France, including identity crisis, loss of historical memory and rising xenophobia. Thus, he declares a 'figure of enemy' as the focus subject of his artistic programming. Migrants, refugees, poor and underprivileged, ethnic and religious others, who have become the scapegoats of neo-liberal economics and politics, of media and pro-nationalist groups, are the 'enemies' who Mouawad desires to bring centre stage. He fights not only the derogatory labels and negative discourses of the other, but also the 'deafness of the educated' (Mouawad 2017–18), because, as Mouawad writes, it is the duty of the 'literary people in France' to ask

> How and to what extent have we become disconnected from those fellow citizens whose voices, words, disarray, anger, and rejection of us we no longer hear? How

can we understand that before trying to bring in those spectators who never come to our theatres, we must realize a degree of disgust we generate with many of them, ... because we no longer see the severity, drought, lack of hospitality and carelessness of our own world and inner-self? ... How can we wake up? How can we reverse the perspective? (2017–18)

Connected to these failures of social and political reconciliation, Mouawad continues, is a necessity of realization that among these enemies are also those who support 'Brexit. Trump. Far right'. Paradoxically, he insists, if in our work 'we desire to show the violence of the world and the way in which this world grinds the most fragile among us, we must realize that those whom we name enemies and who vote for withdrawal, rejection and nationalism are precisely the children, the brothers, the sisters, the parents, of these characters that we claim to defend' (Mouawad 2017–18). The question we must ask is: 'what dramatic texts one must write knowing that those who we want to address, these other enemies, will never read them?' (2017–18).

These concerns are very personal to Mouawad, as he realizes that among spectators of La Colline there are also those who are convinced that he 'squanders public money', and that he, the foreigner himself, has taken 'the place and the job of a Frenchman' (2017–18). His response to such hypothetical but possible accusations is to do theatre, 'to open up to the world' and to plunge 'into the battle, using forces of hospitality, generosity, attention, welcome, listening, speech, fragility, sensitivity, emotions, stories, and beauty' (2017–18). In his plays, Mouawad calls 'to assert that the Other [is] our watchword, lookout and destination, both for ourselves and for the enemy' (2017–18). To support this statement, in his 2017 *Tous des oiseaux*, Mouawad tells the story of one's search for this ultimate other, which must become today's true history.

Tous des oiseaux: On dramaturgy of reconciliation and commemoration

'It has been a long time since we had seen a creation of such a scale', wrote Dominique Poncet when reviewing *Tous des oiseaux*. In this play, Mouawad 'takes us to the heart of political, existential, and religious debates that upset today's citizens' (Poncet 2017). A tragedy of reconciliation, the play argues that to fix the present the truth of the past must be revealed, questioned and justified. A story of today's Romeo and Juliet, it unfolds on the historical backdrop of one Jewish family across three generations and continents, between New York, Berlin and Jerusalem. A multilingual performance, *Tous des oiseaux* continues Mouawad's autobiographical project of exile. It dramatizes the child's disengagement from the land, the language and the customs of their ancestors. In the centre of its philosophical debate is the issue of multiple truths, which can differently apply to and be defended by the members of one family. So, the play builds on the theatricalization of collective and individual memory, as well as objectification and fictionalization of a communal history. Pierre Nora's concept *lieux de mémoire* (sites of memory), 'where memory crystallizes and secretes itself' and where 'a sense of historical continuity persists' (Nora 1989: 7), applies to both the historical spaces of the play's action (including the onstage Jerusalem where the family secrets are uncovered and the off stage of Wahida's newly discovered Ramallah) and the symbolic space of the parable of the Amphibian Bird (as told by Leo Africanus), in which an improbable encounter and a reconciliation of the enemies take place. Seen through the prism of Nora's concept of history as a site of memory, *Tous des oiseaux* presents its characters both as witnesses to the burdens of history and as its victims.

Stylistically, as with Mouawad's other works, *Tous des oiseaux* appears under the influence of Romantic tragedy, which investigated, imagined and staged the struggles of an individual in the face of a collective catastrophe. The tragic conflict that moves the plot of this play forward focuses on the ethical struggles of each protagonist, and thus, it aligns Mouawad's work with Friedrich Hegel's reading of modern tragedy (2000: 323-6). Hegel, a philosopher of German idealism, argues that Romantic tragedy focuses on 'the personal aspect of suffering and passions' (323). This conflict however should be considered within a broader context of 'the family, the State, [and] the Church' (323), although the subject of dramatic scrutiny remains with 'the inner experience of their heart [the heart of each single individual- YM] and individual emotion, or the particular qualities of their personality, which insist on satisfaction' (324). Unlike the characters of the classical Greek tragedy, whose ethical pathos stems from 'their own already formed personality', the characters of the Romantic tragedy emerge from 'within a wide expanse of contingent relations and conditions', so that the conflict they face 'abides within the *character* itself' (325).

Similarly, Mouawad's *Tous des oiseaux* presents its characters responsible for setting their history right but also guilty in their ethical pathos of righteousness and arrogance. Inspired by the author's personal story of the exilic flight, *Tous des oiseaux* also escalates the suffering of its protagonists to the tragedy of abandoned childhood. Mouawad's characters 'bear the heavy legacy of their parents' fate, along with the ethical sense of responsibility and the tragic sense of belonging' (Telmissany 2012: 54). It is not by chance that Mouawad chooses to preface his play with an excerpt from Sophocles' *Antigone*, which Hegel considered an example of an ideal tragedy (Hegel 2000: 322).

In its historical references, *Tous des oiseaux* draws an image of today's world, in which the Israeli-Palestinian conflict acquires a particular significance: not only does it exclusively mark Mouawad's biography of war and determines his political sensibilities, but it is also specific to the Western construction of the post 9/11 figure of enemy (Diaz 2018: 141-7). At the same time, the play elevates a history of today's ethnic and religious hatred to the level of a philosophical parable. To a certain degree, it reminds one of Gotthold Ephraim Lessing's *Nathan the Wise* (1779), in which he put forward the philosophical utopia of the Enlightenment. In *Tous des oiseaux*, much like in Lessing's tale, multiple truths coexist but are impossible to reconcile. These multiple truths not only define the tragic quest of each of the play's characters, but also leave them no choice but explore and mourn their parents' past.

On patricide

The play begins when Eitan, a young German scientist of Jewish background, who wants to dedicate his life to 'understanding the origins of the species' (Mouawad

2018: 11), decides to introduce Wahida, an Arab-American student at Columbia University, who recognizes the concept of shifting identity as 'a dissimulation' (16), to his family. Eitan's father, David, a Jew of traditional beliefs, condemns this love and partnership because of the religious and cultural differences between the young people. To David, Eitan's life duty lies with the guilt of the survivor, which all Jewish people must share. This guilt imposes an obligation: Eitan must marry a Jewish woman to ensure a continuation of his tribe and his family. To David, therefore, Eitan falling in love with someone of a non-Jewish origin and specifically an Arab is an act of a diasporic treason: 'you're participating in the disappearance [of the Jewish people - YM] and you're not ashamed' (32), David says. 'You're insulting us and you're insulting your grandfather's memory' (32), a survivor of the Holocaust. Even more, you are committing a patricide (38).

To the scientist Eitan, this argument does not make much sense: 'suffering cannot be transmitted from one generation to another!' he believes; 'the experiences of a human being during his lifetime do not affect his chromosomes, no matter how brutal those experiences are!' (Mouawad 2018: 35–6). To prove his point, Eitan collects the DNA of his parents only to discover a larger secret that makes up his identity and the story of his family. To untangle these secrets Eitan must travel to Jerusalem. However, as Eitan and Wahida arrive in the country, they fall victims to a terrorist attack on the Allenby Bridge, which connects the Palestinians of the West Bank and Jordan. Eitan ends up in the Israeli hospital in coma, while Wahida is left to bring his estranged family together. In the second part of the play, the history and the truth, different from each character, resurface. They cause repercussions impossible for either of the characters to reconcile, with many of them falling to the tragic guilt of personal arrogance and orthodoxy.

A truth-seeker, Eitan serves as a hero to this modern tragedy. An avenger of his family's name and traditions, he is someone who has sworn the oath of obedience and so is possessed by a singular ethical pathos. This pathos corresponds to Eitan's personality: a typical Romantic hero, he comes to conflict with every other pathos of every other character who surrounds him. These other characters also demand recognition, so *Tous des oiseaux* exemplifies a modern tragedy based on a collision and a collapse of multiple pathos (Hegel 2000: 324–5). The play stages its every character driven by their own moral claims and personal truths.

However, it is Eitan's ethical pathos that moves the action forward. Revealed through the symbolism of his Hebrew name, Eitan emerges as strong and enduring, but may be not too wise. As he initiates his family's collective journey into the past, on his path of righteousness Eitan becomes unstoppable. In his arrogance, he reminds of Sophocles' Oedipus blind to his own sins. His tenacity to bring his family's elders to atone for their past, no matter the sacrifices he needs to make and the suffering they might endure, constitutes Eitan's tragic fault. When he finally discovers the truth, Eitan also commits a patricide: the truth he uncovered crashes the world of his father.

When David learns the truth of his origins – born Palestinian, he was raised as a Jew – he loses his sense of self and suffers a fatal stroke. As stubborn as Eitan, David dies without reconciliation with his family or with his beliefs. Instead, it is Eitan who undergoes a major transformation. Mouawad depicts Eitan at David's funeral delivering a *kaddish* of his own making (Mouawad 2018: 110). Eitan accepts that his own pathos is different from that of his father; but he also admits that the final reconciliation is not possible unless it attains a political dimension. As long as the Jews and the Arabs are at war with each other and as long as Israel and Palestine fight, his personal reconciliation is not going to take place (111). Here Mouawad goes beyond Hegelian views of Romantic tragedy: for him the personal ethos of his tragic character is inseparable from the movements of history, and thus it is always political. Eitan's *kaddish* brings this idea forward:

> I will live my life and it will be what it will be, whole and ardent, but on the threshold of your death, I promise you: as long as your two names entwined in carnage, as long as their two languages battle in blood, I, Eitan, son of Norah and David, grandson of Leah and Etgar, the heir of two peoples who are tearing each other apart, I will not be consoled. (Mouawad 2018: 111)

This personal oath can neither be broken nor brought to fruition, as long as the two peoples – the Jews and the Arabs – who make Eitan's blood continue fighting at each other's throats. Linked to this monologue is Mouawad's view of theatre as a place of metaphysical conflict and reconciliation: a complex triumvirate of memory, forgetting and forgiveness (Ricouer 2004). As Mouawad explains, *Tous des oiseaux* speaks as much about the Israel–Palestine controversies and conflicts, which Mouawad regards personally, as about our new historical condition, with thousands of people on the move, seeking new attachments and histories (Mouawad in Farcet 2017: 11). The true knowledge of one's origin is a possible cure that Mouawad seems to offer, as it can help people stand united as the world is falling apart. At the beginning of the play, all its major characters are deprived of such knowledge. Standing in front of Eitan's apartment and unable to knock at its door to join the family's Seder, which Eitan called into her name, Wahida summarizes their shared sense of historical liminality. She wonders 'whether people [her] age aren't all like that, caught between two storeys, listening to dreams collapse' (Mouawad 2018: 37). When Eitan discovers that David, his Jewish father, was born Palestinian, 'a historical chasm opens, sorrows rise, and the necessity of the truth becomes as hot as a hot iron' (Mouawad in Farcet 2017: 8). To Mouawad, to stay away from this truth is not possible: even if Eitan believes that suffering is not transmissible by the chromosomes, 'history penetrates the very heart of his existence, that thing he thought was his identity' (8).

David's anger towards Palestinians and his thirst for punishment serve as another take on Eitan's theory about suffering and the chromosomes. Raised as a Jew without knowledge of his true origins, David is the product of nurture not nature. During the 1967 Arab–Israeli War, Etgar, a survivor of Holocaust and a soldier in Israeli army, found David in one of the Palestinian villages. He adopted the baby and never looked for his birth parents. Explaining his decision to depict David the way he is, stubborn in his life views and full of hatred, Mouawad cites his own childhood experiences, when he grew up listening to the derogative statements about Jews around his own kitchen table – statements similar to what David says in the play about the Arabs and their world (Mouawad in Farcet 2017: 11). These statements reveal David firmly positioned on one side of the conflict, unprepared for and actively resisting reconciliation. To Mouawad this casual hatred of the Other is the unfortunate reality of today; something that he wishes to challenge in his work. Making theatre is 'to go towards the enemy, against one's tribe', declares Mouawad (ibid.). It is to accept the truth of the other. In the case of *Tous des oiseaux*, it is the controversial history of making and running of the state of Israel that he is trying to accept. Today, Mouawad explains, 'Lebanon still does not recognize Israel. … For a Lebanese citizen to collaborate with an Israeli is to commit treason' (ibid.). For an immigrant writer residing in France this issue of collaboration becomes even more difficult. The questions he asks are 'what should one do? Write against? Write for? Do not write? To write from the position of the sufferings of my own people?' (ibid.) The history tends to repeat itself with the region's constant wars and conflicts, and there are no innocent victims and no hope for its conflicts to come to an end. To resist these wheels of history, one must refuse 'to comfort one's clan' – not to reject one's origins but to 'refuse the amnesia [the clan] shows' (ibid.).

In *Tous des oiseaux*, in other words, Mouawad challenges traditional forms of reconciliation. He refuses reconciliation as a simple and positive solution to the past problems, and he warns of danger to reproduce stereotypes. Mouawad invites his audiences to investigate this enigmatic connection between the past and the present, and he challenges the concept of nationhood as a collective agreement to commemorate who 'we' are and to reject who 'we' are not. Indirectly, Mouawad suggests that both reconciliation and commemoration can also be exclusionary, as he explains.

> My position is to always ask the same question: what were we responsible for during this civil war? The war during which I was taught to hate all those who were not in my clan. Without planning it, when I started writing for theatre, I stubbornly created the characters that were precisely those who made me hate others, I gave them the most beautiful roles, I provided them with the vectors of the strong emotions. So are Muslims in *Incendies* and a Palestinian in *Anima*. Now I want to write and love the characters of *Tous des oiseaux*, those of an Israeli family, those Jews, precisely, that for years, as a child, I was taught to hate. (Mouawad in Farcet 2017: 11)

David remains a controversial figure of reconciliation: after learning the truth of his origins, he proclaims that God sent him his special trial. Before David suffers his lethal stroke, he forgives those who lied to him and declares that he has found his *afikomen*, a symbol of 'the ultimate redemption from suffering, which comes at the end of the [Passover's] Seder' (Lind 2014). Mouawad, however, does not end the play on this elevated note. He takes the action further. For his soul to depart in peace, David needs to face his true self, even if against his will. This self, as Mouawad argues, can be found only in one's mother tongue. David's native language – the language of his biological mother – was Arabic, and hence Mouawad summons al-Hasan ibn Muhammad al-Wazzan or better known as Leo Africanus to converse with David in Arabic, to help him reconcile the impossible, and to die in harmony with his own I.

Leo Africanus (Hassan al-Wazzan)

Protagonist to Natalie Zemon-Davis's book *Trickster Travels: A Sixteenth-Century Muslim between Worlds* (2007), which served Mouawad as inspiration for this work, Leo Africanus was a Berber diplomat from sixteenth-century Granada. Enslaved by the Spanish corsairs, he ended up at the court of Pope Leo X. Leo Africanus spoke many languages, and to save his life he agreed to convert to Christianity. In *Tous des oiseaux*, Leo Africanus emerges as a highly symbolic figure. A subject of Wahida's doctoral research, he connects the characters' past and present. Through his silent presence on stage and by telling David a Persian tale of the amphibian bird, he provides the play's philosophical background.

The bird, as Leo's tale goes, was so drawn to the life of the fish that, despite his family's warning, he plunged into the water to join them. When the bird fell, he grew gills and began to breathe, and so he turned into a fish. 'And breathing, flying-swimming, he moves among the fish with scales of jade, gold and pink, as fascinated with him as he is with them, and the bird greets them, saying "Here I am! It's me! I am the amphibian bird arriving in your midst. I am one of you. I am one of you!"' (Mouawad 2018: 109).

To Mouawad, this tale of ultimate metamorphosis speaks the truth of the migrant's divided self and is called to teach his audiences something profound 'of our world and our relationship to the Other, to the enemy' (Mouawad 2017). By staging improbable historical and linguistic meetings between Leo Africanus, who addresses David in Arabic, and David, who responds to him in Hebrew, Mouawad wishes to overcome political, geographical, linguistic and symbolic borders that make peoples' identities and histories. In this dialogue, he breaks theatrical verisimilitude and invites his characters to converse in the language of improbable, to move beyond the locutionary function of a referential speech act.

To help translating this philosophical and political quest into theatrical terms, Mouawad brought together a team of international actors from geographical regions that historically have been at war with each other. Often in his work, language served Mouawad as a primary artistic vehicle to debate the questions of truth, identity and belonging. This time, however, it was not the poetics of a unilingual encounter that kept this story going, but the aesthetic potential of onstage multilingualism, which finally drove its political message home. Written in French, but performed in English, German, Arabic and Hebrew, *Tous des oiseaux* evoked the multilingual vernacular of today's metropolis on stage.[2] In his response to Charlotte Farcet's question about what constitutes one's identity today, Mouawad speaks of the power of language. The words that 'come out of our mouth and the voice that has its source in our breath' make our sense of self; 'I like to think that identity is emigration and never immigration', he explains. 'The fixed identity is the worst closing of oneself. It forces us to think of ourselves as a center around which other identities rotate' (Mouawad in Farcet 2017: 9). Like Leo Africanus, Mouawad thinks of himself as an eternal traveller 'for whom there is no center, only the voice that becomes home' (9). Identity, he says, 'is a movement, there is no fixed center, only relativity. For a traveler, when he/she is asked "where are you from?", … it is impossible to say – "my identity is my origin" – without denying the road he/she traveled' (9). Disappearance is the traveller's fate: to Mouawad it constitutes the history of exile and the truth, which he also seeks in this play. *Tous des oiseaux*, he explains, is the story not only of fragmentations and paradoxes (8), but also of metamorphosis, specifically when the writer's word reaches his audiences in the most transformed and distant form of surtitles and re-translation (7).

Mouawad connects this artistic process of translation and metamorphosis to his own childhood experiences, when he was losing his mother tongue, Arabic, to his second language, French. In childhood, however, the loss of one's language is not that painful, he explains. 'The language disappears, and the child has no awareness of the consequences of this loss' (Farcet 2017: 7). Understanding significance of this loss comes later and so one can decide to re-learn their mother tongue, although re-learning one's mother tongue can turn into the most ironic and painful paradox of displacement and non-truths that come with it. In *Tous des oiseaux*, David, the victim of this linguistic violence, faces this choice too late. Although he does understand Leo Africanus addressing him in Arabic, the true knowledge of his origins, his mother tongue, and so his own self remains unattainable to him. The character who succeeds on this road of personal reconciliation through language is Wahida: she recognizes and accepts her cultural identity and history, when she experiences a visceral encounter with her mother tongue, as she embraces the smell and the touch of Ramallah, and the sound of her name spoken in the language of her ancestors.

Wahida

Designed as a foil to Eitan, Wahida is another tragic character in this play. She is also a scientist searching for her own truth and reconciliation. Unlike an objectivist Eitan, 'who doesn't waste time indulging in idle daydreaming' (Mouawad 2018: 5), Wahida represents everything that her name stands for. Translated from Arabic, *Wahida* means a singular, peerless, unique and a leader in spiritual matters. At the same time, Wahida is defined by the male gaze: 'men must flock around you', David assumes (61). This juxtaposition of male/female, rational/sensual evokes a somewhat tiered trope of the exoticized or even fetishized femininity, yet heavily criticized by Edward Said (1979: 187). This is what Said writes in his criticism of the nineteenth-century French literature, specifically the writings of Gustave Flaubert, who was simultaneously spellbound and frightened by the Orient:

> The most celebrated moments in Flaubert's Oriental travel have to do with Kuchuk Hanem, a famous Egyptian dancer and courtesan he encountered in Wadi Haifa. He had read in Lane about the *almehs* and the *khawals*, dancing girls and boys respectively, but it was his imagination rather than Lane's that could immediately grasp as well as enjoy the almost metaphysical paradox of the almeh's profession and the meaning of her name. ... Alemah in Arabic means a learned woman. It was the name given to women in conservative eighteenth-century Egyptian society who were accomplished reciters of poetry. By the mid-nineteenth century the title was used as a sort of guild name for dancers who were also prostitutes, and such was Kuchuk Hanem, whose dance 'L'Abeille' Flaubert watched before he slept with her. (Said 1979: 186)

Wahida is aware of such fetishizing gazes and desires. As she claims several times in the play, she is often their victim (Mouawad 2018: 86–8). 'The Oriental woman', Wahida can be imagined as another subject to Flaubert's reflections. Similarly to Kuchuk Hanem, who entranced Flaubert by her 'self-sufficiency, by her emotional carelessness, and also by what, lying next to him, she allow[ed] him to think', Wahida acknowledges her place within the Western imagination as 'a display of impressive but verbally inexpressive femininity' and 'a disturbing symbol of fecundity, peculiarly Oriental in her luxuriant and seemingly unbounded sexuality' (Said 1979: 187). Thus, by reintroducing this trope of the exoticized femininity, Mouawad provides critique of this motive in terms similar to Said's and, at the same time, he commemorates it.

In *Tous des oiseaux*, Wahida emerges as *a double feminine* of Kimberlé Crenshaw's intersectionality: a theoretical and legal lens to discuss how the dimensions of class, gender, and race intersect with and reflect of each other in creating unique forms of discrimination (1994: 95). Thinking of Wahida along the lines of 'a double feminine', a woman of colour positioned as a (potential or even obvious) victim of domestic violence, rape, systemic abuse and an object of fetishism (97), intersectionality helps Mouawad to elevate Wahida to a symbol of rebellion and personal freedom. Written in the language of a political manifesto, Wahida's goodbye monologue to Eitan presents this woman as a double victim: she is not only a female but also an Arab, she is a scholar but does not know her history and she speaks Arabic but was deprived of her culture (Mouawad 2018: 86–7). So, writing Wahida as a character of intersectionality allows Mouawad to break the stereotype of a mysterious and exoticized femme fatale. By acknowledging Wahida's double feminine, Mouawad builds a strong case against Islamophobia and misogyny.

A journey to Jerusalem brings Wahida a new understanding of her subject of research – Leo Africanus. It not only gives her a better view of the reasons he accepted his hybridity, but also helps Wahida to reconcile her own past and the past of her people. Palestine, which she chooses over Eitan and their happy ending, serves Wahida as her personal *lieux de mémoire* – the place of her people and the site of their shared ancestral and modern history. Walking through the streets of Ramallah, sleeping in the houses of refugees and listening to her name spoken in the language of her parents helps Wahida recognize her difference as a product of displacement – half American/half Arab – as sameness. It also aids Wahida in accepting her own story. Describing her visceral encounters with the land of her ancestors, Wahida says, 'I went to the other side of the wall', 'I wandered in the dust of Palestine and I felt I have come home. I slept in the homes of people I didn't know and when they asked me my father's name, I burst into tears. Never since his death had I heard my name pronounced so well' (2018: 86). Thus, when Wahida hears 'the song of her name' spoken in the language of her father (86) and when she realizes that 'all of Ramallah smells like my mother' (88), she performs an act of reconciliation. This physical return to the roots, the sounds, the smells and the dust of the land that she never knew helps Wahida fight cultural stereotypes. All her childhood, Wahida explains, she was trained to hide her identity. 'I am an Arab and no one taught me how to be one. On the contrary, I was taught to find it disgusting and I vomited it out of me' (87). As an academic, she dedicated her life to prove 'how dangerous it is to let the principle of identity dictate your life, how stupid it is to cling to your lost identity' (89). Hearing and speaking her mother tongue, Wahida rejects all these prejudices. 'The reality is simple', she declares. 'This is what I am. I belong to this, and if I want to escape it, I have to start by taking a look at myself' (89). Leo Africanus, she realizes, never 'concealed who he was' (89). In the choices he made, including his conversion to Christianity, Leo Africanus 'chose to reveal himself so he could pursue his passion for the world' (89).

Language plays a special role in Wahida's ethical pathos of reconciliation: it demonstrates that in the case of shifting and hybrid identities, mother tongue still serves as a leading feature of one's own self. A subject to 'a linguistic family romance', mother tongue helps Wahida 'to fantasize a bodily as well as familial grounding in language', something tightly linked to such important manifestations of familial intimacy as 'affect, gender, and kinship' (Yildiz 2012: 14). Born and raised in the United States, Wahida is familiar with her native language and culture only through her parents who are already dead. But she has never claimed it as hers before. Wahida's monologue, in which she explains why she wants to break up with Eitan and stay in Palestine as an activist, spells out one of the major ideological and philosophical focus points of *Tous des oiseaux*. It not only insists on the power of mother tongue to construct one's identity but also, paradoxically, reinforces the paradigm of monolingualism, in which 'individuals and social formations are imagined to possess one "true" language only, their "mother tongue", and through this possession to be organically linked to an exclusive, clearly demarcated ethnicity, culture, and nation' (2). For Wahida the case is different. As she joins the Palestinians, Wahida comes to recognition of her 'true self'. Her reconciliation is both affectual and communal: by accepting her own identity as an Arab and as a woman, she declares her place in the world as a new cosmopolitan. Not only Wahida recognizes the other within herself – the postulate by which Levinas suggested we act ethically towards the other – but she also accepts her mission to carry her own roots on her back, to exhibit the act of 'cosmopolitan patriotism' (Appiah 1997: 617).

Conclusion

Tous des oiseaux, as this chapter argues, exemplifies theatre writing oscillating between the act of historiography, the act of commemoration and the act of performance. Like French philosopher Paul Ricouer, Wajdi Mouawad recognizes the subjectivity of a narrating agent as an experiential act of the past and as an act of interpretative utterance. A written account of the past, Mouawad's theatre emerges as a product of the narrative effort of an artist/historian, whereas the act of writing – characterized by the act of playfulness and invention – serves him as a form of remembering and forgetting (Ricouer 2004: 144). This intermediate position of the act of writing turns a historian, the writer of the living memory, into a philosopher, the maker of a performative narrative, in which 'the opposition between living memory and dead deposit becomes secondary' (144). In this process, a historical account is transformed into the narrative of performative re-contextualization, in which 'history remains a hindrance to memory' (145). Drawing upon the difference in experiencing the act of history and its representation, Ricouer's 'second-order reflection' (333), Mouawad's work reveals his vision of history as a circular network of faults and errors made by individuals; their deeds make monumental history, the consequences of which are carried by their children.

In the case of *Tous des oiseaux*, staging a multilingual play of reconciliation between history, memory and politics, Mouawad investigates each of his characters' unique pathos. To Hegel, romantic heroes can rise beyond limitations of their personal pathos only when they realize that they are fighting for a cause larger than their own. In *Antigone*, Hegel explains, both protagonists are right in their pathos as they represent different and equally important truths (2000: 321). In *Tous des oiseaux*, drawing upon the difference in experiencing the past and its representation, Mouawad reveals his own vision of history as a network of human errors and wrong decisions, and he writes this play aiming to defeat Hegelian understanding of tragic conflict only as a reconciliation of the characters' subjective truths (323–5). He constructs his new modern tragedy, in which a single pathos of each character can be turned into political ethics of encounter. Much like in Hegel's tragedy, the destiny of Mouawad's tragic character is predetermined by the external circumstances of their birth and environment. When his characters suffer or perish, for us, the audience, there is no alternative 'but to lament the pathetic transiency' of their tragic fate as 'this pitiful state of our emotions is … simply a feeling of reconciliation that is painful, a mind of unhappy blessedness in misfortune' (Hegel 2000: 326). Constructing such modern tragedy allows Mouawad, an artistic director of a state-sponsored French theatre, to bring the questions of history, memory and forgetting onto its stage. Staging *Tous des oiseaux* at La Colline, Mouawad fights the long-standing traditions of the French stage, in which 'the figure of the immigrant, as much as that of the French citizen of foreign origin, lives oftentimes at the periphery of the [French] national space, whether spiritual or geographical. He or she remains the subaltern witnessing the unidirectional cultural and historical flow of a "Grande Nation", … that excludes those who reached and redefined France from outside its borders' (Rauer 2018: 412). Producing this work at La Colline, in other words, serves Mouawad as his personal act of reconciliation, because writing this play, Mouawad, the author of *Tous des oiseaux*, supplies Mouawad, the political thinker, with the devices of storytelling that allows Mouawad, the historian, to think about our past and future as a philosopher.

Notes

1. Produced by *Théâtre national de la Colline*, Paris (17 November 2017), *Tous des oiseaux* was written and directed by Wajdi Mouawad, with Jalal Altawil as Wazzan, Jérémie Galiana as Eitan, Leora Rivlin as Leah, Judith Rosmair as Norah, Rafael Tabor as Etgar, Raphael Weinstock as David, Souheila Yacoub as Wahida and Victor de Oliveira and Darya Sheizaf as Eden. It was translated into German by Uli Menke, English by Linda Gaboriau, Arabic by Jalal Altawil and Hebrew by Eli Bijaoui, with French surtitles by Audrey Mikondo and Uli Menke.
2. In this play, members of a nuclear family freely switch from one linguistic idiom to another so their multilingualism – the authenticator of the characters' linguistic

and cultural identity – becomes a tool of Mouawad's theatrical truth. For more on this issue, consult Meerzon, Y. (2021), 'Dramaturgies of Authenticity: Staging Multilingualism in Contemporary Theatre Practices', *European Journal of Theatre and Performance*, 3: 26–73.

References

Appiah, K. A. (1997), 'Cosmopolitan Patriots', *Critical Inquiry*, 23 (3): 617–39.

Crenshaw, K. W. (1994), 'Mapping the Margins: Intersectionality, Identity Politics, and Violence against Women of Color', in M. A. Fineman and R. Mykitiuk (eds), *The Public Nature of Private Violence*, 93–118, New York: Routledge.

Diaz, S. (2018), 'Postface', in W. Mouawad, *Tous des Oiseaux*, 135–78. Montreal: Leméac Éditeur.

Farcet, C. (2017), '*Des langues, une écriture*. Entretien entre Wajdi Mouawad et Charlotte Farcet, dramaturge'. Programme notes for *Tous des oiseaux*, November 2017, 6–11. Available online: https://www.colline.fr/sites/default/files/prog-oiseaux_vdef4.pdf (accessed 26 October 2021).

Foucault, M. (1977), 'Nietzsche, Genealogy, History', in D. F. Bouchard (ed.), *Language, Counter-Memory, Practice: Selected Essays and Interviews*, trans. D. F. Bouchard and S. Simon, 139–65, Ithaca, NY: Cornell University Press.

Giammaria, J. (2019), 'In Conversation with Linda Gaboriau', *The McGill Tribune*, 26 November. Available online: https://www.mcgilltribune.com/a-e/in-conversation-linda-gaboriau-112619/ (accessed 26 October 2021).

Hegel, G. W. (2000), 'The Philosophy of Fine Arts', in D. Gerould (ed.), *Theatre/Theory/Theatre: The Major Critical Texts from Aristotle and Zeami to Soyinka and Havel*, 314–327. New York: Applause.

Hurley, E. (2011), *National Performance: Representing Quebec from Expo 67 to Céline Dion*, Toronto: University of Toronto Press.

Lind, D. (2014), 'What Is the Afikomen and Why Is It Hidden?', *Vox*. 5 August. Available online: https://www.vox.com/2014/8/5/18002032/what-is-the-afikomen-and-why-is-it-hidden (accessed 26 October 2021).

Mouawad, W. (2018), *Birds of a Kind*, trans. L. Gaboriau, Toronto: Playwrights Canada Press.

Mouawad, W. (2017), 'La légende de l'oiseau amphibie', *Tous des oiseaux*. Available online: https://www.theatre-contemporain.net/images/upload/pdf/f-521-5a13b367be75f.pdf (accessed 26 October 2021).

Mouawad, W. (2017–18), 'Ode à l'ennemi', *Manifesto*. Available online: https://www.colline.fr/manifeste-2017-2018 (accessed 26 October 2021).

Nora, P. (1989), 'Between Memory and History: Les Lieux de Mémoire', *Representations – Special Issue: Memory and Counter-Memory*, 26: 7–24.

Poncet, D. (2017), 'Tous des Oiseaux. L'un des grands moments de la saison théâtrale', *Culture-Tops*, 28 November. Available online: http://www.culture-tops.fr/critique-evenement/theatre-spectacles/tous-des-oiseaux (accessed 26 October 2021).

Rauer, S. (2018), 'The Racial Unconsciousness of the Parisian Public Theatre: Borders and Demotions in Francophone Contemporary Drama', *Modern Drama*, 61 (3): 411–35.

Ricouer, P. (2004), *Memory, History, Forgetting*, trans. K. Blamey and D. Pellauer, Chicago: University of Chicago Press.

Said, E. (1979), *Orientalism*, New York: Vintage Books.
Salino, B. (2016a), 'Pour Wajdi Mouawad, l'exil s'arrête à Paris', *Le Monde*, 8 April, Friday: 18.
Salino, B. (2016b), 'Les "quatre versants" de La Colline selon Wajdi Mouawad', *Le Monde*, 19 April, Friday: 14.
Salter, D. (1991), 'The Idea of a National Theatre', in R. Lecker (ed.), *Canadian Canons: Essays in Literary Value*, 71–90, Toronto: University of Toronto Press,.
Telmissany, M. (2012), 'Wajdi Mouawad in Cinema: Origins, Wars and Fate', *CineAction*, 88: 48–57.
Tirley, S. (2018), *The New Nationalism: How the Populist Right Is Defeating Globalism and Awakening a New Political Order*, Virginia Beach: CreateSpace Independent Publishing, Kindle Edition.
Yildiz, Y. (2012), *Beyond the Mother Tongue: The Postmonolingual Condition*, New York: Fordham University Press.
Zemon-Davis, Natalie (2007), *Trickster Travels: A Sixteenth-Century Muslim between Worlds*, Hill and Wang.

6

From difficult pasts to present resonance: Performances of memory and commemorative gestures in contemporary Vienna

Vicky Angelaki

As the 2018–19 theatre season began in Vienna, the banner hanging outside the Theater in der Josefstadt took spectators down memory lane, showing a black-and-white image of two young girls in transit, looking out of a porthole. In the photograph, both girls touch their faces with their hands in reflection and contemplation.[1] One girl's gaze was observant, perhaps even faintly smiling; the other's was withdrawn, concerned. The picture communicated sadness and uncertainty captured in the precarious image of children, perhaps unaccompanied, under circumstances unknown. The ambiguity that the image cultivated was considerately curated as the slogan accompanying it suggested. It read: 'Wer sich seiner Geschichte nicht stellt, entstellt die Geschichte', or 'Whoever does not face up to their history, defaces history.'[2] The Theater in der Josefstadt, founded in 1788, is of profound historical significance to Vienna. In an essay concerned with commemoration and its manifestations such as monuments, memorials and remembrance culture, it is fitting to begin with a reference to the theatre itself, as both a monument and a register of history told through drama and performance. As befits a monument, it not only re-produces history through staging choices that tell of social and political contexts past, but it is also in dialogue with history, through resonant programming. As such, the theatre becomes the ground for commemoration and reflection. The photograph signposting the new season would come to resonate fully when the premiere production, *Die Reise der Verlorenen* (The Voyage of the Lost), opened in September 2018. It is an image that has been circulated with reference to the infamous sea voyage in 1939 that inspired the production, when precarious Jewish individuals fleeing their newly hostile environment embarked upon a journey that would expose the limits of empathy, their ship turned away from countries in the position to offer support.

This chapter concentrates on seminal productions and commemorative events and structures: the theatrical examples are, purposefully, revivals and/or adaptations, tracing how these serve as cultural monuments – concrete, yet transformable sites of memory performing acts of commemoration. Similarly, the architectural interventions I consider allow me to reflect on broader narratives of disruption against cultural amnesia. The examples I have selected, despite differences in genre, all share the same ethical imperative: to reinstate fact at the heart of the inquiry, to remind older generations of what they know, and to acquaint the younger ones with aspects of history that might be all too easily whitewashed.

Encountering the memorial: Site, pedestrianism, performance

Vienna's Second District, Leopoldstadt, holds the largest number of commemorative plaques, or *Steine der Erinnerung*, 'presencing' (Garner 1994) the city's Jewishness. The Verein Steine der Erinnerung (Stones of Remembrance Society) caters to the placement and cataloguing of plaques across the city, highlighting addresses that Vienna's Jewish inhabitants, who fell victims to *Nationalsozialismus*, were associated with. These include *Sammelwohnungen* (Gathering, or Collective Apartments), where Jewish families were placed prior to deportation. The plaques have been paramount to performances of active pedestrianism, namely the pursuit of routes with a social, commemorative and/or ideological purpose, and to a city establishing a dialogue with its past, which it is performing in promenade durational style. In Leopoldstadt one also encounters the Path of Remembrance, or *Weg der Erinnerung*. The numerous plaques, sometimes on buildings, sometimes embedded on the ground, list Jewish individuals, often entire families, along with date of birth and execution, as well as details of deportation. Even though we are not necessarily dealing with architectural ruins, we are dealing with human ruins – with demise. The plaques, therefore, stand as memorials towards an act of 'lament[ing] rather than celebrat[ing] the past' (Arnold-de Simine 2015: 94).

The Verein Steine der Erinnerung assert their intervention as follows:

> By commemorating different facets of the everyday life for Jewish people living in Leopoldstadt, we hope to reconstitute, stone by stone, the existence of Jewish inhabitants who were driven from their homeland and murdered by the Nazis. In so doing, we hope to ensure that a trace of these lives are [sic] left for their descendents [sic]. We also want to ensure that the Remembrance of Jewish life and the culture in Leopoldstadt is kept alive. Our intent is that the 'Path of Remembrance' stimulates reflection among the publ[i]c and contributes to how Vienna manages its difficult past (Verein Steine der Erinnerung, n.d.)

In her edited collection on the subject of intersections in the acts of walking and logging presence through words and performance, Roberta Mock observes that 'the acts of walking, remembering and writing, and thus the construction of narrative self and performance spaces, ... [are] intimately related' (Mock 2009: 7). There are different ways in which these constructions might materialize: the path might be followed – and revivified – by the singular presence of one, or by the collective presence of multiple bodies on an urban pilgrimage to memory. It is an activity that, depending on purpose and time, might unfold over a single day, or, in any case, a limited window; or it might unfold over a longer period, in recurring intervals. In the former case, perhaps, the walker has visited the city with the purpose of paying homage, with the mission of actively remembering. In such a situation, there is likely to have been a root, and/or a heritage connection. In the latter option, there is a different type of walker constructing these narratives: the one who lives in the city, and whose own heritage and past are being commemorated; or yet another type of walker, who encounters by accident, or intentionally, with the purpose of visiting and learning, but with no heritage connection, and who then happens upon these monuments often, as part of leisurely – or in some other cases, daily commuting – experiences. Either way, it is difficult to imagine that, especially due to their welcome increased visibility, the plaques would not affect how we think of – and reflect on – place. The disruptive commands attention. In Leopoldstadt, the plaques startle, as their statements are not easily dismissible.

This holds true of other Jewish memorials in Vienna. In selecting my references, a choice was made regarding impact and visibility, as well as intervention in parts of the city that are, in terms of a walking itinerary, relatively close so that an enhanced experience of participation in commemoration would be fathomable. By this, I mean that a visitor could practically and theoretically engage with a number of these within the space of a day, or of one journey. One prominent example is the Holocaust-Mahnmal (Holocaust Memorial) in Vienna's Judenplatz, also home of a branch of the Jüdisches Museum Wien. Judenplatz is a historical square in a pedestrian zone as central as it is tucked away, so that it unfolds – again startlingly – as the walker's, or the spectator's gaze lands upon it on first contact. Rachel Whiteread's imposing white cube installed on the square (in the year 2000), a large-scale sculpture known as *Nameless Library*, holds, on its base, engravings of locations where Austrian Jews were deported and murdered. As the note, provided also in English on the memorial, reads: 'In commemoration of more than 65,000 Austrian Jews who were killed by the Nazis between 1938 and 1945'. In her study of the memorial, Rachel Carley remarks that through its structure, an inside-out library room holding countless unnamed books, it delivers 'a work of mourning in perpetuity' (Carley 2010: 25).

The spiritual healing that the *Nameless Library* facilitates is, in my view, akin to that of a smaller-scale and somewhat less prominent memorial: the DENK-MAL Marpe-Lanefesch, located in one of the quieter courtyards of the Altes AKH (*Allgemeines Krankenhaus*, or hospital), the former grounds of Vienna's General Hospital in the city's central Ninth District (Alsergrund), which have become home to a number of Vienna University's administrative and academic departments. The structure, built by Max Fleischer, has been on site since 1903, well predating the transfer of the premises from the hospital to the university (in the year 1988). The structure was conceptualized 'as a prayer pavilion for Jewish patients' (Posch 2017). In the brutalities of the decades that followed, however, its sanctity was thoroughly compromised first by *Nationalsozialismus*, which it may have structurally survived, but during which it was 'desecrated', and, later, by its misappropriation as 'an electrical transformer building', leading to both interior and exterior damages (Posch 2017). Rather than accommodating grief, the structure itself became subject to mourning for what it had once been, signifying a further act of erasure. It was only in 2005 that the monument in its current form, bright, colourful and welcoming, making use of the surviving structure and of contemporary construction materials (predominantly glass), as developed by Minna Antova, was inaugurated. This restored to the structure its original significance in the shape of a space that commemorates history, both of the memorial itself and of Austria's Jewish populations, and acknowledges the violence to which both were subjected. The monument, again in a pedestrian zone, receives most of its footfall through the university population or walk-through-campus commuters. The splitting of the word *Denkmal* (denoting a monument, or a memorial) indicates the commonly used wordplay of, effectively, 'stop and think', giving the structure the first part of its name: DENK-MAL. Meanwhile, meaningfully, 'Marpe-Lanefesch', in the Hebrew language, means 'healing for the soul' (Posch 2017).

I am interested in practices of healing through mourning, or mourning for/towards healing, as public gesture and private state and as a momentary as well as durational process. Additionally, my interest lies in the grounds that facilitate the performance of healing, not as a spectacle (whether politicized or not), but as an act of substance, in the sense of tangible social intervention – or at the very least of impetus towards achieving this. There is, of course, mourning for one person and mourning for a collective – and indeed the multifarious reasons for engaging with memorials as a visitor have received their own due attention, as in discussions of trauma tourism (see, for example, the work of Laurie Beth Clark). Here I am concerned with monuments that facilitate the latter, or the former in the context of the latter, primarily directed at not only those who have suffered or inherited trauma, but also being open to those who may wish to commemorate without a heritage connection.

Such are, to an extent, also the parameters that Carl Lavery develops in *Mourning Walk*. However personal the project of Lavery's tribute act to his late father, the critical and contextual framing of the activity, particularly insofar as it concerns mourning as pedestrian performance, is very relevant to this discussion. Lavery's discussion of agency and engagement with landscape, with specific routes and sites and, therefore, with roots, has wide applicability. I find his observation as to 'the essentially performative quality of landscape' (Lavery 2009: 46) thoroughly apt. It is so in the sense that cities, performing their own histories through time, precisely as we perform ourselves as walkers, as active participants in the urbanscape and as interactive entities with memorials, whether permanent or temporary, are not static frames, but are shaped through the bodies and actions of their spectators/participants, who inscribe a presence. And although it needs to be acknowledged that the encountering of the plaques, or the engagement with the architectural memorial structures, is not a pedestrian performance in the sense of a promenade show, this does not render the experience any less spectatorially profound, or performative. Because of factors relating to open access and the intimacy of the encounter, perhaps these traits are even heightened. It equally ought to be emphasized that we come upon these monuments/commemorative gestures as pedestrians, and walking is a cognizant performative act. We are, therefore, part of something bigger than ourselves: an event. In contexts like these, as Lavery's notes, 'it does not seem farfetched to claim walking, as an alternative form of psychotherapy, an activity in which enchantment acts as a bridge between past and present, self and cosmos, life and death' (Lavery 2009: 51). It is in this way that

I propose, through the experiences I have discussed earlier, commemoration leads, beyond mere acknowledgement, to healing – and mourning becomes a dynamic act.

The extraordinariness of durational, site-specific constructions of performance, and of stationary monuments that condition us powerfully, in that way moving and alive, is also to do with the fact that we may never (quite) arrive. The process of commemoration is as momentary and tangible as evolving and fluid. Upon departure, we are prepared to arrive – and discover – again. Remembering, therefore, becomes a continuous act of both self- and landscape performance. To 'walk empathically', as Mock observes in relation to Deirdre Heddon's work, is precisely how I would describe this process, which, in turn, yields a state whereby 'time, space and body fold together through kinaesthesia' (Mock 2009: 10). As to why this constitutes performance, I find a note that Mock makes regarding the relationship between text and performance particularly relevant. Mock observes that it is typically true that we engage with texts written for the stage by performing them. A challenge arises when we take on someone else's autobiographical text and imprint our own performance upon it: the layers deepen (Mock 2009: 16). The unfolding of Mock's argument motivates me to consider that we may perform walking tasks intentionally or unintentionally. In the former case, where there is intentionality, we set out to perform a specific walking task, for which we are prepared. This would entail coming into contact with the commemorative monument in a knowing way. In the latter, there is what we might call a seemingly unconscious intentionality, when, 'on our feet' we favour one route over another. Thereby, encountering – or, otherwise, not encountering – the monument, we are performing the script of our own choice through the act of visiting, or happening upon. Actively choosing to remember is no more bound to memory than to actively choose not to (by avoiding the monument; by choosing an alternative route). In either scenario, we impress our own present agency unto the past lives of others.

That agency, in turn, is a loaded term, as Mock's experience of staging Heddon's autobiographical work reveals (Mock 2009: 19–20). However different the examples, considering Mock's concern as to her responsibility with the material that was so personal to someone else, and the risks associated with identification of performer with material, some questions arise. As a non-Jewish (and indeed non-Austrian) individual, how problematic is my agency in encountering, as well as writing about these acts of commemoration, when they are not a direct part of my own cultural heritage? How might I avoid allowing them to become sensationalized and, therefore, a mere spectacle? Although I would like to think that this rests in exercising what we might call mindful walking – and mindful writing – I remain aware of the problematics. I acknowledge the significance of avoiding the fetishization of memory, or, worse, appropriation, much as I recognize the risks of giving in to forgetting. Nevertheless, I propose that, in the face of these memorials, the latter is not an option anyway, which preserves us, and which leaves us to deal with the former challenge in an honest way. Why the second variable (forgetting) is unlikely is because the monument is always present, insofar as it continues to survive, of course, in times of peace; the memory it triggers is ever renewed. Even when we do not select to engage with it, therefore, by its mere being there, the place of commemoration, and the act associated with it, outperform, and I would argue conquer, mental and emotional withdrawal. It is, ultimately, the same debate as the one concerning an engaged, or disengaged, theatre spectator: the act of finding oneself within a memorially charged performative context leaves an imprint regardless.

The canon writes back: Adaptation and revival

In September 2018 Herbert Föttinger, actor and artistic director of the Theater in der Josefstadt, opened the new season with a commission of Daniel Kehlmann's *Die Reise der Verlorenen* (*Voyage of the Damned*), pivoting towards what, for a venue as affluent and ensconced in one of Vienna's most *bürgerlich* (middle-class, privileged) districts, bordered on activism. The significance of the commission was augmented by the fact that, for a second year running, the Theater in der Josefstadt had chosen, as a season opener, an epic narrative that dealt with histories of anti-Semitism, persecution and violence. In 2017, that place had been reserved for an adaptation of Ernst Lothar's *Der Engel mit der Posaune* (The Angel with the Trumpet) by Susanne F. Wolf. The premiere narrowly predated the parliamentary election held soon after. One year later, the Lothar adaptation remained in repertoire and *Die Reise der Verlorenen* was playing to audiences who were now experiencing the first months of a conservative and far-right coalition government consisting of the ÖVP and FPÖ. Some time later, as the 2018–19 season was drawing to a close, that coalition would collapse due to a scandal enveloping members of the FPÖ leadership (the *Ibiza-Affäre*), including the Austrian vice-chancellor at the time. It had been a particularly politically heated period in Austria, not least because the recently held (and protracted) 2016 election for the office of the Bundespräsident had concerned two candidates, Alexander Van der Bellen, running as an independent candidate, formerly associated with the Green Party, and Norbert Hofer (FPÖ), whose vastly different politics had already exposed underlying tensions now bubbling on the surface.

In one of its most effective strategies, in 2016, the Van der Bellen campaign released a video interview with an eighty-nine-year-old woman called Gertrude Pressburger. The lucid account of a Holocaust survivor, the only member of her immediate family of five (parents and two younger brothers) – deported to Auschwitz along with Gertrude when she was sixteen years of age – to make it out of the concentration camp alive, criticized divisive political rhetoric. It did so by drawing on her memory of how similar wording was used during Austria's darkest days to stoke fear and hatred (*Vienna Vital* 2016; see also Pressburger and Groihofer 2018). In November 2018, the Volkstheater Wien, which this chapter does not discuss due to space restrictions, but which has been a consistent source of activism especially in matters relating to diversity and the refugee crisis, as well as to Jewish Austria, produced a stage reading accompanied by music of Gertrude's memoir (chronicled with the journalist Marlene Groihofer), *Gelebt, erlebt, überlebt* (Lived, Experienced, Survived).[3] Such was the climate in which these adaptation-driven revivals were occurring. As Föttinger himself summarized, 'Politisch korrekt waren wir lang genug' (we were politically correct for long enough) (Trenkler 2017). Because of its inherent adaptability, the method of reworking canonical source material, cross-genre, helped to revive social concerns not only to commemorate, but also to unsettle.

Föttinger's programming of *Die Reise der Verlorenen*, directed by Janusz Kica, was symbolic because of the production's overall theme, as well as of Föttinger's own role. The play (and previous film and book accounts) concerns a sea voyage whereby a group of precarious individuals drift away from a homeland turned hostile. The actual events took place in 1939 when the *MS St Louis*, carrying over nine hundred Jewish refugees, departed from Hamburg towards Cuba promising a passage to safety.[4] This was not meant to materialize. In the Theater in der Josefstadt adaptation, Föttinger played the role of Captain Gustav Schröder. Sources widely report that Schröder's input was crucial to the humane treatment of the Jewish refugees on board the *MS St Louis*, a fact that the production highlighted. Schröder was depicted as sober and benevolent, aware of his own limitations and acting to the best of his abilities to meet his historic responsibility. In a memorable production moment, against a rousing soundscape and in robust voice, Föttinger takes centre stage and in a gesture of fictional, interventionist historical reparation delivers a rallying speech that asserts an unyielding demand for the refugees to be taken in by their would-be transatlantic benefactors. The elation of intervention dissipates when it becomes evident that this is merely imagination and the captain concedes that this is not how events unfolded; on the contrary, the ship was turned back to Europe. The end image of the show and the curtain call, depicting a large number of the Theater in der Josefstadt company with Föttinger at the centre, was a clear semiotic statement as to by whom – and in which direction – the theatre was being steered, but also as to the artistic power of the collective that formed the theatre. Beyond the past unreal imaginary, the production suggested, we need to commemorate by facing history and by being awake to our current responsibilities and agencies.

The outcome of the ship's return to Europe following the refusal of Cuba, the United States and Canada to allow the passengers entry, had been as follows: 288 passengers were allowed into Britain; 214 into Belgium; 181 into the Netherlands; 224 'found at least temporary refuge in France' (*Holocaust Encyclopedia* 2016). However, none of this equalled safety. In a later tally, in addition to the one person of those admitted to Britain that died during an air raid, a staggering 254 were killed in the Holocaust. Otherwise, those who made it to Britain survived: '84 who had been in Belgium; 84 who had found refuge in Holland, and 86 who had been admitted to France' (*Holocaust Encyclopedia* 2016). The production, concentrating on individual plotlines of passengers, while also engaging with members of the crew, was as much a commemoration of facts, as it was a call of warning towards the rising tide of division. As one reviewer commented,

> The most powerful moment ... arrives at the very end: the performers walk onto the ramp and each character narrates what became of them: killed in the KZ [concentration camp], survived in hiding, fallen in the war, cooperated with the Nazis ... One Jewish woman says: 'I was fortunate. I died [the word *gestorben*, used here, implies natural causes].' (Tartarotti 2018)[5]

The fact that the narrative of the play concerned a ship carrying refugees turned away and unable to dock also acted as a historical metaphor for recent events concerning displaced populations seeking asylum in Europe, evidencing the circularity of humanitarian catastrophe, as well as, of course, the fact that no such catastrophe is ever inevitable. The refugee crisis as an issue had been especially contentious in recent Austrian politics, a fact highlighted by a number of new commissions, as well as revivals, particularly in the post-2015 period, following the events of the *Lange Sommer der Migration* (Long Summer of Migration).

Two other productions, again directed by Kica, were crucial to the overall agenda of historicizing through commemoration: the aforementioned *Der Engel mit der Posaune* (initially a 1947 novel, subsequently adapted into film) and the revival of Arthur Schnitzler's play *Professor Bernhardi* ([1912] 2018). As opposed to *Die Reise der Verlorenen* or *Professor Bernhardi*, whose action is more temporally contained, the Lothar piece spans decades as Viennese society moves from its fin-de-siècle bourgeois comforts and quietly brewing tensions to the throes of military conflict as the piece captures both world wars. Those underlying tensions stemming from differences in faith and minority phobias are very much the palette of the Schnitzler piece, which famously takes place in *Wien um 1900* (Vienna in 1900) – revisited by Schnitzler with the benefit of a degree of hindsight, slightly over a decade later. Revived frequently in German-speaking Europe, though largely absent from the English-speaking European realm, *Professor Bernhardi* is one of Schnitzler's – and the entire period's – most significant plays. An important production, the Almeida's liberal adaptation by Robert Icke in 2019 (London), titled *The Doctor* and featuring Juliet Stevenson in the lead, made the play more visible to contemporary audiences. It also delivered a most welcome gender intervention. Additionally, Icke's version made it to Vienna in a new Burgtheater production in 2021–2). Here, I make reference, other than the Theater in der Josefstadt production, to the earlier Burgtheater production, which premiered in April 2011 and was directed by Dieter Giesing.

There is a strategic significance in revisiting a play whose action takes place in Vienna and not only addresses one of the most difficult issues that have arisen in its history, but also transcends locality. There is, moreover, something particularly noteworthy about a text that perceives a social atmosphere and exposes a crisis before it has unfolded. It reminds us our historical responsibility of not only commemorating but also reading the signs and acting preventatively. The play stands out as a vehicle for what Steven Beller describes as 'the uncovering of society's hypocrisies' (1989: 219), including 'the way in which liberalism's promise of the ultimate victory of light and truth was illusory: against the perplexing nature of the Austrian state and society, the only wise counsel was one of retreat' (1989: 218). As Beller also notes, this did not mean passivity, but it did mean highlighting the lack of this essential truth, while defending it (1989: 218–19). For commemoration to serve a purpose, historical fact matters. And as these seasons in the Theater in der Josefstadt were taking place while the term 'alternative facts' was also taking root, Bernhardi's forensic quest for the truth was a helpful tool towards forging a path against manipulation and misinformation.

The plot of the play is as follows: Dr Bernhardi is a respected medical professional and head of the Elisabethinum clinic. When a destitute patient is admitted with sepsis following an illegal abortion, Bernhardi rightly diagnoses impending death as inevitable – and chooses not to upset the young woman's chemically induced euphoria with a revelation of how dire her condition is, so that she can at least die happy. He therefore decides not to allow a Catholic priest to read the patient's last rites. However, a nurse judges the situation differently, allowing the priest access. This causes the patient to realize that she is dying, so her last moments are spent in anxiety. The domino effect of the clash between science and religion escalates, beginning from the micropolitics of the Elisabethinum board and extending into actual politics as Bernhardi is brought to justice and the case draws widespread attention. At the centre of it all lies not only Bernhardi's call of judgement, but also his Jewishness – in a professional and social context where he is in a minority, he becomes doubly an outcast.

Schnitzler's text predates *Nationalsozialismus*, a fact that renders it even more significant for its proactive criticism against silent, condoned prejudice. At the Burgtheater, Giesing and dramaturg Amely Joana Haag updated the image of the play by disturbing the gender picture of the source text, where all doctors are male, casting Caroline Peters in the role of Dr Cyprian, the neurologist who emerges as one of Bernhardi's (here Joachim Meyerhoff) strongest allies and an overall stand-out part in the large cast. Giesing's production established Cyprian as, effectively, a professional partner to Bernhardi, a woman whose power was considerable, and who was on the liberal side of the narrative, committed to the quest for reason and truth. Critics, broadly praising the production, tended to discuss Peters's Cyprian mostly in terms of how she embodies a formidable ally for Bernhardi in her lucid pragmatism. Casting a woman in the role carried significance as the character's agency brings weight that determines developments; she has senior managerial responsibility. As Norbert Mayer observes in *Die Presse*, it is the neurologist who displays the most reasonable handling of the situation from the beginning, retaining her lucidity throughout (2011).

Despite a lack of gender subversion, the Josefstadt production did, however, thrive on one of the play's key elements: the discursive exhaustion of the issue and its unwieldy politics, contrasted with the protagonist's resilience. Föttinger's performance in the lead was, once more, symbolic. Like the Burgtheater production, the Josefstadt one allowed Schnitzler's text to flow unimpeded. However, differently from the vast Burgtheater stage that served to set the clinical tone using a white backdrop that dominated visually, shrinking the individual who is rendered insignificant against the larger frame of society, politics and mores, in Josefstadt the darker hues of the stage created a feeling of claustrophobia. There, Bernhardi became enclosed within a narrowing context of encroaching hostility.

The element of commemoration in the play relates not only to the chronic persecution of Jewishness, but also to the persecution of the vulnerable female. In his monograph *Performing Statelessness in Europe* (2018), Stephen Wilmer discusses both practices of racial and classed marginalization: on the basis of gender, income and falling from grace within a religious context. This produces a fruitful examination as to who, ultimately, comes to be fully considered a citizen of a given country with a given set of rights. Acknowledging that the national and historical contexts differ, Wilmer's helpful commemoration of women suffering under the regulations of the Magdalene Laundries in Ireland is, nonetheless, relevant for understanding how the commemorative gesture of a revival like that of *Professor Bernhardi* at the Burgtheater and the Theater in der Josefstadt might work intersectionally. They both remind the spectators of different historical injustices and methods of victimization. At the heart of Schnitzler's play lie two isolated figures: the patient and the doctor. The overarching issue of care, conceptualized systemically and individually, synchronically and diachronically, emerges as the cornerstone of historical memory. This is care not only towards the vulnerable and precarious, but also towards the one whose social position might have once been deemed as strong, but can quickly come under threat. *Professor Bernhardi* shows us that precarity is a relative and unpredictable signifier given an opportune political moment and reversals of fortune constructed by those in power. Above all, it is profoundly a play about human rights.

Focus on reversals of fortune, is, then, a crucial trope of commemorative performance. In the adaptation of Lothar's novel, which features considerable variation from the source material, we are focused on the Alt family, Vienna piano manufacturers, whose long-established social and financial privilege, strong in the first decades that the narrative covers, diminishes as time wears on and the political climate changes. The story begins in 1888 as Franz Alt is about to marry, not without reservations from his family, Henriette Stein, Jewish by birth. Despite early suggestions that this is a narrative focused on Franz, the patriarch, it becomes increasingly evident that the perspective that will come to dominate, at least in the stage version, is that of Henriette. Her Jewishness is the pivotal theme, not least as her status, parallel to that of her family, becomes increasingly precarious as the grip of *Nationalsozialismus* over Austria grows firmer. As the production evidences, no amount of prior social capital can avert risk when demagogy and propaganda take hold.

When Henriette marries Franz, she is negotiating the grief of a doomed relationship with a prominent figure, Crown Prince Rudolf. That is a nod to the complex weave of Austrian history, given that Rudolf was also the protagonist in one of the most infamous incidents of the country's monarchy – what became known as the double suicide in Mayerling, where both he and his underage lover died. Henriette, always untameable, is a contrast to Franz's steadfast rule; there is infidelity and considerable conflict in the marriage. But when Franz returns from the First World War a broken man, dying soon after, it is she who now officially emerges as the family leader – and in the last stretch of his life, some genuine tenderness develops between them. Amongst their three children – the older son, Hans, an intellectual who clashes with his father, the middle son, Hermann, a rampant nationalist, and a devoted daughter, Martha Monica, the youngest child and product of an affair of Henriette's – we see the different perspectives of society at the time. When Hans marries the Jewish actor Selma, events escalate. It is Selma who delivers one of the production's most striking lines, concerning Austrian identity being an *Erfindung* – that is, a construct that, here, emerges from an empire whose various coexisting entities always had tenuous and contentious bonds. Selma dies suddenly after having experienced difficult-to-diagnose symptoms of ill health, later revealed to be the side effect of gradual poisoning by Hermann, who had otherwise pretended to be a friend. Not long after, Henriette is murdered by the Nazis inside the family home. Although we might be able to predict Henriette's fate, still, her sudden, in-cold-blood shooting lands as a shocking moment, reminding us of the vulnerability of even those who had shown resolve and survival skills under challenging conditions. From that point onwards, it is the storyline of Hans that provides a glimmer of hope. He resists, becoming a political reactionary doubly aware of his moral debt, not only because of his own Jewish heritage, but also because of the tragic loss of his young Jewish wife.

The space required to provide a plot summary for the performance, whose duration was three hours, is reflective of the complexity of events that the narrative takes on – and was commented on in early reviews of the film version as well (*Der Spiegel* 1948). Even though different plotlines emerge and, depending on our priorities, we might place emphasis selectively, the defining moments of the production, in my view, pivoted around the central issue of Jewishness and historical memory. This stemmed not only from the sympathy that the dynamic depiction of Henriette and Selma had cultivated throughout – an educated perspective that by far transcended the *comme-il-faut* bourgeoisie of the Alt family – but especially from the play's final moments. The performance closes with a vivid act of commemoration, as Hans, centre stage, which is bare except for him and a lowered microphone, implying an illegal underground transmission, vocalizes dissent by wondering what Austria would have been without its multicultural identity, presented here, accurately, as the very fibre of the nation. After the prologue, Hans continues by commemorating Jewish contributions to the creation of the Austrian brand across all domains of life. As his voice becomes technologically amplified, we hear a long list of Jewish names. They create momentum, mobilizing memory and exposing the potency of actual historical fact versus misinformation, demagogy and propaganda.

In that moment, especially as the performance quietly but decisively steers itself away from sharp naturalism and into atmospheric abstraction, it also extends beyond its given time and place: we are no longer operating under the façade of the play. What is happening, rather, is a communion between stage and audience: an awakening to the past for which the vehicle of Lothar's narrative provides the frame, but which is, now, almost incidental. It is the physical act of embodying history through voice that matters – a pronouncement, as much as a protest, with the temperature, against the cold light of the stage, notably rising. In my spectatorial experience, the rapturous applause that followed the ending was as much an acknowledgement of the final minutes as of the last three hours. In that sense, I agree with the critic who remarked that 'the [audience] cheers after the premiere might be understood as antifascist avowal and a bow to the cultural and scientific accomplishments of Jewish Austrians' (Haider 2017),[6] though I do not share the further comment that this was a worthwhile moment that did not, however, work well on the stage. In my view, the moment was profoundly affective precisely because it broke with the narrative style of the production. The strategic timing of the verbal release was as structured as it felt uncontainable: the personal and physical became thoroughly political, their energy electric. The piece, ultimately, is a state-of-the-nation drama that speaks to the historical cruelties of the context it is engaging with, but that is also, as a newly commissioned adaptation, pointed towards the risks of neglecting historical memory in our own time. Ahead of the production opening, Wolf commented, 'Only in historical truth there is no pardon' (Pohl 2017).[7] Such was, also, the approach that the production took – at once poetic and sobering.

Conclusion

As Alette Willis helpfully reminds us, there is a fundamental difference between dealing with challenging events, here difficult pasts, effectively and affectively and providing what might be real, albeit temporary, relief.

> Palliation and healing, although often elided in the dominant narratives that circulate through society, represent two very different orientations to well-being. Etymologically, to palliate means to cloak. Palliatives are charged with dampening-down symptoms and emotions regardless of what has caused them. Healing – to make whole, holy, to make sacred – is concerned with underlying causes and their transformation. Painful physical and emotional symptoms can be catalysts for healing transformations. However, if they are cloaked and ignored, they cannot sound their warnings and people may not realize that they require healing until it is too late to affect the needed changes. (2009: 86)

What applies to people also applies to nations. Beyond the examples of memorials and commemorative activities that I have chosen to discuss here due to their character and significance, there are, of course more – and one would hope that these will continue to proliferate. This chapter has taken a more elastic understanding to the concept of performance, drawing on the work of scholars who have engaged with the body in public space as a form of pedestrian performance event, analysing its profound implications. In so doing, it has also engaged with the concepts of mourning and healing through remembrance and has asked how our own agency conditions these processes, arguing that irrespective of motivation, the act of encountering the memorial is unlikely not to leave a mark on the beholder. The chapter then considered three examples of theatrical performances – all in the revival and/or adaptation genre – to ask how the past can inform the present into a vivified process of reflection and dialogue rather than dispassionate instruction. The past, as this chapter has discussed, is an issue to feel passionate about – especially when we are dealing with concerns of persecution and erasure such as the ones that have informed my selection of examples. In dealing with the commemoration of Jewishness in contemporary Vienna through performative gestures and theatrical performances, we have a paradigm for the active embodiment – across different forms of public interventions – of the timeless imperative to engage with the past in the present, as a galvanizing force for our own agency in the making of the future.

Notes

1. This chapter makes reference to a number of commemorative gestures, of which I have first-hand experience, as follows: I have visited all Jewish memorials discussed here multiple times over a number of years; I attended the four theatre productions in Vienna on these dates: *Die Reise der Verlorenen*: 7 September 2018; *Professor Bernhardi*: 28 December 2017 (Theater in der Josefstadt) and 25 April 2015 (Burgtheater); *Der Engel mit der Posaune*: 7 September 2017.

2. Unless otherwise stated, translations are mine throughout.
3. For a discussion of the Volkstheater's political activism in the recent period, see Angelaki (2019).
4. Accounts as to the exact number differ. Numbers are listed as 'more than 900' (Lanchin 2014; Blakemore, 2019); elsewhere the number is more specifically given as 937, with the indication that the vast majority of the passengers were Jewish (Gunkel 2017; *Holocaust Encyclopedia* 2016).
5. 'Den stärksten Moment hat diese Aufführung ganz am Schluss: Die Darsteller treten an die Rampe und jede Figur berichtet, was aus ihr geworden ist: Im KZ ermordet, im Versteck überlebt, im Krieg gefallen, mit den Nazis kooperiert ... eine jüdische Frau sagt: "Ich hatte Glück. Ich bin gestorben"' (Tartarotti 2018).
6. 'Der Jubel nach der Premiere darf als antifaschistisches Bekenntnis und Verneigung vor den kulturellen und wissenschaftlichen Leistungen jüdischer Österreicher verstanden werden' (Haider 2017).
7. 'Nur bei der historischen Wahrheit gibt es kein Pardon' (Pohl 2017).

References

Angelaki, V. (2019), 'Performing Migration in Vienna: The Volkstheater Trilogy', *Performing Ethos*, 9 (1): 9–22.
Arnold-de Simine, S. (2015), 'The Ruin as Memorial – The Memorial as Ruin', *Performance Research*, 20 (3): 94–102.
Beller, S. (1989), *Vienna and the Jews, 1867–1938: A Cultural History*, Cambridge: Cambridge University Press.
Blakemore, E. (2019), 'A Ship of Jewish Refugees Was Refused U.S. Landing in 1939. This Was Their Fate', history.com, 4 June. Available online: https://www.history.com/news/wwii-jewish-refugee-ship-st-louis-1939 (accessed 28 August 2019).
Carley, R. (2010), 'Silent Witness: Rachel Whiteread's Nameless Library', *IDEA Journal/Interior Ecologies*, 10 (1): 24–39.
Clark, L. B. (2011), 'Never Again and Its Discontents', *Performance Research*, 16 (1): 68–79.
Der Spiegel. (1948), 'Der Engel mit der Posaune'. Available online: https://www.spiegel.de/spiegel/print/d-44418970.html (accessed 30 August 2019).
Garner, S. B., Jr. (1994), *Bodied Spaces: Phenomenology and Performance in Contemporary Drama*, Ithaca, NY: Cornell University Press.
Gunkel, C. (2017), 'Irrfahrt eines Schiffs. Wie die Vereinigten Staaten 937 jüdische Flüchtlinge abwiesen'. Available online: https://www.spiegel.de/geschichte/irrfahrt-der-st-louis-wie-die-usa-937-juedische-fluechtlinge-abwiesen-a-1134494.html (accessed 28 August 2019).
Haider, H. (2017), 'Daheim im Haus Österreich', *Wiener Zeitung*, 3 September. Available online: https://www.wienerzeitung.at/nachrichten/kultur/buehne/914638_Daheim-im-Haus-Oesterreich.html (accessed 30 August 2019).
Holocaust Encyclopedia (2016), 'Voyage of the *St. Louis*'. Available online: https://encyclopedia.ushmm.org/content/en/article/voyage-of-the-st-louis (accessed 28 August 2019).
Icke, R. (2019), *The Doctor*, London: Oberon Books.
Lanchin, M. (2014), 'SS *St Louis*: The Ship of Jewish Refugees Nobody Wanted', *BBC News*, 13 May. Available online: https://www.bbc.com/news/magazine-27373131 (accessed 28 August 2019).

Lavery, C. (2009), 'Part 1: Carl Lavery', in R. Mock (ed.), *Walking, Writing and Performance: Autobiographical Texts by Deirdre Heddon, Carl Lavery and Phil Smith*, 25–56, Bristol: Intellect.

Lothar, E. (2016), *Der Engel mit der Posaune: Roman eines Hauses*, Vienna: Paul Zsolnay Verlag.

Mayer, N. (2011), 'Burgtheater: Schnitzler schneidet tief ins Fleisch', *Die Presse*, 18 April. Available online: https://diepresse.com/home/kultur/news/651208/Burgtheater_Sch nitzler-schneidet-tief-ins-Fleisch (accessed 20 August 2018).

Mock, R. (2009), 'Introduction: It's (Not Really) All about Me, Me, Me', in R. Mock (ed.), *Walking, Writing and Performance: Autobiographical Texts by Deirdre Heddon, Carl Lavery and Phil Smith*, 7–22, Bristol: Intellect.

Pohl, R. (2017), 'Susanne F. Wolf: "Ich mache auch vor den eigenen Zeilen nicht halt"', *derStandard*, 1 September. Available online: https://www.derstandard.at/story/200006 3430966/susanne-f-wolf-ich-mache-auch-vor-den-eigenen-zeilen (accessed 30 August 2019).

Posch, H. (2017), 'DENK-MAL Marpe Lanefesch: Ehemaliges jüdisches Bethaus im Alten Allgemeinen Krankenhaus', Universität Wien, 650 Plus – Geschichte der Universität Wien, last updated: 9 September 2021. Available online: https://geschichte.univie.ac.at/de/artikel/denk-mal-marpe-lanefesch (accessed 27 August 2019).

Pressburger, G., and M. Groihofer. (2018), *Gelebt, Erlebt, Überlebt*, Vienna: Paul Zsolnay Verlag.

Schnitzler, A. (2018), *Professor Bernhardi*, Ditzingen: Reclam.

Tartarotti, G. (2018), 'Josefstadt: Gelungene Kehlmann-Uraufführung', *Kurier*, 7 September. Available online: https://kurier.at/kultur/josefstadt-gelungene-kehlmann-urauffuehrung/400111333 (accessed 28 August 2019).

Trenkler, T. (2017), 'Herbert Föttinger: "Politisch korrekt waren wir lang genug"', *Kurier*, 28 April. Available online: https://kurier.at/kultur/herbert-foettinger-politisch-korr ekt-waren-wir-lang-genug/260.820.461 (accessed 28 August 2019).

Verein Steine der Erinnerung (n.d.), 'The Path of Remembrance', *Stones of Remembrance*. Available online: https://steinedererinnerung.net/en/projects/path-of-remembrance/ (accessed 28 August 2019).

Vienna Vital (2016), 'Frau Gertrude – Van der Bellen – warnt vor Rechtsextremer Rhetorik – Untertitel auf Spanisch', *YouTube*, 26 November. Available online: https://www.youtube.com/watch?v=uWzzbmvSpCQ (accessed 28 August 2019).

Willis, A. (2009), 'Restorying the Self, Restoring Place: Healing through Grief in Everyday Places', *Emotion, Space and Society*, 2 (2): 86–91.

Wilmer, S. E. (2018), *Performing Statelessness in Europe*, London: Palgrave Macmillan.

7

Dancing impossible histories: Commemoration, memory and trauma in screendance

Aoife McGrath

This chapter discusses how dance creates sites for the representation and embodiment of women's experiences that have been omitted from official historical narratives underpinning commemorative events. Focusing particularly on untold women's stories connected with commemorative events employed in the perpetuation of exclusionary nation-building narratives, I explore how dancing women's stories into visibility raises troubling questions and uncomfortable affects through the embodiment of memories and traumas that are oppressed and/or forgotten. Yet those stories continue to linger on the fringes of social consciousness to haunt the present (Gordon 2008). Examining two screendance works, *Medicated Milk* (2016) by Áine Stapleton, and *Falling Out of Standing* (2016, 2017) by CoisCéim Dance Theatre and Anu Productions, I discuss how voices of women who have long inhabited cultural blind spots in Irish history are danced into remembrance, lending flesh to unacknowledged, traumatic experiences connected with nation-building commemorative events and cultural artefacts. I also propose that these choreographies create space for alternative and productively troublesome and disruptive sites of commemoration that are located both in the screendance works themselves, and also in their spectators, who carry the experience of the works beyond the performance event to their engagement with future narratives of commemoration.

Both works discussed were created in 2016 as performances for commemorative events linked with Ireland's 'Decade of Centenaries' (2012–22), a programme of annual commemorations of 'events of importance' for the nation sponsored by the Irish government.[1] The programme includes commemorations of significant political and revolutionary episodes leading up to the establishment of Irish independence in 1922, and important cultural events, such as the centenaries of key publications from the Irish literary revival of the late eighteenth and early nineteenth centuries that are closely interwoven with the formation of Irish national identity. In the context of the Irish performance landscape, 2016 can be viewed as a watershed year in Irish theatre history due to controversy surrounding high-profile performance events connected with the commemoration of Ireland's 1916 Easter Rising – a six-day-long armed rebellion led by Irish Republicans who fought to end British rule and re-establish Ireland's independence. In late 2015, Ireland's National Theatre, the

Abbey Theatre, published a programme of commemorative events titled 'Waking the Nation' that included staging ten plays. Only one of these plays was written by a woman, and no plays by women appeared either on the Abbey's main stage, or its second stage, the Peacock. Carole Quigley highlights the deep irony present in the Abbey Theatre's official press release for the commemorative season, which featured a promotional video populated entirely by female theatre artists and that opened with a quote from Abbey Theatre actor and 1916 rebel, Helena Moloney, speaking about the rebellion: 'we saw a vision of Ireland, free, pure, happy. We did not realize this vision, but we saw it' (qtd. in Quigley 2018: 85). A century later, although freedom had been achieved in the context of sovereignty,[2] the Abbey's commemorative programme seemed to underscore the continued immateriality of female theatre-makers' experience of equality and freedom in Ireland. The lack of representation of female theatre artists – condemned as 'exclusive, divisive, and inherently sexist' (ibid.) – was met with widespread indignation within the Irish performance community, culminating in the founding of the Waking the Feminists (WTF) movement in November 2015. This movement sought both to highlight 'the sexist nature of the [commemorative] programme itself, and also to discuss the systemic under-representation of women and minority groups ... as a whole' (ibid.: 86).

In the broader context of commemorative events in Ireland, this under-representation of women has deep roots that are interwoven with the colonial and post-colonial history of the nation. Following the establishment of Irish independence from British rule in 1922, commemoration of the 1916 Rising throughout the following century became deeply entwined with the performance of national identity, and as James Moran highlights,

> after independence, the nationalist response to the colonial caricature of the feminised and childish Celt was to insist on adult Irish masculinity. Women and children were often considered solely in terms of the domiciliary, and when the machinery of the independent state remembered the uprising of 1916, there was a characteristic side-lining of any hints of female experience, child casualties, and the rights of women and children. (2018: 790)

Considering dance performance within this context, it is interesting to note that theatrical dance practice in Ireland has traditionally been aligned with the feminine, and that the history of dance in Ireland also evidences this damaging implementation of sidelining found in the erasure of women's experiences from narratives of commemoration (McGrath 2013). During the formation of a post-colonial 'Irish' identity in the late nineteenth and early twentieth centuries, any genre of dance that was not the republican-sanctioned expression of Irish national identity – Irish step dance – was considered dangerously feminine, 'other' and foreign. This marginalization of theatrical dance within the cultural landscape of Ireland led to the neglect of dance as an artform by state bodies in terms of funding for professional practice and dance education (McGrath and Meehan 2018). Yet theatrical dance's position on the cultural margins can also be seen to have lent it a unique ability to embody and articulate experiences of alterity that question the status quo. Dance performance in Ireland then becomes an elucidative site in the analysis of performances of commemoration, as its inherent positioning in the cultural landscape as the embodied feminine 'other' generates a creative space which affords critical distance from exclusionary narratives, and in which sidelined experiences and memories can achieve a sustained materiality.

There were several performances and events in 2016 that sought to redress the lack of attention paid to women's experiences in the construction of narratives of Irish identity and nationhood through commemoration.[3] Both *Falling Out of Standing* and *Medicated Milk* belong to these, with *Falling Out of Standing* produced as part of the Decade of Centenaries programme, and *Medicated Milk* produced independently, but screened as the 'Irish Focus' event of the 2016 Joycean Bloomsday commemoration programme at the Irish Film Institute.[4] Both works were presented as live performance pieces as well as screendance works.[5] *Medicated Milk* is based on the life of Lucia Joyce, a professionally trained dancer and daughter of Nora Barnacle and Irish writer, James Joyce. The screendance version premiered on Bloomsday, 2016, the annual commemoration of the particular day, 16 June 1904, depicted in James Joyce's novel *Ulysses*, and the day in which his life and work are remembered and celebrated in Ireland and internationally. *Falling Out of Standing* was part of a collaborative project between CoisCéim Dance Theatre and Anu Productions, *These Rooms* (2016), commissioned by the Irish Arts Council as part of the ART:16 programme commemorating the 1916 Easter Rising. Both *Medicated Milk* and *Falling Out of Standing* attempt to choreograph what Adrian Parr describes as the 'ungraspable' nature of trauma memories (Parr 2008: 1), creating a dialogue between embodiments of both collective and personal traumas that span a century of Irish history.[6] Both works also reflect a pressing, current need and trend in Irish society to uncover and recover forgotten voices, particularly those of women and children who have been excluded from official historical narratives of commemoration. This exclusion can be seen to operate both at a public level, in terms of a lack of public recognition, and at the personal level due to the impossibility of assimilating traumatic experience into linguistic narrative structures. When people suffer trauma, they undergo a 'speechless terror' (van der Kolk and van der Hart 1995: 172). As the experience cannot be organized on a 'linguistic level', there is a 'failure to arrange the memory in words and symbols', which leaves it to be organized on a 'somatosensory or iconic level: as somatic sensations, behavioural reenactments, nightmares and flashbacks' (ibid.). As unprocessed memory trauma can then be understood to remain in the body, 'possessing' it (Caruth 1995: 4). Thus, dance performance, an embodied practice, becomes an important site through which to investigate artistic representations of cultural and personal trauma. Both *Medicated Milk* and *Falling Out of Standing* communicate an affective sense of the forgotten or silenced traumas of women whose lives are intertwined with people and events of public commemoration important to the construction of Irish social consciousness. Through dance performance, these works present sites of cultural production that allow for an alternative, corporeal approach to the reshaping of exclusionary narratives of commemoration.

Dance, trauma and public remembrance

In her study of public remembrance, Adrian Parr suggests that the combination of collective traumatic memory and cultural production can help 'peel back the skin and tissue of repression so as to uncover the utopian demand that memory stirs forth' (2008: 3). Understood as 'corporeal movement of memory thinking', memorial culture is a combination of idealism and realism, which allows the 'social field' to approach the 'sociopolitical contradictions that collective trauma exposes' in imaginative ways (ibid.). Memorial culture then becomes a 'social activity that organizes the energies, affects and forces of memory' (ibid.). In both of the screendance works discussed here, I am interested in exploring how their focus on embodying these energies, affects and forces of memory, rather than a more traditional, revisionist, counter-narrative, allows forgotten or repressed voices and their traumatic memories to surface.

Traumatic memories are often understood as 'the unassimilated scraps of overwhelming experiences, which need to be integrated with existing mental schemes, and be transformed into narrative language' (van der Kolk and van der Hart 1995: 176). In both *Medicated Milk* and *Falling Out of Standing*, the choreographers have avoided any attempt to 'make sense' of these memories in a narrative language that works towards a conclusion of holistic integration. Instead, we are presented with the unassimilated scraps of the body memories associated with traumatic experience, and any potential work of integration is left to the part of the spectator. Considering this choreographic choice (i.e. the resistance of any linear retelling of traumatic events within the frame of the relationship between trauma and the creation of historical narratives of commemoration), it strikes a chord with Caruth's assertion that traumatized people 'carry an impossible history within them, or they become themselves the symptom of a history that they cannot entirely possess' (1995: 5). In the following, I explore how the choreographies of these impossible histories in *Medicated Milk* and *Falling Out of Standing* create alternatives to dominant, official commemoration narratives, allowing the dispossessed voices of women to achieve visibility.

Medicated Milk

In *Medicated Milk*, director and choreographer Áine Stapleton sought to 'give Lucia [Joyce] a voice and try and understand what happened to her' (Bolger, Ó Conchúir and Stapleton 2017). Born in 1907, Lucia Joyce was a professional dancer who trained at the Dalcroze institute in Paris, performed in France, Germany and Austria and was a member of a touring group of six female dancers known as *Les Six de Rhythme et Couleur*. Lucia Joyce was also the daughter of Nora Barnacle and internationally acclaimed Irish author, James Joyce. In Ireland, the post-colonial remoulding and rebranding of a masculine Irish identity that escaped demeaning, colonial characterization as feminine was often imagined and performed through literary works. During the Irish Literary Revival movement, which originated in the late eighteenth century, the written word allowed a freedom of imagination outside of stifling colonial and neo-colonial limitations imposed on corporeal expression (especially any form of expression linked with femininity), inevitably placing increased importance on literary articulations of identity (McGrath 2013). Unsurprisingly, the writers of these literary works are overwhelmingly male. The work of James Joyce has been positioned by Declan Kiberd as contributing to the 'invention' of a notion of Ireland, and Kiberd claims Joyce as 'among the great post-colonial writers' of the nation (1996: 327), who 'wanted to mediate between Ireland and the world, [and] most of all explain Ireland to itself' (ibid.: 334). Several of the first publication dates of James Joyce's works are marked in the Decade of Centenaries programme. The year 2016 saw the celebration of the centenary of the first publication of *A Portrait of the Artist as a Young Man* in 1916, and in 2022 several events commemorate the first publication of *Ulysses* in 1922, the same year as the recognition of Irish independence. Bloomsday has been commemorated annually in Dublin since 1954. Bearing this in mind, the premiere of *Medicated Milk* as the headlining 'Irish Focus' event for the Irish Film Institute's Bloomsday programme was a bold one, as it placed Lucia Joyce's story, rather than her father's, centre stage.

Many details about Lucia's life are disputed, but there is general consensus that she had a very troubled relationship with her family, and that following a number of brief but emotionally disturbing romantic relationships (including one with a young Samuel Beckett), she was sent to Zürich by James Joyce in 1934 to receive psychiatric treatment with Carl Jung. After a diagnosis of schizophrenia, Lucia was in and out of psychiatric care for several years until the Joyces had her committed to an asylum outside Paris aged twenty-eight. She would spend the rest of her life incarcerated in asylums until she died in 1982 at the age of seventy-five in an institution in Northampton, England. As Stapleton discovered in her research of Lucia for *Medicated Milk*, there is little historical material either in existence, or at least accessible to researchers, related to Lucia's life. James Joyce's grandson, Stephen Joyce, heir of the Joyce estate, announced at a Bloomsday event in Venice, Italy, that he had destroyed most of Lucia Joyce's correspondence, including letters to her from her father and other people significant in Lucia's life, such as Beckett, in order to prevent scholars prying into family affairs (McKenna 2012).

Stapleton drew inspiration from Carol Loeb Schloss's contested biography, *Lucia Joyce: To Dance in the Wake* (2003) (McKenna 2012), and her work is quoted in *Medicated Milk*. However, Stapleton's work is less interested in Schloss's project of recuperative historiography, focusing instead on portraying the difficulties and pain inherent in grasping and retelling memories of traumatic experiences, especially those that are unacknowledged or forgotten by others. To do this, it connects danced responses to fragments of Lucia's life and writings with Stapleton's own experience of childhood trauma (hinted at throughout the work, but never made explicit). Scenes danced at locations that Lucia visited during holidays in the Irish seaside town of Bray in the 1930s are followed by scenes filmed in Stapleton's own childhood home in Ireland, in which she recounts her Obsessive Compulsive Disorder symptoms in the family bathroom. Connecting Lucia's past trauma with her own, current, personal trauma, Stapleton positions Lucia's story within the broader, continuing history of women's traumatic experiences of oppression. This is of particular relevance to experiences of incarcerated, forgotten women within the Irish-specific context of 'architectures of containment', which saw the institutional incarceration of 'fallen' women in psychiatric facilities and laundries (Smith 2007).[7]

Trauma and danced contractions of time

In addition to the merging of historical and personal stories, Stapleton also collapses the past and the present in scenes in which she dances together with her niece, Ayla Stapleton. In these scenes, they both wear clothing that is reminiscent of the styles worn during Lucia's childhood in the early 1900s, and Ayla plays with objects from the past, such as a gramophone and a china doll. Throughout the film these objects take on a dreamlike and often nightmarish quality. In one early scene, Ayla dances on a beach wearing an extraordinary gramophone costume, which includes a large gramophone horn worn around her neck like a ruff, and a long, bronze tail that is attached at the base of her neck, and which she uses to 'plug' herself into an actual gramophone while she cranks its handle. The cranking of the gramophone produces no sound or 'voice', but Ayla's beach dance communicates in the absence of recorded sound, evoking the articulative power of the body in the absence of the narrative of 'his master's voice',[8] understood here as the habitual narratives circulating around Lucia's life that position her story only in relation to that of her father's. In a later scene, Stapleton and Ayla row out to sea in a small boat dressed in antiquated nightdresses. Stapleton uses safety pins to attach their nightdresses together, creating a joining side-seam that connects their bodies and underlines the embodied contraction of past and present in the experience of trauma. Analysing the ability of artworks to contract moments of feeling linked with trauma and separated by the distance of time into a 'direct proximity with one another', Brian Massumi suggests that

> the contractile abilities of feeling are most dramatically evidenced in trauma. The response to a traumatic event tends to reerupt in the present, often through what appears to be a random visual trigger bearing no formal resemblance to any part of the event. The automatic triggering brings ages as different in kind and as unthinkably far from each other as childhood and adulthood into the absolute proximity of repetition. Moments of time contract into the dynamic identity of a reliving. (Massumi 2006: 206–7)

In *Medicated Milk*, Stapleton experiments with affectively potent visuals such as a gramophone on a beach and pinned-together nightdresses.[9] She makes visible an experience of contracting time spanning the century that has elapsed between Lucia's childhood and Stapleton's own childhood, while also bringing the embodied memory of trauma from childhood into dialogue with adult choreographies of memory. The century that is spanned in this work maps directly onto the century at the heart of the commemorative programme of Ireland's Decade of Centenaries. Moving carefully side by side in their pinned-together nightdresses, Stapleton and Ayla embody not only the attempted suturing of feelings from past experiences with present realities (as performed by commemorative events), but also a suturing of women's stories across time that performs a kind of reverse excision in its stitching over of the gap in knowledge of women's experiences created by patriarchal histories that have kept women's stories separate from official commemorative narratives.

Sondage – Probing an open wound

Medicated Milk shows the struggle to piece together an alternative commemorative narrative for Lucia Joyce out of disparate fragments of memory and evidence. Many of its dream-like scenes could be connected with the protective, anaesthetizing function of disassociation, as experienced by trauma survivors. However, the work also shows the pain and suffering endured through trauma. In one scene of the film, the text, 'Sondage – the probing of an open wound', appears superimposed over the image of a sheep's carcass hanging in a slaughterhouse during the butchering process. As the carcass hangs on the hook, the camera focuses on the eviscerated body cavity of the sheep through a cut in its flesh that is a long oval shape, narrow at both ends and wider in the middle, resembling, disturbingly, a vagina. As the carcass sways gently side to side, the camera's focus switches back and forth between the sheep's pearlescent spinal column in the background and the shorn, bare skin framing the oval wound opening in the foreground. The following shot is of Stapleton, standing naked, making slow, constrained movements in the corner of a concrete bathing shelter, head down and hands braced up against the wall in front of her. The colour palette in both of these shots is a similar blend of fleshy pink and grey, visually connecting the slaughtered sheep with Stapleton's body. She pushes against the wall, trapped in the corner, but always resisting. During these two scenes, we hear a voiceover by Stapleton giving details of treatments that Lucia Joyce endured during her incarceration: 'sea water injections, seven weeks in bed, animal serum injections, straight jacket, solitary confinement'.

The connection of the gory slaughterhouse scene with Stapleton's body is a reminder of the pain inherent in performing a sondage of traumatic memory – a probing of unresolved, open wounds – and a reminder that the pain of others can be difficult to comprehend. In her seminal discussion of pain, Elaine Scarry suggests,

> when one hears about another person's physical pain, the events happening within the interior of that person's body may seem to have the remote character of some deep subterranean fact, belonging to an invisible geography that, however portentous, has no reality because it has not yet manifested itself on the visible surface of the earth. (1985: 3–4)

As memories of physical and psychological trauma remain 'trapped' in the body and invisible to others, the visual connection with the sheep's butchering wounds offers the spectator a visible geography of the pain of trauma and the pain experienced by trauma sufferers when their stories are doubted or unacknowledged. The foregrounding of the body and pain in this scene can be read as a response to the history of disbelief and doubt surrounding not just Lucia Joyce's experiences, but also the many stories of abuse and oppression of women and children in Ireland that have come to public awareness over the course of the past decade following the publication of several government commissioned reports investigating abuse in state-run institutions such as industrial schools and mother and baby homes.[10] *Medicated Milk* introduces a discomforting viewpoint to the annual cycle of commemoration of Bloomsday that threatens to disrupt its celebratory tone. Scarry writes of the contradictory viewpoints inherent in the consideration of pain that

> for the person in pain, so incontestably and unnegotiably [sic] present is it that 'having pain' may come to be thought of as the most vibrant example of what it is to 'have certainty', while for the other person it is so elusive that 'hearing about pain' may exist as the primary model of what it is 'to have doubt'. Thus, pain comes unshareably into our midst as at once that which cannot be denied and that which cannot be confirmed. (1985: 4)

Through its focus on the embodiment of the pain of traumatic memory, *Medicated Milk* dances this interlinking of doubt and certainty, and the 'unshareability' of Lucia Joyce's experiences and history, into visibility. Lucia Joyce continues to haunt official narratives surrounding James Joyce and the commemoration of his life and works. In attempting to recover Lucia's voice in *Medicated Milk*, Stapleton has created an evocative, and necessarily fragmented and dreamlike portrayal, that provides an embodied sense of an alternative commemorative legacy for Lucia herself.

Falling Out of Standing

Falling Out of Standing (filmed in 2016, premiered in 2017) is a screendance work choreographed by David Bolger that was developed out of the performance collaboration, *These Rooms* (2016), between dance theatre company CoisCéim, and theatre company, Anu Productions. *These Rooms* and *Falling Out of Standing* commemorate the North King Street massacre, which took place in the final days of the Easter Rising in the early hours of 29 April 1916 in Dublin. During the massacre, fourteen men and one sixteen-year-old boy, all unarmed civilians, were shot and/or bayoneted to death in their homes by members of the second and sixth South Staffordshire Regiment of the British Army during their search for rebels in a row of three-storey houses in North King Street, Dublin 7. Upon the discovery of two bodies buried by the soldiers in a cellar of one of the houses a few days after the massacre, an internal enquiry by the British Army was conducted in late May 1916. The enquiry found no one responsible for the murders and a public enquiry was never conducted. Perhaps due to this lack of official attention and record keeping, or due to the fact that the event concerned the private lives of civilians not aligned politically or ideologically with the rebels, the massacre has not featured prominently in the official narrative of the 1916 rebellion as it took shape over the last century, and consequently, it has fallen out of public consciousness. However, a collection of eyewitness statements of the massacre survives in a document assembled by Irish Republican party, Sinn Féin, a few years after the event (*c.* 1919). Titled *A Fragment of 1916 History*, the document includes statements by thirty-eight women, mostly the wives and mothers of the men killed in North King Street.[11] These women's eyewitness statements inspired and formed the dramaturgical basis of the commemorative work by CoisCéim and Anu. During the massacre, which was conducted over several hours, the women were separated from the men in each house and held in rooms away from the parts of the building in which the killings took place. In their testimonies, the women describe hearing the deaths of their husbands, sons and fellow tenants, without knowing what was occurring, and then they describe finding their bodies after the soldiers departed. Instead of attempting a recreation of the narrative formed by the statements, choreographer Bolger, director Louise Lowe and visual artist Owen Boss were interested in trying to give a sense of what the massacre felt like for the women who could not see what was happening to the men. As Lowe explains about the creative process,

> I was thinking about the impact of what was happening on their other senses. They couldn't see what was happening. They were listening to it. Feeling it. ... That seemed to be a good opportunity to *consider* how might we *ever* kinaesthetically respond to it [the 1916 Rising] [original emphasis], rather than in a robotic piece of theatre, the easy way to look at the testimonies. But that is not what we want to do. We are not trying to recreate the testimonies. But want to consider how we can interrogate [the testimonies] in terms of the trauma on the body, let's say, or the place, or the architecture of the space? (in Bolger et al. 2016)

Similar to Stapleton's work in *Medicated Milk*, Bolger and Lowe were interested in interrogating material related to forgotten histories and voices through an embodied lens that paid attention to the impact of trauma. The narrative of the 1916 Rising is foundational to the creation of Irish national identity and sovereignty and the stories of the Rising's leaders and fighters are well known. However, the stories of the civilians affected by the fighting have only recently begun to be unearthed. The actual number of civilian casualties – 485, which accounted for 54 per cent of all deaths caused by the Rising – was only very recently established by a necrology project undertaken by the Dublin Cemeteries Trust (Glasnevin).[12] The women's experiences that emerge in *These Rooms* and *Falling Out of Standing* give insight into private memories of war not accounted for in the creation of official historical narratives of national commemoration. Bolger and Lowe's project works to shift the focus of commemoration from a celebration of military action to an archaeology of corporeal experience. Memories of traumatic events buried within collateral statistics are re-figured through a contemporary choreographic lens sensitized to the gender-political effects of post-colonial re-imaginings of national identity, and the role of commemoration within this process.

Site and memory

Bolger, Lowe and Boss were originally interested in creating a site-specific piece on the original site of the massacre. However, after researching historical maps of the site in North King Street, they discovered that the houses no longer existed. After decades of being left to decay, the row of ten houses in which the massacre took place had been demolished, and after years of the site being neglected as a wasteland, it had recently undergone regeneration to become a public green area. Considering how social production of a 'sense of the past' is created through public representations such as monuments, memorials and statues, and how these 'official representations affect individual or group conceptions of the past', C. Nadia Seremetakis uses the term 'dominant memory' to refer to the 'power and pervasion of certain historical representations, their connection with dominant institutions, and the part they play in winning consent' (2000: 308). In forging social consensus of what is worthy of commemoration, public sites of memory 'select what is to be remembered and how it is to be remembered', and, in doing so, 'can also generate forgetfulness and inattention' (ibid.). Many of the commemorated events and figures connected with the dominant memory of the 1916 Rising have connections with buildings and memorial statues. The General Post Office, a key battle site on Dublin's O'Connell Street and headquarters of the rebellion, for example, houses Oliver Sheppard's *Death of Cúchulainn* statue, chosen by Éamon de Valera, a surviving commander of the Easter Rising and subsequent Taoiseach (head of parliament) and president of Ireland, as the official memorial of the Rising for the twentieth anniversary commemorative celebrations in 1932. The North King Street massacre involved the deaths of citizens, not rebels, and the site was left unmarked for nearly a century until a commemorative plaque was erected in the run up to centenary celebrations in 2016. In response to the limitations of dominant memory, Seremetakis points out the importance of private memory (which also may be collective and shared) in the creation of an 'enmeshed memory' of a place that is sensory and embedded in matter (2000). Using the example of a city destroyed by the catastrophe of an earthquake, she argues that excavations of private memories can create an alternative cultural legacy, built from a 'poetics of fragments' when monuments of memorial are absent. In reconciling the distance between official historical narratives and private memories, she suggests that the human body can function as a site that bridges this gap.

In the absence of official memorialization of the massacre site, and the subsequent erasure of the buildings where the event took place, Bolger, Lowe and Boss constructed their commemoration of the event using the private memories of the thirty-eight women as the foundational structure. The women's memories of the event, embodied through dance, functioned as the corporeal bridge for an act of commemoration in the absence of the buildings in which the massacre took place. Creating an enmeshed memory of the massacre embedded in matter, the team of *These Rooms* used details from the women's private memories to reconstruct their vision of the houses of the original site in an architecturally similar house in 85/86 Upper Dorset Street (a twelve-minute walk from North King Street), in which they combined features from the original time of the massacre in 1916, with features from 1966, the fiftieth year of commemoration. In layering three separate time periods (1916, 1966 and 2016), *These Rooms* brought attention not only to the multi-layered processes of memory sedimentation at work in the building of commemorative narratives over time, but also to their potential malleability through the embodiment of alternative perspectives within seemingly solid structures.[13]

Vertigo and entrapment in split-screen choreographies

Similar to Stapleton's focus on creating an affective environment and avoiding a linear narrative approach in *Medicated Milk*, Bolger was also more interested in investigating the sensations and feelings evoked and transmitted through time by the women's memories of the massacre. Due perhaps to the physical erasure and subsequent forgetting of the original buildings where the traumatic event took place, there is an increased focus on the function of site in commemoration in *Falling Out of Standing*, and the building used to house the piece becomes an important dancing body in its own right. As Bolger explains, the work is 'a non-linear exploration of how memory and the energy of dramatic events is retained in the walls of buildings themselves and how this anguish is encountered through ghost like sensations in locations of conflict' (2017). The use of split-screen in the choreography of the film's editing also functions to present a multiplicitous view of action, destabilizing any attempt to read a single, homogenizing, narrative thread. The split-screen choreography is disorienting, (re-)creating an affective environment of confusion and dread. In the opening of *Falling Out of Standing*, we see the door to the same building in both split-screen frames. The camera then takes us on two different journeys through the door and up the stairs, travelling up and down the stairwell at great speed. The contrasting tempi and directions afforded by the split-screen create a vertiginous sensation – the bannisters whizz by, and the speed of motion is accentuated by the accompanying sound of a soft, bodhrán drum roll. A sensation of vertigo is played with throughout when objects are dropped from a high floor, and the drop is then echoed by men's bodies performing forward falls to the stairwell landings, holding their bodies horizontal to the floor. The choreography also works with the sensation of entrapment. In one scene, a woman dances in a window frame behind a lace curtain, performing frantic, flailing arm movements, reminiscent of a trapped moth drawn to light (or in this case, the sounds of the massacre) that will harm it, but which it cannot resist moving towards.

In another scene, the split-screen shows a different woman in each frame, pinned in corners of stairwell landings, a floor apart. They raise their arms again and again in protective, defensive movements as they perform slow circles, rotating their bodies on the spot, moving through postures of grief and horror in a seemingly unending, repeated pattern. These repeated movements and phrases make visible the trauma that possesses the bodies of the women survivors. Bolger's choreography of repetition dances the 'behavioural reenactments' (van der Kolk and van der Hart 1995: 172) of unresolved and unacknowledged trauma memories in the body. The spectator witnesses the corporeal effects of the sidelining of women's experiences in the creation of narratives of commemoration and national identity in Ireland; the silencing of women's stories condemns their traumatic experiences to be repeated until they can be resolved through integration into the commemorative narrative of the 1916 Rising.

Concluding thoughts

In her illuminating discussion of staging trauma, Miriam Haughton speaks of the 'silencing or "shadowing" of trauma and abuse directed at the female body and female experience in public discourse and representation' (2018: 5). Haughton's concept of 'shadowing' encompasses narratives and events that have not been 'fully silenced' or censored, but that have become 'de-escalated in urgency, isolated from public points of discourse, and somehow associated with threat or danger so that any individual or institution that may interact with them is at risk of becoming tainted by association' (ibid.). The women represented in both *Medicated Milk* and *Falling Out of Standing* can be seen to have undergone this shadowing process. In response, the choreographers of these works have not only sought to create alternative sites of commemoration allowing embodiment of their stories, but have also drawn explicit attention to their tenebrosity.

In communicating forgotten memories and traumas through sensation and the building of affective environments in dance performance, the choreographers of both *Medicated Milk* and *Falling Out of Standing* present an alternative, embodied lens through which commemorative events and figures can be viewed. In both works, the focus is on the embodiment of a poetics of fragments (Serematakis 2000), rather than the integration of these into dominant memories of commemoration. And so, in both works, the trauma memories remain unresolved and perpetuated without resolution for the viewer, remaining productively problematic, and discomforting, with the potential to disrupt 'official' commemorative narratives. Simultaneously, in seeming contradiction to the works' embracing of the ungraspable and tenebrous, it is interesting that both Stapleton and Bolger created an artwork of (relative) permanence in screendance that would exist after performances of the live version of their pieces ended; an artwork of memorialization. As the press release for *Falling Out of Standing* states, 'a fundamental aim of this project was to create a permanent legacy, a long term marker relevant to the present day that will live well beyond 2016'.[14] In the context of commemoration, the permanence desired can perhaps be reconciled with the ungraspable nature of the work's content through the ability of spectators to connect with movement and perform the work of integration into existing narratives themselves, carrying the memories of forgotten voices forward to be included in encounters with future commemorative events.[15] Alternative sites of commemoration produced can then be seen as living both within the choreographic cultural artefacts and in the bodies of the spectators who witness the works.

Considering the operation of spectators' feelings in relation to artworks of commemoration that deal with traumatic histories, Katherine Hite proposes that 'memorializing is a conjunction of affect and awareness', and that 'abstract commemorative art is that which moves viewers to react, but perhaps in a less immediate, more contemplative way that recognizes their distance, that acknowledges that viewers can connect and feel even when they cannot really know what it was to experience such trauma' (2012: 57). In retaining the unfinished, tenebrous and abstract nature of the women's stories represented in *Medicated Milk* and *Falling Out of Standing*, the choreographers hold on to their ability to both connect and move spectators, and to continue to haunt problematic and exclusionary imaginings of nationhood and commemoration. Dancing experiences omitted from official narratives of nation-building enable a corporealization of alternative realities within seemingly ossified narratives of commemoration, making them productively unfamiliar. Lending flesh to these voices, in a spirit of indeterminacy, creates sites where traditionally exclusionary and homogenizing commemorative narratives can be questioned for their impossibility.

Notes

1. See the 'About' section of the Decade of Centenaries website: https://www.decadeof centenaries.com/about/ (accessed 17 November 2022).
2. This freedom was only achieved for the twenty-six counties of the Republic of Ireland following the partitioning of the island to create the separate legal entity of Northern Ireland in 1921, which remains part of the UK.
3. A further significant dance performance foregrounding women's experiences for the Decade of Centenaries commemorative programme was *Embodied* (2016), a series of solos created by female choreographers in response to the first reading of the proclamation of Irish independence at the General Post Office in 1916.
4. Several of the first publication dates of Joyce's works are part of the Decade of Centenaries programme, with centenary celebrations in 2016 of the first publication of *A Portrait of the Artist as a Young Man*: https://www.decadeofcentenaries.com/6-december-2016-published-in-1916-james-joyces-a-portrait-of-the-artist-as-a-young-man-national-library-of-ireland-dublin-2/.
5. The live performance that provided the origins of *Falling Out of Standing* was *These Rooms* (2016). The analysis provided here is based on the screendance versions of the two works.
6. Parr links the difficulty of narrating trauma memories with an understanding of memory as always in motion, writing that, 'memory is dynamic and its movement is largely ungraspable' (Parr 2008: 1).
7. James M. Smith uses the term 'architecture of containment' to describe how the Irish state used imprisonment in institutions, such as Magdalen Laundries, to contain and discipline 'deviant' women, removing them from public visibility. He also suggests that this architecture continues to be present in how these women are remembered: in stories (artistic representations and survivor testimonies), rather than official histories (see Smith 2007).
8. 'His Master's Voice', or HMV, is an international recording industry trademark (originally used as the unofficial title of the British Gramophone Company Ltd., established in 1901) associated with a painting by Francis Barraud from the 1890s that depicts a terrier dog listening to a gramophone recording of his master's voice.
9. The images used in *Medicated Milk* were inspired by Stapleton's research of Lucia Joyce's dream diaries that she wrote during her time at St Andrew's Psychiatric Hospital in Northampton, England, between 1952 and 1982.
10. These reports include the *Ryan Report* (2009) by the Commission to Inquire into Child Abuse (CICA), investigating child abuse from the 1930s to the 1970s in religious industrial schools; the *Murphy Report* (2009), investigating the (mis) handling of clerical child sex abuse allegations by state and religious institutions between 1975 and 2004; and several interim reports by the Commission of Investigation into Mother and Baby Homes (2015–21), examining the (mis)treatment of women and babies in religious and public institutions between 1922 and 1998.
11. Available on the Decade of Centenaries website: http://www.decadeofcentenaries.com/30-april-1916-commemoration-of-north-king-street-massacre-dublin-7/ (accessed 10 November 2017).
12. The Glasnevin Cemetery is Ireland's national cemetery.
13. This house was also the location for *Falling Out of Standing*, which was filmed in the middle of the run of the live performance.

14. Quoted from the press release for *Falling Out of Standing* available on the CoisCéim website: http://coisceim.com/falling-out-of-standing-press-release/ (accessed 10 November 2017).
15. Recent developments in neuroscience are echoing and substantiating dance therapy practices founded on the knowledge that memories can be stimulated and accessed through one's own or another's movements (see Harris 2007).

References

Bolger, D., O. Boss, L. Lowe and K. E. Till (2016), 'From "Uninvited Rebellion" to "Collective Dreaming"', 10 February. Available online: http://theserooms.ie/wp-content/uploads/2016/06/BolgerEtAl2016_THESEROOMSbooklet_EdTill_w.pdf (accessed 23 November 2021).

Bolger, D. (2017), 'Director's Note for *Falling Out of Standing*', Limerick: Light Moves Festival, unpaginated programme notes.

Bolger, D., F. Ó Conchúir and Á. Stapleton (2017), 'Bodies in Time: Embracing History in Screendance', interview by Aoife McGrath for Light Moves Festival of Screendance, Limerick.

Caruth, C., ed. (1995), *Trauma: Explorations in Memory*, London: John Hopkins University Press.

Falling Out of Standing. (2016, 2017), Directed by D. Bolger, O. Boss and L. Lowe. Premiere: Dublin.

Gordon, A. (2008), *Ghostly Matters: Haunting and the Sociological Imagination*, London: University of Minnesota Press.

Harris, D. (2007), 'Dance/Movement Therapy Approaches to Fostering Resilience and Recovery among African Adolescent Torture Survivors', *Torture*, 17 (2): 134–55.

Haughton, M. (2018), *Staging Trauma: Bodies in Shadow*, Basingstoke: Palgrave.

Hite, K. (2012), *Politics and the Art of Commemoration: Memorials to Struggle in Latin America and Spain*, London: Routledge.

Kiberd, D. (1996), *Inventing Ireland: The Literature of a Modern Nation*, London: Vintage.

Massumi, B. (2006), 'The Voice of the Grain', in Bracha L. Ettinger (ed.), *The Matrixial Borderspace*, 201–13, London: University of Minnesota Press.

McGrath, A. (2013), *Dance Theatre in Ireland: Revolutionary Moves*, Houndmills: Palgrave.

McGrath, A., and E. Meehan (2018), *Dance Matters in Ireland: Contemporary Dance Performance and Practice*, Houndmills: Palgrave.

McKenna, M. D. (2012), 'In the Wake of Fair Use: Incest, Citation, and the Legal Legacy of *Finnegans Wake*', *Journal of Modern Literature*, 35 (4): 56–72.

Medicated Milk. (2016), Directed by Á. Stapleton in collaboration with J. M. Jiminez. Premiere: Dublin.

Moran, J. (2018), 'Children of the Revolution: 1916 in 2016', in E. Jordan and E. Weitz (eds), *The Palgrave Handbook of Contemporary Irish Theatre and Performance*, 783–98, Houndmills: Palgrave.

Parr, A. (2008), *Deleuze and Memorial Culture: Desire Singular Memory and the Politics of Trauma*, Edinburgh: Edinburgh University Press.

Quigley, C. (2018), 'Waking the Feminists', in Eamonn Jordan and Eric Weitz (eds), *The Palgrave Handbook of Contemporary Irish Theatre and Performance*, 85–90, Houndmills: Palgrave.

Scarry, E. (1985), *The Body in Pain: The Making and Unmaking of the World*, Oxford: Oxford University Press.
Seremetakis, N. (2000), 'The Other City of Silence: Disaster and the Petrified Bodies of History', in G. Brandstetter and H. Völckers (eds), *ReMembering the Body*, 302–32, Ostfildern-Ruit: Hatje Cantz Publishers.
Smith, James M. (2007), *Ireland's Magdalen Laundries and the Nation's Architecture of Containment*, Indiana: University of Notre Dame Press.
Van der Kolk, B., and O. Van der Hart (1995), 'The Intrusive Past: The Flexibility of Memory and the Engraving of Trauma', in Cathy Caruth (ed.), *Trauma: Explorations in Memory*, 158–82, London: John Hopkins University Press.

Part 3

Challenging the Nation/the State: Performing Affective Critiques

8

Performing/mourning Marikana as affective critique of a nation in crisis

Miki Flockemann

The Marikana massacre on 16 August 2012, when a task force of South African police shot thirty-four striking miners, exposed South Africa as a nation in crisis. The massacre continues to generate public debate and reverberates across other forms of cultural expression, especially theatre and performance. Of interest is how the reverberations of this crisis are manifested in the spectrum of events commemorating Marikana, which also illustrate the diverse intentions and performance modes associated with commemorative theatre. For instance, the notion of reverberation is evident in a response to a site-specific production, *Mari and Kana* (2015), which was staged against a backdrop of white crosses planted on the well-tended lawns of the historic Company Gardens in the heart of Cape Town three years after the massacre, in close proximity to the Houses of Parliament, but far away from where the massacre happened. In his review of *Mari and Kana*, Liduduma'lingani Mqomboti concludes his discussion by describing the lingering personal effect that the production had on him as a spectator.

> Long after the actors had left the stage, the audience had dispersed, and the stage was cleared of its props, I was left staring into the empty space where the play had taken place, reimagining it, dismissing it, attempting to abandon it there and not take it with but the play is still replaying in my mind, over and over again, action by action, haunting me to remember the Marikana Massacre. (Mqombothi 2015: 4)

While the intention of the playmaker was to enact a process of healing, Mqomboti questions whether the production does not in effect enact a reiteration of trauma – a haunting rather than a healing – where the scenes are replayed over and over again in the mind's eye. One notes the interplay between past and present captured in the tense shift, from the actors who 'had' left, to the image that 'is still replaying'. This reaction speaks to some of the problems associated with commemorative theatre in relation to a disjuncture between intention and effect.

In light of this, one aim here is to explore how commemorations of a singular event, in this case the Marikana massacre, encompass the different ways in which theatres of commemoration can be employed, and how the choice of aesthetic strategies shapes audience responses. At the same time, as noted by the tension between healing and haunting, some of the problems associated with commemorative theatre and performance are also foregrounded when looking at different commemorative productions of the same event in relation to one another. In addition, since a crisis is what brings matters to a tipping point, one needs to ask what (if any) changes are posited through these commemorations, and what future scenarios might be envisioned? Is it the nation that is in crisis, or is it the concept of South African nationhood itself that is under scrutiny? Or are we simply stuck in the replay of the same event, over and over again, as the past is repeated in the present?

As shall be demonstrated, the performance events dealing either directly or indirectly with the Marikana massacre can be read as illustrative of the continuum between the promise and the pitfalls of commemorative theatre and performance outlined in the introductory chapter. These range from spectacles which provide political critique through contestation, to productions drawing on the Marikana event as a source of nation rebuilding, or alternatively, as a means of uncovering hidden or marginalized histories of exclusion in the (not yet) post-apartheid state. Moreover, there is a strong emphasis on the therapeutic and healing aspects of commemoration via affective affinities with victims and a focus on relational notions of belonging, as well as how an extraordinary event can reveal the everyday. My focus, however, will be on the performative modes employed in works which can be described as mourning Marikana. These will be explored in terms of the synergies that have been identified by Mark Fleishman between what he terms the 'African mourning play' and Walter Benjamin's notion of the *Trauerspiel* (or sorrow/mourning play). Of particular interest is the affective impact of how, in the *Trauerspiel*, 'mourning breaks, as it were, into language, at the same time breaking apart the unity of sound and sense, sound and meaning' (Weigel 2015: 9), while in the African mourning play words are minimal or replaced by 'a vocabulary of gestures, physical images and choreographic sequences set against some kind of musical score' (Fleishman 2016: 8–9). Before looking at the performances in terms of the modalities outlined earlier, and then exploring possible implications for future scenarios in terms of the politics of nationhood and belonging, it is first necessary to sketch a brief background to the claims that the Marikana event marks a turning point in recent post-apartheid history.

Marikana as tipping point

After an unprotected strike[1] at the platinum mine run by Lonmin (a British-owned multinational company) escalated into violence following an impasse in negotiations during August 2012, Lonmin called on state assistance to end the strike. When the protesting miners collected with makeshift traditional weapons on a hill now named Marikana Mountain in the area formerly known in Afrikaans as 'Rooikoopies', or red hills' near Rustenburg, they were corralled by police using razor wire and thirty-four miners were shot as they tried to flee. However, following an inquiry into the event by the Farlam Commission, neither Lonmin, nor the minister of police and mine unions were held fully accountable. (Cyril Ramaphosa, the current South African president, was implicated as he was also on the board of Lonmin at the time, and apparently supported the use of force to bring the strike to an end.) Despite recommendations from the commission that Lonmin improve the 'appalling living conditions' of its workers and their families, to date not much has changed.

Commenting on the repercussions of the Marikana massacre as a 'turning point event',[2] Peter Alexander claims it signalled a 'rupture' leading to further occurrences, which include annual commemorations, both at the site of the shootings and elsewhere across South Africa. According to Alexander, 'We have not yet reached the end of this chain of occurrences, and the scale of the turning point remains uncertain' (2013: 605). He adds that as with other historical turning point events, 'Marikana has revealed structures unseen in normal times, providing an exceptional vantage point … and enabling actors to envisage alternative futures' (2013: 605). Alexander's claim speaks to the question posed earlier about what changes or future scenarios might be envisaged through commemorative performances, particularly given that the footage of the shootings went viral. In addition, the footage invited deeply disturbing parallels with images of the apartheid-era massacre in 1961, when police fired on the inhabitants of Sharpeville protesting against the infamous pass laws, as well as the 1976 Soweto student uprising. The most immediate 'occurrences' included increased and more militant strike action at other mines and across other sectors of labour, and the formation of a new political party, the Economic Freedom Front (EFF), led by expelled former youth leader in the African National Congress (ANC), Julius Malema. The new party, which situates itself left of the ANC (and comprises a number of its former members), claims that they are the mouthpiece of the disaffected working class. The EFF subsequently became the third largest party elected to Parliament in the general election of 2016.

The question prompted by the Marikana event about whether the apartheid era crisis of discrimination and inequality is repeating itself in the so-called post-apartheid present has become the subject of a number of documentaries, as well as the visual arts and theatrical performances which engage with the shootings from a variety of perspectives (see Lucy Graham, 'Representing Marikana', 2016).[3] At the same time, Marikana continues to haunt the news media in relation to service delivery and other protests. Further to this, a report published in August 2021 notes that no police, state nor mine official has yet been convicted. Instead, 'for nine slow years, this litany of injustices over Marikana has lain like a ghoulish incubus on our nation's soul, with the government failing to apologize, the police refusing to accept responsibility, and the mines putting money over life while the lives of the victims decline' (Forbes 2021: 4–5).

Performing cultural trauma as nation rebuilding spectacle, institutional contestation or sensory archive

One of the reasons that South African theatre can offer a useful vehicle for considering responses to historical events is that, as Yvette Hutchison points out, in dramatizing, narrativizing and reconstructing memories of what happened in the post-apartheid era, official narratives which favour 'coherence and consensus' can be challenged. In such cases, the theatrical work 'asks not what happened, but what can be drawn from the implications of the happenings' (2010: 68). Similarly, Sofie de Smet, Marike Breyne and Christel Stalpaert (2015) point out that the multiple narratives that can be played out in performance when dealing with cultural trauma such as Marikana provide scope for resisting a unilinear or master narrative of the event.

As shall be shown in the following section, these multiple narratives are evident in the spectrum of performative reverberations of the Marikana shootings. These range from political to artistic performances. In fact, initially the most common commemorations of the Marikana massacre took the form of nation rebuilding spectacles, as well as performances that celebrated recent heroes of post-apartheid struggles. This emphasis was in keeping with attempts to provide the kind of homogenizing narrative of the traumatic event that de Smet, Breyne and Stalpaert caution against. Although a number of other trends have emerged, this initial focus still has traction.

Arts festivals undoubtedly offer a productive index for identifying what can be seen as perhaps predictable responses to the Marikana event, in addition to offering unusual vantage points, making visible previously 'unseen' structures (Alexander 2013: 605). A case in point is the 2014 National Arts Festival with its somewhat misplaced triumphalist ethos celebrating twenty years of democracy, and marking the fortieth anniversary of the festival (the largest in the southern hemisphere), which happened to host the largest number of works which dealt either directly or indirectly with the Marikana massacre. From the outset it was striking how even at the same festival, performative responses approached the Marikana massacre from diverse vantage points. These included naturalistic and often rather schematic approaches which focused on issues of reconciliation, culpability and complicity (like *Marikana – the Musical* by Aubrey Sechaba, which attempted to use song and dance to present an even-handed portrayal of both the striking miners and the police),[4] to works which reclaimed the humanity and individuality of the miners as unsung heroes (such as *The Man in the Green Jacket* by Eliot Moleba, based on one of the slain strike leaders).[5] However, in tandem with these more predictable responses that focused on 'the shooters and the shot', other vantage points also emerged which revealed a shift of focus from the event, the place and the players involved (miners, police, Lonmin mine and state officials) to a more generalized and often ritualized aesthetics of mourning. As I shall suggest, this deepens the context of the massacre by offering a sensory archive of what miners go through to make a living.

As suggested earlier by de Smet, Breyne and Stalpaert, the value of performances dealing with the Marikana event is that by offering multiple or layered perspectives, they can generate a counter-narrative to the Truth and Reconciliation Commission's 'master discourse of forgiveness, reconciliation and disclosure' (2015: 228), which would locate a traumatic event like Marikana in the past. One of the consequences of creating a rupture between the past and the present is that it allows one to evade the acute reminder of how the images of the Marikana shootings replay the traumatic shootings of the apartheid era, and thus trouble current notions of nationhood and belonging in a democratic South Africa (de Smet, Breyne and Stalpaert 2015: 228).

While the performances dealing with the shooters and the shot used mainly naturalistic performance styles, another commemorative performance mode which gained considerable traction in later productions was also already in evidence at the

2014 National Arts Festival, as illustrated by a short but compelling performance by Tebogo Munyai, *Doors of Gold*. What was distinctive about this performance was that it did not address Marikana directly or attempt to make sense of that specific event. Alternatively, it was a mourning ritual that functioned as an embodied and intangible archive (Taylor 2003) of the experiences of those miners for whom, as Munyai puts it, 'there is not even a trace of it in the archive' (2014: 26). While Munyai's work did not receive the same recognition as works like *Marikana – The Musical* or *The Man in the Green Jacket*, his performance offered a vantage point that subsequently gained considerable momentum by producing an affective commemorative aesthetic.

Performing/mourning Marikana: *Doors of Gold*

Munyai's *Doors of Gold* was presented in the Performance Art category, one of four works that were part of a site-specific production, *20/20 Vision*. The piece was performed in a dingy unlit basement room with the mostly standing audience crammed into an uncomfortable and discomforting airless space, while Munyai, naked except for a miner's torch flickering from his groin, moved spasmodically on a grave-like area covered by a thick black shiny plastic sheet surrounded by gold skulls. There was an uncanny ritual feel to the production, reminiscent in terms of the music and movement of a shamanistic San trance dance[6] while the space evoked a sense of suffocation caused by being trapped underground. The vulnerability of the miner was exacerbated by his nakedness as well as by the tortured movements that designated yearning and fear. During his performance, the skulls and stones positioned around the grave space were lifted at intervals and an incantation performed. The focus of this work was not on what happened at Marikana but turned inwards to what it is like to be a miner, to be down a mine shaft, to lose one's life there.

Munyai's affective performance aesthetic, as I shall show in the next section, has synergies with a number of other works produced subsequently. This focus on the everyday trauma experienced by miners (as well as their families), which keeps resurfacing in public spaces as in *Door of Gold*, thus refuses to be relegated 'safely' to the past and situates the spectator as complicit witness. Looking at Munyai's piece in relation to a series of performances at the landmark 2014 National Arts Festival suggests that one of the reasons that his wordless performance lingered was because, as argued by Deleuze and Guattari (1988) and Massumi (2002), affect travels between human and material bodies, in this case the bodies of the spectators and the performers. In addition, Munyai's performance anticipated a series of works developed subsequently, which can be described as mourning Marikana, and thus serves as a prompt for tracking some of the diverse perspectives and performance strategies employed in a performative mourning.

A year after the 2014 National Arts Festival, several Cape Town-based works employed similar affective performance aesthetics as *Doors of Gold* in engaging with the Marikana massacre. Some examples include *Ashed* (2015) performed at the Artscape Theatre by the Unmute dance company choreographed and directed by Themba Mbuli,[7] and two site-specific productions at the annual Infecting the City Festival which focuses on public art forms, *Mari and Kana* (2015) by Mandisi Sindo,[8] which was followed by a companion piece, also dealing with Marikana, *Iqhiya Emnyama* (2015) by Cindy Mkaza-Siboto. *Ashed* begins with a percussive soundscape that is shattered by volleys of gunshots as the lights come up to reveal a landscape of devastation as bodies lie scattered amongst sculpted wire figures, to illustrate Mbuli's comment: 'here is what was done in the past (i.e., Sharpeville/Soweto) and here is what is being done again' (Marikana) (2015: n.p.).[9] On the other hand, in *Iqhiya Emnyama* (the title refers to the black headscarf worn by women in mourning), the spectators follow a group of women walking along the wide leafy path called government avenue in the direction of the Parliament buildings, carrying mattresses (signifying past baggage as well as the mattrasses that mourning women sit upon). As a framework for approaching such works (but with a focus on *Mari and Kana*) as 'mourning Marikana' I shall engage with Fleishman's description of what he calls 'the African Mourning play', as well as de Smet, Breyne and Stalpaert's discussion of the potential of performance to avoid replicating master discourses that relegate trauma to the past.

Mari and Kana: Commemoration as *Trauerspiel*

Both Fleishman and de Smet, Breyne and Stalpaert emphasize the interrelatedness of present and past as common to South African performance practice. Performances such as *Mari and Kana* and *Iqhiya Emnyama* as de Smet, Breyne and Stalpaert point out (2015), in effect speak to the presence of the past, given that performance is a live event witnessed by spectators who in some cases become participants. Fleishman (2016) makes a similar point in his discussion of the dramaturgical implications of how, as a neo-apartheid society, South Africans are still haunted by the unsettled ghosts of a traumatic past (also recalled in David Frank's reference to Marikana as a 'ghoulish incubus on our nation's soul'). This extends to a remembered, cross-generationally inherited, but not personally experienced, past. Fleishman uses Michael Ignatief's claim that societies undergoing rapid and often violent social transition 'are not living in a serial order of time but in a simultaneous one in which the past or the present are a continuous agglutinated mass of fantasia, distortions, myths and lies' (in Fleishman 2016: 4). Ignatief's claim acts as an incentive for artists to find performance practices 'that engage in an active way with the persistence of the past in the present lest it block the emergence of a desired future' (Fleishman 2016: 5). At the same time, Fleishman's description of performance practices that attempt to give expression to (unspeakable) trauma as characteristic of 'the African mourning play' has synergies with de Smet, Breyne and Stalpaert's description of the two site-specific works *Mari and Kana* and *Iqhiya Emnyama* as 'requiems' (2015: 222), in which the performers make us aware of the 'unfinished' aspect of the Marikana massacre.

Commemorations of Marikana as African mourning plays prompt further questions on some of the issues touched on earlier, such as how the modes of commemoration selected shape notions of nationhood and belonging, and what (if any) changes are posited through these commemorations, as well as what future scenarios might be envisioned. As a point of departure for this discussion, it is useful to look more closely at Fleishman's description of characteristic features of the African mourning play in which he takes up Walter Benjamin's distinction between the conventions of tragedy and the *Trauerspiel*.

In his treatise on *The Origins of German Tragic Drama*, Benjamin contrasts the classic tragic form involving sacrifice and catharsis embedded in mythic consciousness, and the *Trauerspiel*, which unlike classic tragedy, does not offer textual closure, but is open-ended, resulting not in reconciliation, but agitation. It can be argued that there are significant parallels between the wordless ritualized and ceremonial performance mode of *Doors of Gold*, and Benjamin's claim that while tragedy does not require an audience, *Trauer* signifies sorrow, and the lament, as well as the ceremonies and memorabilia of grief, 'demand audience' (Steiner 1998: 17). Moreover, Benjamin sees classic tragedy as operating outside history, whereas the *Trauerspiel* is a response to events that occur in history and evokes a sense of the 'still-open future' (Eiland 2019: xii). As a side note to the notion of *Trauerspiel*, it is noteworthy that official accounts refer to Marikana as a tragedy rather than a massacre as a way of avoiding institutional culpability. At the same time, accounts that are highly critical of official reports of the event also describe it as a tragedy, not in the way referred by Benjamin as 'outside history', but in keeping with contemporary engagements with tragedy which stress the critical and strategic function of the concept of tragedy as a way to think through the post-colonial present (Scott 2014). Similarly, Simon Critchley stresses tragedy's vital revelatory function in showing how we 'collude, seemingly unknowingly, with the calamity that befalls us" (2019: 2); while Martha Nussbaum argues that tragedy provides an important space for grappling with an ethics of responsibility (2003).[10]

According to Fleishman, in the African mourning play, communication or the desire for a common understanding is not the primary objective; rather, there is an attempt to generate an experience that is immediate, sensual, felt, and somatic' (2016: 9). Fleishman explains that the notion of 'collective mourning' is in keeping with African mourning rituals in that the performances as it were served as a 'proxy' for stages of mourning that have been missed (2016: 13), and this requires the presence of an audience. This is in keeping with Benjamin's description of the *Trauerspiel* as 'a quasi-musical hybrid form, characterized by the endlessly resonating "word in transformation"', whereas, 'the irrevocably closed form of classic tragedy [is] grounded in the "eternal immobility of the spoken word"' (Eiland 2019: xii). Similarly, as Sigrid Weigel points out, for Benjamin, the lament encompasses the endless resonance of sound, and what emerges from the failed attempt to verbalize is music. As noted earlier, as mourning breaks into language it at the same time breaks apart 'the unity of word and sense, sound and meaning' (Fleishman 2016: 9). This again has a bearing on the African mourning play where, as Fleishman explains, spoken language is limited or replaced by a vocabulary of physical images and gestures, as well as 'choreographic sequences set against some kind of musical score' (2016: 8–9). The focus on music and sound and the fluidity of 'words in transformation' has synergies with the affective aspect of Munyai's *Doors of Gold*. Similarly, a continuous musical soundscape is integral to, and resonates with, the embodied communicative acts of the performers in *Mari and Kana* and *Ashed* where sound and movement combine to establish the semiotic landscape of both productions.

At the beginning of *Mari and Kana*, two widows clad in deep-blue dresses and headscarves move frenziedly, as if driven by the push and pull of a strong emotional force, across a graveyard of white crosses facing the Iziko Art Museum in Cape Town's Company Gardens. They move, by turns stopping, collapsing, clutching each other, cupping their hands over smouldering bunches of *imphepo* (a herb used in cleansing rituals), or moving agitatedly to opposite sides of the graveyard in what seems like a search, a yearning. Their movements embody a sense of loss, of chaos, of disbelief that seems at odds with the symmetry of the classic colonial architecture of the building behind them, as well as the ordered patterning of the landscaped gardens, where the pleasing geometric layout obscures its colonial history of violent dispossession. By situating the performance in this historic site, the Marikana massacre is thus superimposed on an older history of colonialism and slavery in Cape Town as well as juxtaposed with the 'official' versions of that history archived in the Natural History Museum adjacent to the performance site. After the two young men, Mari and Kana, dressed in orange prison uniforms, are brought in by two khaki-clad policemen, it emerges that they are the sons of the husbands the women are searching for. The continuous grieving ritual of the women evolves into cleansing ceremonies for the sons as they prepare for their own mourning rituals for their fathers.

At the same time, as de Smet, Breyne and Stalpaert observe, the interchangeability of roles is apparent in the transition from perpetrator to victim, which is in stark contrast to the opposing communities of miners and police in *Marikana – The Musical*. In an interview, Sindo explains that his aim was to heal and that his focus was not on the dead miners but on 'those left behind' (2015: n.p.). However, he also notes that the performance did not necessarily have that effect and acted instead as a provocation, adding that while reports on Marikana are constantly featured on television, he was struck by how the spectators ('of all colours') shared the grief of those left behind. This is also borne out by the reaction of the spectator quoted in the epigraph, whose words echo both Sindo as well as Benjamin's notes on the *Trauerspiel*. In response to Sindo's comments that the purpose of his theatre is 'to help people to heal' (2015: 3), Mqombothi notes that 'to an extent the performance does this but also it does something else, something more terrifying than helping people to heal. It opens wounds that have not healed', and instead, 'one did not experience the feeling of healing but grief, anguish and the spirit of the dead circling around' (2015: 3). This evokes not only the dead miners, but also the additional sedimentation of unmourned dead dating from the first colonial encounters.

This response resonates with the description of the sorrow/mourning play as outlined by Benjamin, which results not in reconciliation, but agitation. This agitation dominated the movements of the performer in *Doors of Gold* as well as the grieving women in *Mari and Kana*. In the case of the latter, agitation dominates despite the fact that, at the end, as the mothers/widows are led away, their movements are slowed from the restless anguish of before to a gently rhythmic dance-like step as the chorus sing, 'The day of the sun is coming / The heaven is not going to rain and thunder forever / Heal my son. Calm my son' (trans. Mqombothi 2015: 3–4). Nevertheless, the resonance of the music of the lament referred to earlier continues to linger, a sound that haunts. This is captured in Mqombithi's claim that, 'the text of the music still haunts me many days later after the show. It echoes and echoes in the back of my mind like a voice yelling in the dark' (2015: 4). Instead of attempting to find closure or a single, consensual account (as attempted in *Marikana – The Musical*), the ephemeral nature of such site-specific works, as de Smet, Breyne and Stalpaert (2015: 221) point out, enables the construction of multiple narratives which avoid and question a unilateral account of the event.

The ubiquitous presence of female figures in mourning clothes, as both Fleishman and de Smet point out, signifies unfinished mourning. For instance, the grieving women in *Mari and Kana* embody the collective aspect of the African mourning play, characterized through their restless interactions with the graves of their slain husbands and their living sons, and with one another. In *Ashed*, a woman dressed in flowing robes is present on stage throughout, by turns a choric, ancestral or prophetic figure who sings and chants to an evocative soundscape. At the end she too becomes a mourning figure as she circles a pile of living and sculpted bodies, while singing the national anthem as a minor key lament. However, in *Mari and Kana* kinship bonds are created by the connectedness between 'those left behind' referred to by Sindo, who share a common grief. It can also be argued that even if they cannot change the nature of the events, these female figures can affect how they are remembered. Moreover, as Irene Stengs claims, public (rather than private) commemoration 'is always a political act' because public commemoration demonstrates that 'the significance of a deceased person reaches beyond his or her direct social environment' (2009: 102). This is borne out in the 'unfinished' nature of the mourning processes performed here, which, as will be discussed in the next section, can be read as a form of political critique.

Final remarks: The possibilities and problems of commemoration as mourning

From what has been discussed so far, the performances engaging with the Marikana massacre can be seen to travel in two broadly different directions, some opting for closure (and it seems that these have gained the most popular traction as in *Marikana – The Musical*), while the two works referred to above are representative of more ephemeral events of unfinished mourning. The resonance referred to by Fleishman between the African mourning play and Benjamin's *Trauerspiel* invites further questions about the implications of such aesthetics of mourning. One could ask: does this emphasis on mourning in works like *Doors of Gold* and *Mari and Kana*, as well as the reductive focus on forgiveness and social cohesion in *Marikana – The Musical*, allow the neo-liberal South African state and its multinational allies to, literally, 'get away with murder'? Yet again? Moreover, does the focus on mourning, rather than challenging the events that led to the massacre, not feed into the continuing marginalization of those communities, who should be claiming, in Henri Lefebvre's terms, their 'Right to the City' and citizenship (1996), but instead remain stuck in a loop of poverty and exclusion, unable to move forward? That could certainly be one way of looking at it. However, a counterargument could be that the refusal of closure is itself a dissent, a form of resistance that refuses to speak back to power using the state's own discourse in attempting to challenge, to critique or to explain the massacre. Instead, the focus on the acts of mourning forces onlookers (but of course only those onlookers open to the experience) to be complicit witnesses to an unsettling and discomforting sensory and affective archive of commemoration, rather than being kept at a 'safely' abstract distance from the presence of those without trace in the official archive.

Given the claim that theatre is where nations can be scrutinized (Holdsworth 2010), and that as noted earlier, the Marikana massacre exposed South Africa as a nation in crisis, what can one infer (rather than conclude) about notions of nationhood and belonging from these commemorative performances? For instance, in considering what the Marikana massacre means for the post-apartheid state, Vishwas Satgar wryly observes that maybe the question should be rephrased, 'Is the Marikana massacre simply a manifestation of what the state has become in South Africa'? (2012: 34). This comment speaks to the questions posed earlier about how the aesthetic modes employed in commemorative theatre and performance might shape responses, and what, if any, future scenarios are posited. As noted, the approach that sets up spectacular contestations between miners and police in *Marikana – The Musical* backfires as a nation rebuilding event. In the end, it plays into problematic notions of South African exceptionalism and autochthonous belonging in terms of rural, urban and ethnic identities, rather than challenging the exclusion of those marginalized by economic inequality who are now also citizens. It is telling that Sindo remarks in an interview (2015) that he does not see the Marikana massacre as a unique event that will not happen again. He links Marikana to the ongoing xenophobic attacks on fellow 'foreign' Africans that are fuelled by similar notions of South African exceptionalism and autochthonous belonging – despite the claim by Magaziner and Jacobs (2012) that Marikana in effect marks the end of notions of South African exceptionalism.

One way out of such an impasse would be to recognize the fluidity of the concept of citizenship itself, and to accept that citizenship should be viewed not in terms of status, but as an 'act'. For instance, drawing on Isin (2009), Christopher Stroud distinguishes between acts of citizenship and citizenship as a legal status: 'acts of citizenship are the processes whereby new actors, seeking recognition in the public space in order to determine a new course of events, shift *the location of agency and voice*' (emphasis in original, 2018: 21). As we have seen, *Marikana – The Musical* simply replays familiar oppositional tropes, which also explains its ongoing popular appeal. Nonetheless, in terms of the alternative vantage points offered by works like *Doors of Gold, Ashed, Iqhiya Emnyama* and *Mari and Kana*, it could be argued that the practices of unfinished mourning can themselves be seen as acts of citizenship through the way the 'unfinished' and apparently private everyday effects of the Marikana massacre are inserted into the public realm again and again by 'new actors', thus 'shifting the location of agency and voice' (Stroud 2018: 21). It is also important to remember that considering the fact that the majority of miners and their families have been legal citizens with voting rights since 1994, this serves as a further indictment of their ongoing exclusion in the post-apartheid era. Moreover, by situating spectators as both witnesses and fellow citizens ('of all colours' as remarked by Sindo earlier), the Marikana event offers a challenge to the very notion of South African citizenship.

While these commemorative performances of unfinished mourning do not necessarily envisage future scenarios, such performative practices, as Fleishman claimed earlier, nevertheless fulfil an urgent need to engage with 'the persistence of the past in the present lest it block the emergence of a desired future' (2016: 4). In tracking performative commemorations of Marikana, I have shown how works employing a performance mode of unfinished mourning open up a form of affective critique of notions of post-apartheid nationhood, citizenship and belonging by placing those generally excluded centre stage. The intersubjective performance event as a live encounter between performer and onlooker lingers in the memory of the onlookers, and as pointed out, despite attempts 'at dismissing it, attempting to abandon it there and not take it with' (Mqombothi 2015: 4), the event continues to resonate and to affect the spectator. Performative commemorations that opt for closure, however, close off potential critique or alternative scenarios. On the other hand, as argued here, the affective encounter generated by the performance modes of unfinished mourning function as an affective critique of the Marikana massacre, persisting as discomforting after-images, or as reverberating sound echoes that refuse to stay safely relegated to the past, and in the process unsettling prevailing notions of nationhood and belonging.

Notes

1. The strike was considered illegal because the miners who felt largely dissatisfied with union representation had not followed the protocols outlined in the Labour Relations Act of 1996.
2. Alexander is drawing on the historian William Sewall who equates a historical turning point with an 'event', often identified in hindsight.
3. Lucy Graham focuses on three documentaries (Rehad Desai's *Miners Shot Down*, Stephen Kaganof's controversial *Night is Coming: A Threnody for the victims of Marikana* and *Mama Marikana*), as well as Ayanda Mabulu's satirical painting, 'Yakhal "inkomo"', to show how the landscape of structural violence characterizing the State's response to the striking miners needs to be read in relation to a history of rural resistance.
4. Sekhaba adapted the play from the book *We Are Going to Kill Each Other Today – The Marikana Story* (2013) and defended his choice of musical to tell the story, arguing that the miners themselves tell their stories through song; he noted that, since 'we' have forgiven the apartheid government for shootings from Sharpeville to Mamelodi, 'surely we can forgive each other for shooting each other in Marikana' (2014: 3).
5. Mgcineni 'Mabush' Noki from rural Pondoland was a popular strike leader, well-known for wearing a bright green blanket.
6. The San are indigenous inhabitants of South Africa, and have First Nation Status in the United Nations.
7. Unmute is an integrated dance company drawing on both abled and non-abled performers.
8. Mandisi Sindo choreographed and directed the work which was presented by Theatre4Change Therapeutic Theatre.
9. For a more detailed discussion of *Ashed*, see Flockemann (2019).

10. See Flockemann, 'Antigone's Return: When a One-Told Story Is Not Enough', *English in Africa* (2022).

References

Alexander, P. (2013), 'Marikana, Turning Point in South African History', *Review of African Political Economy*, 40 (138): 605–9.

Critchley, S. (2019), 'Simon Critchley on Tragedy: Colluding in Our Calamity. From *Oedipus the King* to *Breaking Bad*, We Do It to Ourselves', *Literary Hub,* 18 April. Available online: lithub.com/simon-critchley-on-tragedy-colluding-in-our-calamity/ (accessed 9 August 2021).

de Smet, S., M. Breyne and C. Stalpaert (2015), 'When the Past Strikes the Present: Performing Requiems for the Marikana Massacre', *South African Theatre Journal*, 28 (1): 222–41.

Deleuze, G., and F. Guattari (1988), *A Thousand Plateaus: Capitalism and Schizophrenia*, trans. B. Massumi, London: Athlone Press.

Eiland, H. (2019), 'Translator's Introduction', in W. Benjamin, *Origin of the German Trauerspiel*, trans. H. Eiland, xi–xxiii, Cambridge: Cambridge University Press.

Fleishman, M. (2016), ' "Peeling the Wound": Dramaturgies of Haunting on the Neo-Apartheid Stage', Unpublished keynote address, Re-moving Apartheid Symposium, Ghent, Belgium, 29 September.

Flockemann, M. (2019), ' "What the Body Can Do": Creating Space for Critical Hope through Affective Encounters with a Different Kind of Otherness', *International Journal of Critical Diversity Studies*, 2 (1): 10–23.

Flockemann, M. (forthcoming), 'Antigone's Return: When a One-Told Story Is Not Enough', *English in Africa*.

Forbes, D. (2021), 'The Unfolding of a Never-Ending Tragedy', *Daily Maverick: 168 Commemoration*, 14 August. Available online: https://www.dailymaverick.co.za/article/2021-08-14-marikana-the-unfolding-of-a-never-ending-tragedy/ (accessed 5 January 2022).

Graham, L. (2016), 'Representing Marikana', *Journal of Postcolonial Studies*, 18 (6): 834–51.

Holdsworth, N. (2010), *Theatre and Nation*, Basingstoke: Palgrave.

Hutchison, Y. (2010), 'Post-1990s Verbatim Theatre in South Africa. Exploring an African Concept of "Truth" ', in C. Martin (ed.), *Dramaturgy of the Real on the World Stage*, 61–71, Basingstoke: Palgrave Macmillan.

Isin, E. F. 'Citizenship in Flux: The Figure of the Activist Citizen', *Subjectivity* 29: 367–88.

Lefebvre, H. (1996), *Writings on Cities*, trans. E. Kofman and E. Lebas, Cambridge, MA: Blackwell.

Magaziner, D., and S. Jacobs (2012), 'The End of South African Exceptionalism', *The Atlantic*, 27 August. Available online: theatlantic.com/international/archive/2012/08/the-end-of-south-african-exceptionalism/261591/ (accessed 3 May 2019).

Massumi, B. (2002), *Parables for the Virtual: Movement, Affect, Sensation*, Durham, NC: Duke University Press.

Mbuli, T. (2015), 'Choreographer Themba Mbuli on *Ashed*', *SABC Digital News*, 26 February. Available online: http://iono.fm/e/144394 (accessed 12 May 2019).

Mqombothi, L. (2015), 'Stirring the Spirits of the Dead Miners of Marikana', *Africa Is a Country*, 19 March. Available online: africasacountry.com/2015/03/stirring-the-spirits-of-the-miners-a-review-of-the-play-mari-kana (accessed 16 June 2018).

Munyai, T. (2014), *National Arts Festival Programme*, 3–13 July, Grahamstown.
Nussbaum, M. C. (2003), 'Tragedy and Justice: Bernard Williams Remembered', *Boston Review*, 1 October. Available online: https://bostonreview.net/articles/martha-c-nussbaum-tragedy-and-justice/ (accessed 13 November 2021).
Satgar, V. (2012), 'Beyond Marikana: The Post-Apartheid South African State'. *African Spectrum*, 47 (2–3): 33–62.
Scott, D. (2014), *Omens of Adversity: Tragedy, Time, Memory, Justice*, Durham, NC: Duke University Press.
Sekhaba, A. (2014), *National Arts Festival Programme*, 3–13 July, Grahamstown.
Sindo, M. (2015), 'Mandisi Sindo & *Theatre4change Therapeutic Theatre* – T3 Mari and Kana, Director's Notes', *YouTube*, 4 May. Available online: youtube.com/watch?v=6FcCzS7Anko (accessed 30 April 2019).
Steiner, G. (1998), 'Introduction', in W. Benjamin, *The Origin of German Tragic Drama*, trans. J. Osborne, 7–24, London: Verso.
Stengs, I. (2009), 'Death and Disposal of the People's Singer: The Body and Bodily Practices in Commemorative Ritual', *Mortality*, 14 (2): 102–18.
Stroud, C. (2018). 'Linguistic Citizenship', in L. Lim, C. Stroud and L.Wee (eds), *The Multilingual Citizen: Towards a Politics of Language for Agency and Change*, 17–39, Bristol: Multilingual Matters.
Taylor D. (2003), *The Archive and the Repertoire: Performing Cultural Memory in the Americas*, Durham, NC: Duke University Press.
Weigel, S. (2015), 'Brunhilde's Lament: The Mourning Play of the Gods: Reading Wagner's Musical Dramas with Benjamin's Theory of Music', *The Opera Quarterly*, Advance Access (18 April): 1–18.

9

Resonances of mnemonic community: Turkey's Kurdish Question in European opera

Pieter Verstraete

For the last decade, Turkey is said to be at a historical crossroads. Underneath the rapidly changing sociopolitical climate, there is a more fundamental epistemological and cultural shift taking place, affecting Turkey's 'communalist' consciousness, which is deeply rooted in Turkey's history of the public sector and state institutionalism, but it also manifests culturally on the music and theatre stage.[1]

Historically, communalism developed out of a movement of solidarity between social groups, usually in a context of dynamic opposition between communities and a colonial state, which under the development of independent nation states gave further rise to the emergence of the usually ethnically based question: which group can claim national identity? In the case of Turkey, besides the communalism that defines the 'Turk' based on Kemalist principles (i.e. founding father Mustafa 'Kemal' Atatürk's fundamentals of the Turkish Republic: republicanism, populism, nationalism, secularism, reformism or revolutionism, and statism), communalism is historically even more associated with the Kurds who, as dispersed people scattered across different state borders, at certain times have claimed cultural and political legitimacy.[2]

Communalism has then more revolutionary connotations for the Kurds who identify today with the Kurdish liberation movement, as a political way of organizing and/or practicing a way of living together based on federated communes. This defies the historical 'Turkish contract' so central to the Kemalist nation-building project, despite decades-long concomitant efforts by many Turkish Kurds to assimilate. It is within this tension that cultural practices of memory and commemoration for individuals who do not feel represented by the state culture or who are deliberately silenced are highly instrumental, particularly in times when these practices are little endured and even prohibited.

Theatre has played an essential role in commemorative practice for centuries in this respect. Ever since Aristotle's mimesis concept in his *Poetics* avowed theatre's essential role in learning through repetition, it became a tool for communities to relive past events and express their common identity, thereby (re)producing it time and time again as a communal practice and ritual. Among the performing arts, music has perhaps even more potential to evade censorship and appeal to communities in terms of a common imagined identity and a shared, embodied and commonly understood experience. In the present chapter, I therefore propose to look at one particular form of theatre, namely music theatre, for its potential to express issues of identity, memory and commemoration in one of the historically most censored mnemonic communities in Turkey, the Kurds. Given the current context of state coercion in Turkey and the international consternation it has caused, particularly in areas of Turkish and Kurdish diaspora, it is unsurprising that the most thought-provoking productions that support the Kurdish identity and memory culture are produced outside of Turkey.

According to Eviatar Zerubavel (1996), language and narration play significant roles in the constitution and preservation of identities and communities under threat that define their existence on a mnemonic basis, or what he calls, 'mnemonic communities'. By means of a case study of the first Kurdish opera *Tosca* (2019)[3] which addresses the concerns of such a community divided over many countries, I aim to challenge Zerubavel's suggestions of mnemonic socialization and community by reading them against Nancy's (1991) philosophical considerations on the unmaking of community, or as he calls it, an 'inoperative community'. The latter is significant in a larger argument that questions the risk of such critical commemorative music theatre practices of falling into the trap of creating new myths for the sake of political propaganda or for an industry around memory and commemoration.

Besides language, I will claim that the staging of collective memories and mnemonic acts of 'musicking' (Small 1998) play a significant role too, not only from within but also in solidarity with Turkey's subaltern communities, particularly the Kurds. Musicking will be discussed as an extension of Zerubavel's theory and criticism by means of the case study. As verb and action, musicking refers to the full musical experience as social process, in line with Small's original definition that stressed the taking 'part, in any capacity, in a musical performance' (1999: 12), be it by performing, rehearsing, listening, dancing and so on. Musicking is not so much about music as sound or as execution of a score, but as social relationship (Kun 2000: 11). Small deliberately coined this all-inclusive term to talk about precisely the grey area between what 'performers are doing and what the rest of those present are doing' (ibid.), thereby circumventing the traditional dichotomy between the act of music production and what Kant once called 'disinterested contemplation'. This will prove to be most fruitful to discuss commemoration in music theatre where all present are welcomed to *do it together*. It is my contention that musicking plays a vital role in transgressing national borders to allow expression of underrepresented identities, while taking part in celebrating and commemorating them.

Context: Turkey, an odd case

Turkey is an odd case as music theatre and opera are not indigenous art forms in the strictest sense, apart from Atatürk's attempts to introduce this European art form into the newly established modern republic by means of commissioned operas. These include *Özsoy* (a neologism meaning, *Pure Ancestry*, 1934) and *Taşbebek* (*The Doll*, 1934) by Ahmed Adnan Saygun as well as the unfinished *Bayönder* (*The Leader*,

1934) by Necil Kazım Akses and *Ülkü Yolu* (*Path of Idealism*, 1935) by Ulvi Cemal Erkin, all to which Atatürk is claimed to have personally provided dramaturgical notes. Significantly, as Ryan Gingeras (2019) remarks, the state's energies at the time were directed towards supporting the creation of a new, national style of music, which according to the then leading Turkish sociologist and political activist Ziya Gökalp meant a 'marriage of folk and Western music' (1968: 99; qtd. in Gingeras 2019: 274) through which Atatürk's pan-Turkic dream of nationalism and modernization would find its antagonistic cultural expression against the old Ottoman historical, cultural and geographical alliances. Though started almost a century ago, the resonances of this modernist cultural project, also called a 'Turkishness' contract (Ünlü 2016), continue to have wide-reaching implications today, including for Kurds historically minorized under this doctrine.

Turkey is also an odd case as new music theatre works are produced within the Turkish diaspora in Europe, while a critical project like the first Kurdish *Tosca* is today virtually unimaginable in Turkey's current political climate. Its rehearsals had to be moved unexpectedly from Diyarbakir to the basement of a burned down theatre in Istanbul because of a sudden mayor switch ('Kanun' in Turkish). Because of Turkey's military operations in Northern Syria, its Turkish premiere was first postponed and eventually cancelled. A previous project by the same director, Celil Toksöz, namely the first Kurdish adaptation of Shakespeare's *Hamlet*, which already included sung parts in the Kurdish dengbêj tradition (more on that later), met with a different fate then. As a result of a brief reform period in 2013 called the Kurdish Opening or Kurdish Initiative, peace talks between the Turkish government and the Kurdistan Workers' Party (PKK) were reopened, which brought instant fame to the theatre tour with subsequent broadcastings of the play on television and occasional visits by respected politicians across the political spectrum. With this contrast in mind, Toksöz's main question today cannot be relevant any more: 'Do we need to forget our culture or to keep on struggling to keep it alive?' (Beeckmans 2012; my trans., qtd. in Verstraete 2018: 65).

Furthermore, Atatürk's historical nation-building project created a very powerful mnemonic community of Kemalists in Turkey who form the backbone of Turkey's secularist 'communalist' consciousness in the state's administrative and educational culture (Turkish *laikık*), which for a long time in history impeded the means of cultural existence of a Kurdish identity. Since state theatre artists are historically associated with the Kemalist project, the political climate today has amplified the need for more cautious dramaturgical approaches that are not potentially seen as harmful by the state, particularly after the post-coup emergency law was lifted, on 25 July 2018, when all state theatres including opera and ballet were placed under the direct control of the newly installed presidency. For the Kurds, however, dramaturgical hints amidst state-organized censorship practices were already a fact of the stage from 1987 onwards when the then emergency situation was declared permanently in the Kurdish regions to restrain armed conflict. Special security forces would make occasional checks in spaces that would attract large crowds. Occasional curfews would limit audience attendance, according to a *Siyah Bant* report in 2012. The state had even forbidden the use of Kurmanji in official events, in public spaces including theatres, and in songs since the 1960s and as early as 1925.[4] It was not until January 1991, when President Turgut Özal and Prime Minister Yıldırım Akbulut lifted the ban on Kurmanji; it would take even longer to be implemented and it was in the 2000s, when Kurdish drama and song in Kurmanji started to flourish again (Verstraete 2018: 52).

Turkey is then an ideal case for the discussion of the role of music and theatre in collective memory building and commemoration of sensitive past events as well as its socializing effects on communities and identities. Of particular interest are performances that try to win the approval of the authorities to avoid political reaction or polarization, notwithstanding opera productions that were imbued historically with a great social and critical function to advance Turkish nationalism. A more recent example of the latter is the 2021 opera *Sinan* by composer Hasan Uçarsa, based on an unrealized film concept by Halit Refiğ in 1978 (libretto by Bertan Rona), staged at the inauguration of the newly rebuilt iconic opera and ballet house, the Atatürk Cultural Centre (AKM) in Istanbul, on the 98th anniversary of the Republic of Turkey. The fact that the opera took a celebrated Ottoman architect as its protagonist is well in tune with President Erdoğan's pan-Ottoman architectonics to re-establish the greatness of the former empire under his vision of a 'New Turkey'. Producing a critical music theatre production for Turkish and Kurdish communities in both Turkey and Europe, whilst evading such state narratives and censorship, suddenly makes a whole lot of sense.

Music theatre as tool for mnemonic socialization

Now that a larger cultural and historical context has been established, this analysis will elaborate on the theoretical foundation for analysing music theatre's role in commemorative practices, starting with Zerubavel's (1996) notion of 'mnemonic community'. In his sociological work on communities, he has demonstrated how commemorative acts, rites and sites can affect what he calls a 'mnemonic socialization'. By this, he considers the workings of collective memory in relation to our material culture, influencing social behaviours, habits of mind, assumptions, values, belief systems, practices, traditions and perceptions of the world – in other words, our pervasive cultural discourse. He distinguishes personalized manifestations of a mnemonic community's collective memory from personal recollections.

> The collective memory of a mnemonic community is quite different from the sum total of the personal recollections of its various individual members, as it includes only those that are commonly shared by all of them ... The notion of a collective memory implies a past that is not only commonly shared but also jointly remembered (that is, 'co-memorated'). (Zerubavel 1996: 293–4)

We shall see later how music theatre, through celebrating language and cultural artefacts that are plagued by long stretches of censorship, can also trouble a collective memory that is inherently incoherent and only comes into existence by re-imagining and co-memory. Moreover, for Kurdish communities, reimagining the dengbêj tradition through an in essence 'European' art form like opera and staging it outside Turkey creates wider opportunities for *co*-memorating. According to Zerubavel, such newly established commemorative practices always engage in mnemonic battles over the social legacy of the past, thereby underscoring their social role in a larger politics of remembrance that affects not only individuals but also entire communities. These battles often bring along discord regarding what the 'correct' way is to interpret the past, which narratives ought to be remembered and *how* they should be remembered, which often corresponds to major social changes that are discussed in the public realm.

Zerubavel discusses mnemonic socialization through narrative structures and *narrativization*. He speaks of a narratological pluralism that underlies the discord in society regarding essentially *what* events should be remembered and *how* these events should be commemorated. For the Kurds, however, the foundational narratives of their communal identity and memory have long been hampered by expression in their language, despite the substantial efforts of Kurdish poets to produce literary works in Kurmanji since the 1970s, many of whom were writing and translating outside Turkey (with the Kurdish Institute of Paris as a significant supportive centre). Since (self-)restriction of speech and writing, and thus of narrative, in the public arena also affects theatre artists and audiences in the theatre, more affective ways are sought to facilitate mnemonic socialization around sensitive topics. Music is then one of such tools to circumvent it as it has the power to reach audiences more directly, affecting them both bodily and cognitively.

In narratological discussions, instrumental music is often described by its problematic *tellability* in contrast to its great propensity for *narrativity*. The former is defined by a medium's ability to recount an event or configuration of events that are (relevantly) reportable, or 'tellable', in a given communicative situation, which music essentially lacks. Labov and Waletzky (1967) contributed to the notion while discussing performative narratives that may be considered 'empty or pointless' when they only recapitulate experience, though they may still enable a 'stimulus in the social context in which the narrative occurs' (13). In narrative psychology of the 1970s, the notion of 'narrativization' was developed to explain how for all music's semiotic ambiguity, it can strongly appeal to a cognitive mode of experiencing the self through music in a narrative interpretation. Zerubavel draws from these same insights when he acknowledges narrativization as a mnemonic tool: 'In order to satisfy their desire for cognitive closure, people tend to mentally transform the flow of more or less unstructured events into relatively coherent narratives' (Zerubavel 2003: 13). Music has that potential to incite the listener finding closure and relief through narrativization in order to maintain a holistic self.

Music theatre's framing mechanisms as well as lyrics in songs (and supertitles) or concomitant gestures of the performers help the spectator to construct a narrative traction by appealing to their familiarity and cognitive ability to make narrative connections. These are defined by contextual clues and socially shaped identifications. We, therefore, should give attention to the full musical context, which is what Christopher Small (1998) denotes with the term 'musicking' as a form of socialization. If, following Zerubavel, we regard narrativization as one significant aspect of this social relationship which the total musical performance situation can bring about, then we have to acknowledge music theatre's significance in mnemonic socialization, particularly in works that address communal issues. Yet Zerubavel has also acknowledged the role narrativization plays in myth-making, for instance in founding myths and ethno-nationalist narratives that foster a sense of common descent and commonality in sharing a common present (Zerubavel 2003: 63). Yaël Zerubavel, Zerubavel's spouse, has added that such myths also fulfil the social function of 'demarcating the group's distinct identity vis-à-vis others' (Zerubavel 1997: 7). This is an important point to look out for when discussing community building through music theatre as a form of mnemonic socialization.

One important aspect has not been fully addressed in this context: the role of identity and the address of self. The social aspect of memory as constitutive in the process of identity formation and selfhood has been well researched since the 1920s by Maurice Halbwachs (1980). He introduced the term 'affective communities' already in 1925 to discuss the role of emotion in the production of social groups. He believes that music, both in production and reception (the production of musical meaning), has correlations with our capacities of memory: it is dependent on a history of replications, previous performances of the music, which is then mediated by the listeners' (and musician's) relations to one another. He uses a comparison to the image of footprints in Defoe's novel *Robinson Crusoe*, as Mowitt (1987) recounts:

> musical signs ... are indices of the action exerted on a performer's brain by the 'colony' of other brains. The significance of these signs arises within the horizon established by this structuring of memory – a memory that is at once fundamental to music and profoundly social ... The social history leaves its traces, its footprints, in the brains of musician and listener alike. (Mowitt 1987: 181)

Since both musician and listener are participating in social history's footprints, one could assume that *musicking*, in all its aspects of performance and reception, is also always shaped by these traces. However, Halbwachs believed that social frameworks pre-exist and shape people's memories by filtering narratives according to their social significance for the group (1939: 7–8). Since the prolific expansion of cultural memory studies in recent years, we have seen studies that show how remembrance is also a cultural force that can help to redefine social frameworks, and, as will become apparent in the following case study, to connect hitherto unconnected communities with differing understandings (Rigney 2018). The latter is particularly of importance if we want to understand the empathetic links to Kurdish communities outside of Turkey, not only within their own diasporic groups but also within the intercultural communities of Europe. In this regard, cultural memory that is reproduced and communicated through formative (and often normative) cultural texts plays an important role and should be acknowledged as a site of new experiential perspectives that could work against the rigidity of foundational myths.

Music has a double role to play in this identification process. Simon Frith (1996), for instance, has been central in the debates surrounding music's ability to address identity, by reminding us first that identity is mobile, a process not a thing, a becoming not a being; second, that our experience of music – of music making and music listening – is best understood as an experience of this *self-in-process*. Music, like identity, is both performance and story, describes the social in the individual and the individual in the social, ... ; identity, like music, is a matter of both ethics and aesthetics. (Frith 1996: 109; qtd. in Verstraete 2013: 191)

As Frith remarks, music – or better, musicking – sustains the social connection between the individual and the collective memory, precisely because of its propensity, just like identity, to stay mobile, unfixed, perpetually *becoming* but never arriving.

When we extend this argument to our discussion of music theatre's purposefulness for mnemonic socialization, the identity question requires a deeper look into the complexity of the audience as temporary community. This is even more complex in bi- or intercultural situations. The Deleuzian/Spinozian idea of the self as pure becoming has inspired philosophers to rethink community, not as a well-defined, coherent social group, but as George Bataille called it, a 'community without community' (Derrida 1997: 48; Nancy 1991: 71). Bataille's notion became the cornerstone of the community debate initiated by Jean Luc Nancy's *La Communauté desoeuvrée* (1986; transl. 1991). The underlying idea is that community should be regarded negatively as the 'antithesis to a notion of community that always already knows who and what it is speaking of' (Kosnick 2011: 28). Community is then 'inoperative' to the extent that it cannot be regarded as 'a project of fusion, or in some general way a productive or operative project – nor is it a *project* at all' (Nancy 1991: 15). Instead, it is 'unworkable' or 'unworking';[5] it is not an 'oeuvre' because it is un-objectifiable. This notion of community is in a state, which Bataille called the absence of myth, or, in Nancy's words, the 'interruption of myth' (1991: 47). Although Nancy meant particularly the Nazi myth and its relentless desire to regenerate the 'old European humanity' (46), it can mean to refer to any foundational myth. It is the latter discussion that will help us to argue for music's ambiguity in appealing to a community's collective memories while that community is by and in itself, 'inoperative'. Hence, we should ask ourselves the question: to what extent does the music contribute or resist the interruption of myth?

Case study: A Kurdish *Tosca*

I propose to discuss the developed argument on music theatre's potential role in mnemonic socialization further through the case study of the Kurdish adaptation of Pucinni's *Tosca* (2019), translated into Kurmanji by exiled Kurdish author, Kawa Nemir. This adaptation was set to a new musical score by the emigrated Armenian-Turkish composer, Ardaşes Agoşya, in a staging by the Turkish-Dutch director, Celil Toksöz. This noteworthy production was produced by the Amsterdam-based Theater RAST in collaboration with artists from the Diyarbakir City Theatre, now called *Amed Şehir Tiyatrosu* in Turkey. This music theatre production comes at a significant political moment in time, when newspapers and petitions speak of another 'genocide' taking place involving Kurds in north-eastern Syria (Dag 2020; Stanton 2019). Amidst this geopolitical crisis and its atrocities, the opera commemorates the Kurdish language, culture and its long history of state oppression and betrayal in different historical contexts, much in line with the main dramaturgical themes of Pucinni's *Tosca*.

On a narrative level, it is perhaps a surprise that this Kurdish musical drama is not based on a Kurdish story but on the libretto of Puccini's 1900 opera, which was in its turn based on a French melodrama by Victorien Sardou. Kawa Nemir got most of the original poetry translated by the librettists, Luigi Illica and Giuseppe Giacosa, with some poetic additions in Kurmanji where appropriate. The choice of Puccini's most political lyrical drama is, however, no coincidence. Inspired by Emile Zola's naturalism in French literature, Italian *Verismo* at the beginning of the 1900s gave Puccini opportunity to put stories of common people with more mundane desires and passions on the stage. In the Kurdish *Tosca* adaptation, however, the figures of political refugee Cesare Angelotti (played by Hediye Kalkan), the insurgent painter Mario Cavaradossi (Dodan Özer) and his rather politically ignorant lover, Floria Tosca (Gülseven Medar) seek a very different 'veristic' truth as they do not necessarily portray Puccini's original admiration for Napoleon Bonaparte and the Italian dissidents who supported the Napoleonic revolutionary wars in Italy. Rather than set in Rome, where Napoleon's battle of Marengo against the Austrians takes place, the fictional world is now 'situated in Diyarbakir, a city on a steep, high basalt rock on the banks of the Tigris', according to the programme brochure.

Moreover, the brochure reveals 'Puccini's 200-year-old story is a metaphor for the suppression that the Kurds experience until today'. In interviews, Toksöz highlighted the theme of 'betrayal' which is very meaningful in the context of the Kurds, particularly in the context today with the Turkish incursion in northern Syria. This sparked international outrage and numerous newspaper articles referencing a long history of betrayal. Historically, that betrayal goes back to the 1920s when Kurds were promised a state under the Treaty of Sèvres, which marks the ending of the First World War and dismantles the Ottoman Empire, a promise never fulfilled by the involved pledging parties, Britain, France and the United States. When the new republic of Turkey was established in 1923, national borders were drawn in such a way that would leave out the fulfilment of an independent (greater) Kurdistan. Kurdish tribes and revolting tribal leaders were quashed by the military.

Each year in November, a related historical event is commemorated among Kurdish communities from Turkey, the Dersim massacre, in which *c.* 20,000 to 30,000 Zaza-speaking Kurds were gassed and killed in the years 1937–8 because they did not comply with Ankara's efforts of centralizing power in the early republican period. The commemoration recalls the hanging of one of the Kurdish rebel leaders, Seyed Riza, on 15 November 1937. The Dersim massacre is seen today by internationally acclaimed academics, like Martin van Bruinessen (1994), as a genocide. It was followed by decades of repressive policies of ethnocide that would curb Kurdish rights to identity in Turkey. Although the creative team of *Tosca* never referenced such harsh historical events directly, neither in media interviews, nor the programme or the staging, they do refer in the brochure and on their website to the context of censorship and linguicide when revealing the production's central metaphor: 'the Kurdish language refers to the language of oppressed, of the refugee, of secrecy. ... This language also searches like a refugee for a home in this opera'. Ironically, the opera's premiere in Turkey, where it would come home, could not take place and it is uncertain if it would ever be produced there.[6]

When one tries to decipher the adaptation's narrative as an allegory for Kurdish political history or for the contemporary situation, the reading always falls short. Neither the storyline nor the characters ever completely fit. It rather circumstantially wants to resonate with bigger metaphors of power (abuse), subjugation, exile and liberation, which anybody can relate to. Since the opera is produced for a very diverse audience in the Netherlands and potentially Turkey, the work is kept open, without clear symbols or cues, so that anybody can read their own story, in other words, 'narrativize' the musical events on stage.

There are, however, some clear dramaturgical changes that have political relevance. One is that a woman, Hediye Kalkan, plays the originally male political refugee Cesare Angelotti, who is a member of the pro-Napoleon dissidents who just escaped prison. Toksöz explained this dramaturgical choice: 'Kurdish women are so combative. ... They have always been under pressure by both the government and the family, and they always have to be strong. It is now often the Kurdish women who protect their land, organize demonstrations and take up arms' (interview with Beeckmans, 16 October 2019). Given the contemporary context, the reference seems then to allude to the all-female Kurdish Women's Protection Units in Northern Syria, which are reported to have become a pawn in a bigger, male-dominated, geopolitical game (Temelkuran 2019). This creates perhaps more tension around the politically unaware Tosca, who later gives up Cesare's hiding place at her lover's safehouse.

A second, less noticeable, dramaturgical change is that the overall focalization has shifted from Tosca to Mario Cavaradossi (Dodan Özer), apart from the scene where Tosca is alone with the corrupt chief of police, Baron Scarpia (Ali Tekbaş). However, one could argue that Cavaradossi is still presently perceiving the scene while being interrogated under torture offstage. This shift in focalization may be the result of some cut scenes, which makes Cavaradossi present in most of the songs. When he sings the legendary 'E lucevan le stelle' aria in a new composition by Agoşyan, it is clear that the audience are meant to feel more connected to the tragedy of the Kurds, who have gone through systematic torture historically. Most known in that regard is the Diyarbakir Prison, established in 1980 as a martial law military prison to interrogate political dissidents after the 1980 Turkish coup d'état, notoriously exposed to horrifying acts of torture. So, when Dodan Özer elongates his musical gasp, 'Oh', it crosses time and space with much historical resonance, until he pronounces: 'I have never loved life like this before.'

It is clear from these two noticeable changes in the adaptation that, in commemorating Kurdish liberation efforts, the overall dramaturgy works around a duality in the recognition and narrativization by diverse audience members. On the one hand, certain narrative elements as well as visual motives are kept deliberately open to interpretation, which invites audiences to feel along with the main dramatic arch close to the original opera, while on the other hand, certain images claim political traction and symbolism. For instance, the painting that Cavaradossi was preparing in the church is in this production a more generic photograph of *Sculpture Woman in a*

Russian Dress[7] by the Soviet sculptor Sergei Konenkov, clearly chosen for its pensive, commemorative bending of a woman's head slightly backwards rather than any direct historical or political connotations. Yet the image of an eagle tied to a tree, which dominates the scene halfway the performance, is clearly suggesting more political significance. The eagle is not only a mythological animal that works as a catalyst for a lot of Kurdish folk stories, but it is also a primary national symbol on the coat of arms for the Kurdistan region in Iraq where the eagle holds a sun on its wings. The fact that it is tied to a tree is a rather obvious political symbol for the capture of Cavaradossi and Angelotti and for the Kurds who want to have sovereignty over their land, a democratic federation and an internationally recognized society, rather than a dispersed, homeless and diasporic community.

Debate: *Tosca*'s problematic mnemonic socialization

This chapter's main question of mnemonic community through music theatre invites us to look at the full musical experience in *Tosca*. The composer admits in a privately conducted interview[8] that he composed the music with the purpose of commemoration in mind. His identity as a previously Istanbul-based Armenian composer is not insignificant: he grew up as a Christian in a cosmopolitan environment with Turkish, Kurdish, Assyrian, Jewish, Greek and Armenian people around him. He claims to have taken his roots from pre- and post-Christian Armenian culture with a 5,000-year-old history, so as a classically trained composer, the music of the Kurds was never foreign to him.

In his composition, he uses famous Kurdish songs and tunes, some of which were compiled by the Armenian composer-singer, musicologist and priest, Soghomon Soghomonian, better known as 'Gomidas' or Komitas Vartabed (1869–1935), whose 150th anniversary was celebrated in 2019. During the Ottoman Empire, Gomidas travelled through Anatolia to notate over four thousand Kurdish, Armenian and Turkish songs in search of a 'pure' Armenian music. By way of commemoration, composer Agoşyan rearranges a tune that Gomidas preserved throughout this opera adaptation in what he calls a 'music of Mesopotamia'. It is perhaps historical irony that music, which was once collected to find the true 'Armenian sound', is now used in a Kurdish opera to identify with Kurdishness. It says a lot about how the timeworn music of Mesopotamia is culturally hybrid. Moreover, Agoşyan left room in the rehearsal process for improvisation for the dengbêj singers –they could choose a region in Mesopotamia and improvise according to the singing techniques associated with each individual region. Through guided improvisation, the composer places a great amount of trust in the singers and instrumentalists to express themselves by adopting new singing techniques while using their own instincts and memories of Kurdish musical cultures.

The reference to 'Mesopotamia' is ideologically significant, as Çağlayan (2012: 6) confirms in her study about the ideological discursive strategies of the Kurdish liberation movement: it may 'emphasize the historical continuity from the pre-historic peoples of Mesopotamia … and thereby allow the construction of a continuous identity of Kurdishness' (Smets and Akkaya 2016: 86). So, by bringing to memory an often-unrecognized Middle Eastern culture, the opera resonates with a micro-nationalist fantasy of the Kurds that gives them existential rights against what is generally imagined as 'Anatolian' within Turkey's national and literary history. In a way, the mnemonic community that identifies itself here by means of a collective memory around some of the songs and tunes can have nationalist undertones. This became very clear when some of the songs were recorded by audience members on their smartphones and shared through Twitter. Social media then reinforced a sense of an imagined community (Anderson 1991) across national borders, which breathes new life into the myths that underpin it.

Nonetheless, the collective memory of the Kurds, particularly those of the diaspora in the Netherlands, is waning. The long censorship history in Turkey (as well as in Syria and Iraq) has had significant influence. Therefore, commemorative citation of their ancient forms of music is always in a sense (re)producing new myths on which the community rediscovers its identity in a continuous process of *becoming* (cf. Frith 1996). One particular Leitmotif that the Kurdish(-Dutch) community can recognize is the repetitive use of two Kurdish wedding dance songs (*düğün halayı*), 'Lorke' and 'Welleh govend ranabe', around which Agoşyan composed his melodies as reflections of these songs. The first time it is heard it signals the thoughts of the villainous chief of police, Scarpia, when he is blackmailing Tosca to share the bed with him in return for her lover's mercy from the death penalty. The wedding 'halay' could then prompt an extra narrative layer for Kurdish listeners, signalling that Scarpia thinks of the situation as his wedding. We hear 'Lorke' for the first time when Tosca accepts Scarpia's deal. Consequently, we continue to hear 'Lorke' after Scarpia is killed by Tosca, which may mean that all his powers are transferred to Tosca in some kind of Shamanic way of thinking. To symbolize this, we hear 'Lorke' again in its amodal transformation: this now symbolizes the wedding that has gone astray. After Tosca kills Scarpia, during the execution scene of Cavaradossi, Tosca imagines for herself a wedding scene just like Scarpia did. Before the execution, we hear 'Welleh govend ranabe' because Tosca will have the same destiny as Scarpia: she thinks she will elope with Cavaradossi because he will be freed safely. However, when she finds out Cavaradossi is killed, we hear the amodal transformation of 'Welleh govend ranabe'. This is her song for a wedding that has gone astray because the groom is now dead.

Even when Dutch audiences, through musicking, would not recognize such cultural meanings of a Kurdish wedding dance song, usually performed as a circle dance by the community in wedding parties, the repetition of the 'Lorke' and 'Welleh govend ranabe' tunes as leitmotifs make the audience part of a collective memory with the Kurdish singers, musicians and audience members. Moreover, the cultural transferences and appropriations of Agoşyan's composition (which, according to him, is also based on one melody in his own oeuvre, namely a Kurdish harvest song) creates enough cultural and mnemonic distance to detach any tendencies in the making of a community through musical recognition and collective memory in a nationalist programme. Such cultural referencing 'necessarily stretch[es] the meaning of national belonging by disengaging it from its presumed territorial and linguistic imperative, and decentering it in relation to any putative "core" values or markers of greater or lesser "authenticity"' (Flores 2009: 45). The 'authenticity' question, according to Lo and Gilbert (2002) quoting Griffiths (1994), can 'easily become a fetishized commodity that grounds the legitimacy of other cultures "not in their practice but in our desire"' (46).

Thus, the authenticity in the musicians' engagement with traditional halay songs and the dengbêj tradition in this opera adaptation marks a chasm in the address of commemorative communities through music: on the one hand, the Kurdish audience members may find themselves trapped in a desire for recognition of their culture in a fantasy that sharing some of their collective musical memories produce a temporary community in listening. On the other hand, the white Dutch audience members may marvel at what they read as an 'authentic' vision of Kurdish traditional music performed by non-Western 'others' producing their (folklore) *culture* on the stage. But then, they may miss the mythologizing aspects that this production engages in its reproduction of a phantasy of a 'music of Mesopotamia' – much similar to the 'memory industry' (Klein 2000) that the newly established House of Dengbêj in Diyarbakir initiated.

The layering of these potential connotations in the different engagements with the music in its production and reception disrupts Jacques Attali's impression that 'all music, any organization of sounds, is then a tool for the creation or consolation of a community, of a totality' (1985: 6). The sense of totality in the musical experience is then more of a temporary illusion, and the community that is produced as much on stage as in the auditorium is rather an 'inoperative' one (Nancy [1986] 1991). The potentially (micro)nationalist connotations of a remythologization of Kurdish cultural 'authentic' traditions through the performance are open enough to sustain a larger appeal and cultural reading by the different communities represented in the context of this theatrical experience and social ritual that traditionally comes along with opera-going. Similarly, its visual symbols may pinpoint nationalist connotations but are open enough to appeal to a hybrid community in a process of *becoming* but never quite realizing as a totality through the musical experience. The in-*operative* community that this opera produces is then rather an apparent paradox under question: a chasm between communities that are always in themselves imagined and whose boundaries are more porous than its constituting individuals may believe.

Concluding remarks

The music theatre production discussed in this chapter sets out to address and commemorate a transnationally dispersed mnemonic community of Turkey in the multicultural contexts of Western Europe, in this case, the Netherlands, but this equally concerns Germany, Sweden, France or Belgium. They showed the importance of opera's commemorative function in translocal and transcultural situations where an 'inoperative' community through commemorative practice in its own national context is prohibited.

In its appeal to memories of individuals and communities, sometimes fabricated, sometimes deliberately ideological, *Tosca* gave rise to questions on the very notion of what the community defined by memory is. Notwithstanding nationalist connotations and aspirations that music may provoke in its appeal to Kurdish collective memories and political imaginings, the mnemonic community is opened and decentralized to such an extent that it drives the attention away from a national belonging. It sets out to include outsiders to that community in a more inquisitive and indefinite way, while commemorating the perpetual deaths and historical betrayals of the Kurds – including cultural and linguistic knockbacks – through protagonists who are borrowed from the European dramatic canon. This multifaceted cultural appropriation consisted of Turkish-Kurdish cultural agents reclaiming Puccini's opera to claim recognition for their culture, the Turkish-Armenian composer reclaiming the hybrid musical-cultural archive of the Kurds and the Dutch diverse audiences reclaiming something of an 'authentic' cultural experience through the familiar narrative format of the opera (by itself, also a cultural hybrid of a French melodrama in an Italian veristic opera form). This hybridity – call it a living 'barbarism' – challenged the total musical experience as an experience of community that, in itself, is a constructed totality. Even more so, it presented itself as a problematic paradox, a myth of a temporary community through musicking that may desire commonality but never arrives there.

Through commemoration, whether it is of language, of music or of political narrative, music theatre reminds us that the coming of communities, be it through mimesis or collective experience, would always somehow necessarily fail short. Its repetitions and aimed restored socializations make the contours of communities more than ever reflective and mistrusted. Yet it is exactly this troubling of community from which mnemonic practice in the theatre draws its communal strengths.

Notes

1. This work was supported by a Marie Skłodowska-Curie grant (project nr. 893827) in the Horizon 2020 research and innovation programme of the European Union. I thank my partner, Görkem Akgöz, for her never-ending support, critique and inspiration throughout the entire research and writing process.
2. Even more so, due to decades of political repression and denial of the Kurdish identity in Turkish society many Kurds have historically felt as 'an active "colonial project"' that is continuing up to the present (Houston 2009: 20). This has fueled the 'Kurdish Question' or 'Kurdish Issue' which has been essentially about either separation of the Kurds from Turkey to create an independent Kurdistan or about more autonomy and rights for the Kurds inside Turkey.
3. The production was advertised as the *first* Kurdish opera, but there have been earlier occasions where Kurdish musicians and singers performed in different Kurdish dialects on the international classical music stage. One notable example is Dilshad Said (in Kurdish, Dilşad Seîd), a Kurdish musician (classically trained in Baghdad and now residing in Austria) who conducted his own symphony, titled *Peshmerga* in 2015 with the Czech National Symphony Orchestra and the Kühn Choir of Prague. The composition was commemorating the massacre of Yazidi Kurds and the capture of Sinjar by ISIS. It was sung by six celebrated Kurdish vocalists in different Kurdish dialects (texts by Edib Chalki). Another famous Kurdish soprano on the international concert stage is Pervin Chakar (born in Turkey's Mardin; studied in Diyarbakir and Ankara), who lives nowadays in Germany's Baden-Baden and sings classical renditions of Kurdish folk songs, mostly with the Junge Philharmonie in Cologne.

4. Kumanji was banned under the Orient Reformation Report, *Şark Islahat Raporu*, sometimes referred to as the Plan, which was enacted in 1925. Particularly, Law No. 2932,8 banned conversing and singing in Kurmanji.
5. 'Inoperative' is the term that Nancy's translators, Peter Connor, Lisa Garbus, Michael Holland and Simona Sawhney came up with in 1991.
6. The premiere was first planned in Diyarbakir and then provisionally set to happen in Izmir and Istanbul after its first run in Dutch theatres but all performances in Turkey were finally cancelled.
7. Sergei Kronenkov is sometimes nicknamed the 'Russian Rodin' and his sculpture perhaps depicts his wife Margarita Konenkova, who allegedly had a brief affair with Albert Einstein when Sergei came down to Princeton University to do his sculpture. Margarita was rumoured in the United States to perhaps be a Soviet spy. Whether Toksöz was aware of this historical reference is unclear, but certainly, the audience is not given a context to read this image in such a way.
8. The author of this chapter conducted the structured interview on the basis of five questions and the responses were delivered on 20 November 2019 in written electronic form.

References

Anderson, B. (1991), *Imagined Communities: Reflections on the Origin and Spread of Nationalism*, London: Verso.

Attali, J. (1985), *Noise: The Political Economy of Music*, trans. B. Massumi, Minneapolis: University of Minnesota Press (Theory of History and Literature, Vol. 16).

Bayönder (1934), [Opera] comp. Necil Kazım Akses, libr. Münir Hayri Egeli, Turkey: Ankara Halkevi, 27 December.

Beeckmans, J. (2012), 'Hamlet spelen is kiezen er te zijn', *NRC Handelsblad* (16 October), https://www.nrc.nl/nieuws/2012/10/16/hamlet-spelen-is-kiezen-er-te-zijn-12564893-a1281546 (accessed 24 April 2020).

Beeckmans, J. (2019), 'Koerdische "Tosca" wordt steeds actueler', *Theaterkrant.nl* (16 October), https://www.theaterkrant.nl/nieuws/koerdische-tosca-van-rast-wordt-steeds-actueler/ (accessed 24 April 2020).

Çağlayan, H. (2012), 'From Kawa the Blacksmith to Ishtar the Goddess: Gender Constructions in Ideological-Political Discourses of the Kurdish Movement in Post-1980 Turkey. Possibilities and Limits', *European Journal of Turkish Studies*, 14(2): 2–23.

Dag, V. (2020), 'The Looming Genocide against the Kurds: History Should Not Repeat Itself', *openDemocracy*, 17 July. Available online: https://www.opendemocracy.net/en/north-africa-west-asia/looming-genocide-against-kurds-history-should-not-repeat-itself/ (accessed 23 February 2022).

Derrida, J. (1997), *Politics of Friendship*, trans. G. Collins, London: Verso.

Flores, J. (2009), *The Diaspora Strikes Back: Caribeño Tales of Learning and Turning*, New York: Routledge.

Frith, S. (1996), 'Music and Identity', in S. Hall and P. du Gay (eds), *Questions of Cultural Identity*, 108–50, London: Sage.

Gingeras, R. (2019), *Turkey in the Age of Atatürk*, Oxford: Oxford University Press.

Gökalp, Z. (1968), *The Principles of Turkism*, Leiden: E. J. Brill.

Griffiths, G. (1994), 'Myth of Authenticity: Representation, Discourse and Social Practice', in C. Tiffin and A. Lawson (eds), *De-scribing Empire: Post-colonialism and Textuality*, 70–85, London: Routledge.
Halbwachs, M. (1939), 'La mémoire collective chez les musiciens', *Revue philosophique* (March–April): 136–65.
Halbwachs, M. (1980), *The Collective Memory*, trans. F. J. Ditter and V. Y. Ditter, New York: Harper & Row.
Houston, C. (2009), 'An Anti-History of a Non-People: Kurds, Colonialism, and Nationalism in the History of Anthropology', *The Journal of the Royal Anthropological Institute*, 15(1) (March): 19–35.
Klein, K. L. (2000), 'On the Emergence of Memory in Historical Discourse', *Representations* 69, Special Issue: Grounds for Remembering: 127–50.
Kosnick, K. (2011), 'Out on the Scene: Queer Migrant Clubbing and Urban Diversity', in G. Stahl (ed.), *'Poor but Sexy': Reflections on Berlin Scenes*, 27–41, Frankfurt: Peter Lang.
Kun, J. (2000), 'The Aural Border', *Theater Journal*, 52: 1–21.
Labov, W., and J. Waletzky (1967), 'Narrative Analysis: Oral Versions of Personal Experience', in J. Helm (ed.), *Essays on Verbal and Visual Arts*, 12–44, Seattle: University of Washington Press.
Lo, J., and H. Gilbert (2002), 'Toward a Topography of Cross-Cultural Theatre Praxis', *TDR*, 46(3) (Autumn): 31–53.
Mowitt, J. (1987), 'The Sound of Music in the Era of Its Electronic Reproducibility', in R. Leppert and S. McClary (eds), *Music and Society: The Politics of Composition, Performance and Reception*, 173–97, Cambridge: Cambridge University Press.
Nancy, J.-L. (1986), *La communauté désœuvrée*, Paris: Christian Bourgois Editeur.
Nancy, J.-L. (1991), *The Inoperative Community*, Minneapolis: Minnesota University Press.
Özsoy (1934), [Opera] comp. Ahmet Adnan Saygun, libr. Münir Hayri Egeli, Turkey: Ankara Halkevi, 19 June.
Rigney, A. (2018), 'Remembrance as Remaking: Memories of the Nation Revisited', *Nations and Nationalism*, 24(2): 24–57.
Siyah Bant (2012), 'Siyah Bant Research Reports 2013: Report I: Developments in Cultural Policy and Their Effects on Artistic Freedom of Expression in the Arts, Ankara and Report II: Freedom of Expression in the Arts and Censorship in Kurdish Region Diyarbakır, Batman', Istanbul: Friedrich-Ebert-Stiftung. Available online: http://www.siyahbant.org/wp-content/uploads/2012/01/SiyahBant_Research_Reports-1.pdf (accessed 24 April 2020).
Small, C. (1998), *Musicking: The Meanings of Performing and Listening*, Hanover, NH: Wesleyan University Press.
Small, C. (1999), 'Musicking – The Meanings of Performing and Listening. A Lecture', *Music Education Research*, 1(1): 9–22.
Smets, K., and A. H. Akkaya. (2016), 'Media and Violent Conflict: Halil Dag, Kurdish Insurgency, and the Hybridity of Vernacular Cinema of Conflict', *Media, War & Conflict*, 9(1): 76–92.
Stanton, G. H. (2019), 'Genocide Watch: Turkey Is Planning Genocide and Crimes Against Humanity in Northeastern Syria', *Genocide Watch*, 8 October. Available online: https://www.genocidewatch.com/single-post/2019/10/08/genocide-watch-turkey-is-planning-genocide-and-crimes-against-humanity-in-northeastern-sy (accessed: 24 April 2020).

Taşbebek (1934), [Opera] comp. Ahmed Adnan Saygun, libr. Münir Hayri Egeli, Turkey: Ankara Halkevi, 27 December.

Temelkuran, E. (2019), 'Kurdish Female Fighters Are Once Again Pawns in a Bigger Political Game', *The Guardian*, Opinion Kurds, 22 October. Available online: https://www.theguardian.com/commentisfree/2019/oct/22/kurdish-women-ypg-isis-tur key-trump-erdogan-putin (accessed 24 April 2020).

Ülkü Yolu (1935), [Opera] comp. Ulvi Cemal Erkin, libr. Münir Hayri Egeli, Turkey: Ankara Halkevi, n.d.

Ünlü, B. (2016), 'The Kurdish Struggle and the Crisis of the Turkishness Contract', *Philosophy and Social Criticism*, 42(4–5): 397–405.

van Bruinessen, M. (1994), 'Genocide of Kurds', in I. W. Charney (ed.), *The Widening Circle of Genocide*, 165–91, New Brunswick, NY: Transaction Publishers (Genocide: A Critical Bibliographic Review, Vol. 3).

Verstraete, P. (2013), 'Turkish Post-Migrant Opera and Music Theatre in Europe', in C. Risi, M. Eigtved, D. Symonds and P. Karantonis (eds), *Music/Theatre: Experience, Performance, and Emergences*, 185–207, Amsterdam: Rodopi.

Verstraete, P. (2018), '"Acting" under State of Emergency: A Conversation with Kurdish Artists about Theatre, the Dengbêj Tradition and the First Kurdish Hamlet', *Performance Matters*, 4(3): 49–75.

Zerubavel, E. (1996), 'Social Memories: Steps to a Sociology of the Past', *Qualitative Sociology*, 19(3): 283–300.

Zerubavel, Y. (1997), *Recovered Roots: Collective Memory and the Making of Israeli National Tradition*, Chicago: University of Chicago Press.

Zerubavel, E. (2003), *Time Maps: Collective Memory and the Social Shape of the Past*, Chicago: University of Chicago Press.

10

Post-colonial imaginations: Afro-Asian dialogues in the past and the present

Bishnupriya Dutt

This essay reconstructs a history with the description and analysis of a commemorative performance that took place in 2015 in India as a case study. The performance and its analysis offer a close reading of the Third India–Africa Forum Summit, a cultural event centred on commemorative performance that undertook varied strategic functions. I argue that the apparent celebrations worked to camouflage the redundancy of cultural politics and reference its own historical past. This in turn allows one to reminisce about the past, not merely wallowing in nostalgia but adapting a post-colonial critical approach, historicizing such practices and exploring critical paradigms to analyse what seems to be a lost spectre from the past.

The present as remnant of the historical past

Flags of fifty-one African nations, with an Indian flag between each, lined the main thoroughfares of Delhi between 25 and 30 October 2015 to create a public display for the Third India–Africa Forum Summit. Fluttering in the wind and colourful, the flags captured the attention of citizens on their daily commute. Occasionally the regular commuters were stopped to let the cavalcade of limousines pass, while police sirens and security personnel drove adjacent to them, indicating the travelling delegates going from one venue to another for talks mainly around trade and economics. The streets had a deserted air, heightened by the local population appearing apathetic and indifferent. International visits seemed a relic of the past when delegates and world icons could rouse people to line the streets, hailing and welcoming them. Those were the times from the newly post-independent India, where the initiatives to reach out to other post-colonial nations, from which organizations such as the Non-Aligned Movement (NAM) and specifically Afro-Asian collaborations emerged, were exhibited on the streets and highly acclaimed by the public. One may regard this not solely within the framework of a particular foreign policy tradition but also as a way of connecting culturally as it exhibited a larger rubric of post-colonial affiliations.

The summits were part of a 'Nehruvian vision', named after Jawaharlal Nehru, the first prime minister of independent India from 1947 to 1964, and played a key role in building a strong transnational network particularly amongst the nations that attained independence after a prolonged anti-colonial nationalist struggle. At those events, each dignitary was an iconic figure because of the movements they had led. Recent political developments in India, which in 2014 saw the coming of the right-wing Bharatiya Janata Party (BJP) to power, resulted in the October 2015 summit seeming like merely a performative display, an irony or anachronism. The Nehruvian era legacy was held on to by the Congress party that faced an electoral defeat in 2014 and subsequently in 2019. Most importantly, India appeared to be desirous of moving away from what was once seen as cosmopolitanism amongst the post-colonial nations to promote an ethnic culture bordering on xenophobic populism. The irony of this nostalgia that the event was meant to construct can be perceived in the cultural performances that ended up disclosing what was systematically being lost and forgotten.

The October 2015 event, in addition to a cultural programme, was a spectacle of Indian and African performers, comprising commemorative performances that spoke to heightened 'national' histories. The intention of this analysis is to unravel the histories of such collaborations and the cultural manifestations that rely on commemoration as a key performative tool. I argue that these manifestations are embedded in the core of the nation's original cultural imagination and formations, emerging from energetic nationalist struggles of many of the Asian and African nations. Rooted in values of democracy and secularism, particularly highlighted in its cultural expressions, the summit was not an unproductive idealism that stood out only from the disputes akin to the Cold War and those of superpower politics, but it also explored aesthetics through performances that initiated solidarities and collaborations between nations. This is an integral aspect of a post-colonial nation's history of cultural formations. At its foundation, factors that contribute to a more cosmopolitan and international outlook often referred to as 'multi-nationalism' remain even today, along with the oft-cited homogeneity of a nation's imaginations.

This essay historicizes and critically conceptualizes the role of the Third India–Africa Forum Summit, and, in particular, the role that commemoration plays in framing memories of nationhood via performance and what this signifies in terms of the power of embodied histories. This is meant to offer the reader a critical means of formulating a history–practice interface and a critical historiography of a nation's cultural formations. It reminds us that if the nation's constructions remain a significant domain to be explored/examined, then these moments of historical reinvention may serve to question how traditions are 'invented' and/or account for producing narratives.

The theatrical staging of collaborations through embodied performances

Against the backdrop of one of the most impressive colonial structures – Rashtrapati Bhavan (the president's palace) in the haloed Mughal gardens – lit up for the occasion with colourful lights, the dance and music spectacle was staged. The president of India in 2015, Pranab Mukerjee, an old Congress-affiliated politician, hosted this event.[1] In Mukerjee's inaugural speech, he pointed explicitly to the colonial legacy. In connection with the gathering, he mentioned how it would have been unbelievable a century ago to think of a meeting with independent nations of Africa and India, and highlighted the need for both economic collaboration and economic growth as a direct outcome of the summit.

A wide range of musical and dance renditions followed, coalesced into an unbroken and continuous flow with one episode blending into another. It was the coming together of various ensembles from India comprising categories of what are deemed as classical, traditional, folk and modern (Odissi, Chhau, Manipuri, Kathak, Gotipua, Theyyam, Rajasthani folk)[2] with Africa represented by dancers, performers and musicians from Ethiopia, Ghana, Kenya, Nigeria, Rwanda, South Africa, Uganda and Morocco. There were approximately two hundred and fifty artists performing on the occasion and one hundred artists from various African nations. The artists were contacted with the help of the high commissions and embassies.[3]

One singer from India and one from Nigeria opened the programme with a short vocal recital, while the soundscapes of two orchestras (one African and one Indian) filled the space, setting the stage for the dances. Lights on the singers and musicians faded into silhouettes once the vocal recitals receded into the background, while the dancers were brought under the limelight and foregrounded.

The Indian dancers of each ensemble entered the stage, matched by an ensemble from one of the African countries displaying their particular mnemonic movements, postures and gestures of the particular genre. The short duration of each episode allowed glimpses and a few formal idioms rather than exploration of any art practice. These were literally itemized as performances along with costumes, accessories and props that identified each genre. The rhythmic soundscape held the various groups together to create a coherent performance despite the obvious differences and distinctions in the dance styles that had no historical or geographical connections.

The performance was choreographed in such a way that at first each ensemble had their own zones marked out on the stage with one Indian and one African ensemble occupying two distinct spaces. These were to mix and come together either circling each other or in horizontal lines, with the bodies meeting and the dancers melding with each other and subsequently leading to their exits. A whirling spectacle of colour, moving bodies and fast rhythm concluded each episode. All the dances were thought of as duets. After the *Darvesh*, the Rajasthani *Kalbela* and *Odissi*, and dances from West Africa, the *Kathak* and the Ethiopian ensembles were performed, various performances bound by their similarities and resonating with rituals and fertility dances began. The genre of folk dances thus created a more circular choreography. The commemorative signals inherent in these performances as pertaining to each specific nation were explicit and heightened by pace and sound. The rhythmic tempos for the folk dances increased as the *Chhau* matched the masked dances of the Voodoo rituals of Rwanda and West Africa. This was intercepted by its climax with the magnificent entry of the *Theyyam* performers in full regalia who took the centre stage while the other dancers circled around them. Though *Theyyam* as a healing ritual has performative elements, it has no particular dance or performance associated with it and the performer circled the state showing his costume. This was followed by the *Manipuri* performers entering the stage with drums around their necks, doing horizontal somersaults, joined by dancers from Ghana and Uganda. The circles around the performers grew larger and larger.

In addition to the characteristic dancing bodies, steps, gestures and postures, costumes were distinct and identifiable, and all of this not only added to the spectacle as well as brightness, but also marked their origins. Tall vessels from both Africa and India (Rajasthan) were balanced on the heads of the performers, who made slow rounds, in contrast to the fast rhythm of the music. The bells on the feet of each dancer were different. For example, the Indian bells followed their convention while African bells were much larger with a variety of sounds such as the cow-bell and other sounds symbolic of agricultural cultures. Masks, headgear and other such markers were also prominent.

The soundscape in the background maintained continuity throughout the fragmented pieces of performance, ensuring various musical pieces blended with wind and string instruments, and a wide variety of percussions. The vocals of the Indian and Nigerian singers were followed by an Egyptian singer who was joined by other Indian classical vocalists. The folk music ensembles, including the Manganiyars, performed group singing. Vocalists in three or four episodes took the lead in the resulting soundscape, while the dance on stage stopped to make space for them. Since rhythm and beats were the most important elements, there were a range of both Indian percussion instruments (tabla, dhol, magaro, pakhawaj and mridangam) and various forms of African drums, mostly of royal heritage.

The finale was possibly the ideal symbolic coming together of the entire cast in celebration. While the final episode played out, the ensembles entered one by one, taking specific allotted spaces, performing a few steps with the characteristic posture and gestures of the form, again and again, till the stage filled up, spilled over with the artists joining in. A sea of bodies and faces responding to a symphonic orchestrated piece of a repetitive refrain and ending with a burst of fireworks from the frames of the makeshift stages concluded the performance. In summary, this collision of national symbols, sounds and embodied rituals reaffirmed the role commemorative performance plays at such key ceremonial events of national significance. However, it can also operate in unintended ways such as raising awareness to the weaknesses and threats faced by both the conceptual and political power of nation states in the neoliberal moment.

Cultural histories: Reminiscences of the nation's cultural formations

The performance by itself could not effectively narrate or commemorate its own historical processes nor address the loss of memory around such events. There was no attempt at any citations or references evident in the performance per se. Yet this was a culmination of long histories of cultural dialogue between India and Africa throughout the twentieth century, which saw the passing of these nations from their status as colonies to independent nations, and subsequently their emergence in their present entities. Dialogues that began with the League against Imperialism in Brussels in 1927 continued to the post-Second-World-War period. At that time, the Cold War took over from where the hot war ended and the emergence of the superpowers was to some extent countered by the emergence of the new independent nation states in Asia, Africa and Latin America. The subversion of the idea of the nation inherent in a Cold War bipolar world was effectively challenged by the aspirations of the independent nation states seeking to construct the nation according to their original and creative imaginations. Vijay Prashad sees this imagination anchored in robust energetic anti-colonial nationalist struggles that took place due to the large-scale participation of multiple groups of the population including the peasants and workers. This culminated in an attempt to formulate ideas of the nation on the basis of plurality and heterogeneity (Prashad 2007), which reflected in tensions along with the tendencies of homogenization. By 1955 at Bandung and 1957 at Accra, Ghana, where recently independent nations met and the Non-Aligned Movement was conceived, a transnational network of collaborations particularly between African and Asian nations emerged. The subsequent landmark summits and meetings at Cairo (1960), Belgrade (1961), Havana (1966) and many other formal and informal meetings not only reinforced these aspects of sharing cultures but also garnered a number of their national ensembles and cultural reconstruction projects to reflect this collaborative spirit of Afro-Asian dialogue. The Afro-Asian nations coming together were united through key components – common opposition to colonialism, detestation due to racism and common determination for peace and stability in the world. These, based on a post-colonial utopia, were shaping the new nation's cultural imaginations and impacted the formations of national canons. Singers, dancers, musicians and performers who formed the national canons were performing at these international celebrations and visits of the heads of states to each other's countries, which were as important as the summits. By performing national concerns, such as (real or imagined) originary rituals and traditions, commemoration as performance tool once more played a central role in this intersection of nationhood, memory and how the present utilizes the past as a future-orientated tactic.

Implicit in these frameworks, in view of the international collaborations amongst the Afro-Asian nations, lay an articulation of the objective to promote or explore means of 'principled multinationalism', which was totally not unpragmatic as it emphasized the identities of composite cultures and syncretism among cultures. Vijay Prashad finds that these conversations created an environment where the 'multinational states would need to evoke this historical dynamic and fellowship and produce the adoption of an official policy of diversity in religion (secularism), racialism (anti-racialism) and language (multilinguism)' (2007: 84). The ethos of multinationalism was, therefore, based on long-term friendships, maintenance of the collaborative spirit and the exploration of the history of an aesthetic that fostered dialogue. It was the task of the nationalist intelligentsia to reinterpret the post-colonial practices in a new light and add a raft of institutions to 'formulate, craft and disseminate the history, artistry and indeed self-perception of the nation' (87).

The Rashtrapati Bhavan, where the performance was held, also houses the annual photographic albums from the 1950s onwards documenting such celebrations: mostly posed black and white photographs of the Indian and international dignitaries and some iconic dancers such as Yamini Krishnamurthy, Damayanti Joshi, Indrani Rahman, Jyotishmati and many others who were regarded as the ones who were at that point shaping the classical dance repertoire. The dancers were in full traditional regalia with make-up and costume and they were intermingling with international delegates from Africa, popular distinguished figures such as Gamal Abdel Nasser (1918–1970), Anwar Sadat (1918–1981), Kwame Nkrumah (1909–1972), Jomo Kenyatta (1897–1978) and others known for their roles in the anti-colonial nationalist struggles and post independence as heads of their states. The general atmosphere captured in the photographs was one of congeniality and social proximity, in an indoor setting, devoid of any outside audiences; or of a distinct stage space displaying the dancer's grace, beauty and aesthetics of the dance form that had just been performed.

These were images circulated extensively in a world evoking what Achille Mbembe describes as 'circuits from affect to emotion and from emotions to passions' meant to stimulate desires 'to reconfigure not only "the everyday" but also the physical, political and psychic conditions of embodiment in our time' (2016: 218). Not accessible to the public, the archive had till date not lapsed into what Mbembe would regard as 'image capital' or pathways of commodification (ibid.).

The canons were undoubtedly reflecting a majoritarian and elitist view. What is often overlooked, however, is the pressure on the post-colonial networks to promote ideas of plurality and heterogeneity such as through international cultural collaborations. In the larger critique of the historical process of the nation's canon formations, these aspects of internationalism – particularly within the space of the Afro-Asian network of cultural exchanges – has often been overlooked. Although problematic in cultural and other contexts, these were the root of the intellectual quandary and the means to create the new self in the new nation and articulate it through the cultures thus being created. It is closely related to the production of new subjectivities, particularly in this context of citizen-artists. This created what we then envisaged as an additional compulsion, which intervened in the nation's formation and prevented it from becoming the homogenized pristine cultural manifestation of its artist citizens.

By 1983, the NAM summit held in Delhi marked the decline of both the movement and the cultural projects associated with it. Amidst large-scale cultural celebrations and performances, the rifts between the various nations of the NAM were evident. The fissures were dependent on economic choices of the member states, who were abandoning socialist principles and opting for rule of capital. Indira Gandhi, who took over the chairmanship of the NAM from Fidel Castro, was slowly moving towards liberalization and her commitments to democracy had been seriously compromised with the one and a half year of Emergency (1975–77) where all fundamental rights of Indian citizens were suspended. With Mrs Gandhi's assassination in 1984, her son Rajiv Gandhi became the prime minister of India and also the chairman of NAM. It was under Rajiv Gandhi that India's processes of liberalization and globalization were expedited and matched by the erosion of social welfare measures inherent in the Indian constitution and policies. It was bound to impact the cultural practices in the way which Prashad described: 'low economic tariffs and high cultural boundaries formed the contours of the new legitimate strategy for the future visions of the alternate movements towards a post-colonial network of conversations' (216).

Few disagreed on paper about the principles of secular democracy, diversity or economic autarchy, but the new cultural principles were based on economic gains, profit motifs, consumer pleasure and free markets. The older notions of multinationalism came to be replaced by macho traditions based on patriotism and nationalism in the narrowest possible sense with an overarching framework of majoritarianism. By the 1990s, there was the new envisaging of the nation as one entity, one majority community and the rise of right-wing ideology, which regarded the criteria of belonging to the nation as determined by religion and notions of blood, soil and nativism of the narrowest possible kind. The summit in 2015, however, while reflecting these political shifts, still aimed to show their own genre of origin as well as the anomalies in both historical and contemporary manifestations.

Return to the performance

The most significant aspect of the 2015 summit was the coming together of the African and Indian performers. Given the Pan-African and Pan-Indian scope of one continent and one subcontinent, it is a large space expected to accommodate a large diversity of cultural forms. The various representative forms, therefore, were squeezed in to provide a sense of the enormous field of cultural practices with all of them presented along and beside each other into an ever-expanding horizontal choreography. The dance forms, particularly the Indian ones – given the inclusion of classical, traditional, ritualistic and folk dances – lacked any attempt to create a choreography that would represent any marked distinctions. No performer or particular style could monopolize the central vision of the audience. The large stage with the overflow of artists could barely create any marked segregated spaces. Thus, touching bodies came together to create a visual impact that signified a congregation of multiracial performers where differences were effectively diffused and, in the finale, performatively dissolved.

The obvious critique of such a simplistic show of celebrating interculturalism, particularly given its official nature, cannot be ignored. The performances from both Africa and India indicated the current trends where the nation itself had stopped its investment in developing and promoting national cultural manifestations. Influences of neoliberalism and globalization could also be detected in how the dances and performers were 'packaged' in colourful costumes, authentic props and references to royal and aristocratic heritages (royal drums and dance forms associated with monarchy and aristocracy). Traditions are still being reinvented, but without the earlier interventions and engagements that focused on 'multinationalism'. The earlier concerns and debates around cultural formations, which we saw being discussed and debated in global forums by the greatest intellectual minds, are no longer the practice. The exploration of how these formations could be adopted into a national culture with all its tensions has no place and could only lapse into an entertaining show of some form or another. The formalistic approach of these spectacles is devoid of rationality and secular democratic ethos that would give these forms significance and relevance while creating the new, artistically self-representing nations which conversed across their own borders and limitations. It may now be only a museum or an archive that still cites the past to commemorate its own histories; yet it remains important for scholars and communities to understand the systematic degradation of these trends of cultural practice.

Theorizing multinationalism

In the course of chronicling the twentieth-century history of what Prashad regarded as the 'Darker Nations' with a non-Eurocentric perspective, or what other scholars like Mbembe would read as 'South-South' dialogue, significant conceptual frameworks like 'multinationalism' and 'radical cosmopolitanism' emerged. These are rooted in the actual material and social conditions of the times and have proved invaluable in turn for framing the cultural practices emerging out of them. They argue not only for the relevance of these aspects of histories but also for the debates reflected in actual practices of cultures that were showcased to illustrate some key critical debates, allowing one to look at the nation's history with that of dialogue across continents. The nation was regarded as the key mediator worthy of its celebratory expressions, while holding out to dominance by the first and the second world in the way it upheld and reinforced narratives of nationalism. This became apparent in the mode of hyper-nationalism that resulted in nuclear armament and aggressive expansion of spheres of influence or opportunistic dismissal of the very principles of nationalism when the post-colonial nations were being compelled to align with one camp or the other. In contrast, the post-colonial world was symbolically exhibiting how it was possible to effortlessly perform national belonging while conversing with other nations. Although such cosmopolitanism is replete with universalism and multiculturalism, as Helen Gilbert and Jacqueline Lo in *Performance and Cosmopolitics* highlight, it offers a 'middle path alternative between ethnocentric nationalism and particularistic multiculturalism with the general aim of remaking cosmopolitanism into a more worldly and less elitist concept – a kind of cosmopolitanism from below' (qtd. in Knowles 2010: 57). Though Gilbert and Lo see these as alternate practices, it can also be seen within the inherent cosmopolitics of multinationalism.

Multinationalism is not a category that can, justifiably, altogether escape the larger criticism in the field of theatre and performance studies pertaining to interculturalism, multiculturalism and cosmopolitanism. While it allows, as Ric Knowles (2010) formulates, 'new ways of thinking about theatrical flow across cultures and the way in which human subjectivity and identity are constituted – brought into being – through performance' (3), it is also subjected to the critique of what it adheres to: multiculturalism. Thus, the critique against multiculturalism, in this case, is also applicable to multinationalism and would include statist intervention, control and micro-management of cultural practices framed by liberal pluralism, cultural differences paraded as ethnic accessories, apoliticized and ahistoricized, universal assumptions about human conditions, a false sense of cohesiveness and reifying cultural differences (44–5). At the same time, it is difficult to ignore the historical role it played, particularly in the transition from colonial to post-colonial cultural practices, and the enormous state investment in cultures and resources provided to reconstruct and foster practices across genres, performers and locations and make its presence felt from the 1950s onwards. Rustom Bharucha, one of the most outspoken critics of interculturalism and multiculturalism, also acknowledges these practices because of their sheer magnitude and impact. As a post-colonial scholar, he engages with these practices, but asks one to exert caution regarding the state support involved for traditional performances, viewing live performances as national heritage, the deployment of tradition within a nationalist agenda and often taking on 'culturalist assumptions about differences that efface material inequities' (Bharucha qtd. in Knowles 2010: 33).

Unfortunately, conceptual frameworks like 'multinationalism' have received very little attention or have not been theorized adequately by scholars, particularly in the field of theatre and performance histories. The discursive turn that originated amongst post-colonial literary scholars and historians in the United States in the 1990s and the first decade of the twenty-first century prioritized theories and perspectives that looked at post-colonial cultural practices through the lens of the local or the global. Mbembe eloquently lays out the problem of such a discursive turn that legitimized certain methodological approaches in relation to perceiving Africa though relevant for most post-colonial nations. The parameters of the global and the local often dismiss the mediation of the nation and result in either looking at post-colonial nations in isolation as studies in ethnography or 'test sites' of theorizing by scholars from the global North. (2016: 214). Both perspectives, according to Mbembe, spawn from philanthropic global projects and compel a need to theorize in abstraction. These also tended to read historical problems and phenomena as 'crisis-entity' since theories emerging from such fields of production inevitably are 'haunted by melancholy or hysteria' (ibid.: 216). The movements considered here have exactly the opposite impulse, namely of celebratory optimism. Yet, when the discrepancy between politics and culture intensified, they revealed their own contradictions. What these collaborations prioritized then were not ethnic but civil ties, and cultural manifestations of multinationalism aimed to do just that. At the core of the argument lies the idea that this version of the nation could challenge symbolically the more dominant trend of philosophical and moral universalism that lapsed into imperial globalization.

Radical cosmopolitanism or multinationalism allows one to rethink the need and modes of performances at display around these landmark events. If they are indeed embedded in national cultures as an 'opposition to moral equality' to deliberately foreground hierarchies of power in contrast to transcendental moral orders, they also incorporate a deep sense of cosmopolitanism, shared systems of meaning and common languages that connect the colonized across spaces. The celebratory mode of the cultural expressions, such as the summit, was deliberate but not devoid of criticality in amalgamating the idea of the nation's cultures to a cosmopolitan world view that did not demand transcendence of geographical locations, discrete cultural traditions and political constructs such as the nation and nationalism. These modes and vocabulary of performance expressions did create vibrant debates around the local, the national and the international, pervading as much of the construction of national cultures at international fora. What happens in the field of actual performance practices if we shift the focus from the larger historical and conceptual arguments to its negotiations in terms of performance idioms and vocabularies is that we can readdress these cultural sites as examples of radical cosmopolitanism based on civic ties rather than ethnic manifestations.

I will now discern some of the residual features of the genre, the duets and the entire ensemble coming together to bear witness to it in the finale of the cultural performances of the 2015 summit. The sensorial expression of different bodies in rhythmic motions and touching one another in an uninhibited manner recalled through muscle memories an aesthetic of solidarity and politics of neocolonial resistance.

In contrast to the general choreography, often seeming a melee of dancing bodies were the duets of the classical and folk Indian dancers with their African counterparts. The Kathak ensemble of seven dancers entered with the characteristic Kathak swirls, following the swirls of the Moroccan Darvesh dances. Amidst the swirls entered three folk performers from Rajasthan (Kalbela) who also swirled until they sat in front of the Moroccan dancers. The stage was filled with twirling dancers of the three genres until the exit of the Moroccan and Rajasthani dancers. At this time the Kathak dancers paused their twirls for the intricate footwork characteristic of their form. At a certain point while continuing with their footwork, they stepped backwards and jumped while running dancers from Ethiopia once again took over the stage, with their entire bodies in rhythmic motion and particularly the extensive use of their heads. Men behind and the women in front performed intricate movements with their entire bodies and heads, until the two groups divided up the stage with the Kathak dancers on the right-hand side of the stage and the Ethiopian dancers on the left-hand side. Each challenged the other through alternate pieces, the intricate beats and leg work of Kathak was followed by Ethiopian rhythmic dance. While one group danced, the others looked at them, pointing at them and enjoying the dialogue and conversation that ensued from such duets, until the Ethiopian dancers exited with a similar agility as the Kathak dancers with their twirls.

A similar short piece was a duet between Odissi dancers with diyas or lamps in their hands and African dancers balancing four vessels on their heads. The Odissi dancers displayed the intricate postures of Odissi in swift movements and some basic steps until they opened up the space for the African performers who were holding tall vessels on their heads and swaying gracefully while keeping their heads absolutely still. The Odissi dancers followed the swaying rhythm with their own lamps.

This scene was cleverly followed by a folk-popular gymnastic form, which is closely linked to Odissi, but not regarded as a classical form. Young boys, dressed in similar costumes like the Odissi classical dancers, performed the Gotipua[4] and presented a few gymnastic formations till they were joined by the Ethiopian dancers, exhibiting the more gymnastic side of their performances, which were in sharp contrast to their duets with the Kathak dancers.

Other than the duets, which I have described briefly, all of them had at least another dance form that they were supposed to engage in dialogue with. After the entry of each genre style, the presence of two or more distinct forms unraveled the beginning of a conversation with bodies and codified performances to hold on to their distinct characteristics while responding to the other forms. The codified repertoire so eulogized and made sacrosanct pushed its limits to what resulted in actual bodily expressions that bordered on transgressions. A number of the artists confessed to similar experiences and how the movements and gestures in this dialogue attained new meanings, and trying to translate them into further bodily movements required extension of the repertoire and evoking kinesthetic impulses to push the bodies into creating new bodily gestures.[5] These conversations between bodies for the dancers and the musicians in terms of sounds were liberating. They talked of visceral feelings where bodies come into vibrant conversations and in these moments, new possibilities of democratizing spaces opened up. The stage is never empty of bodies and the mnemonics of such performance manifestations are the many bodies standing beside each other.

By way of a conclusion, I would like to recall the need to revisit such historical moments, including the events and cultural manifestations that make up the core of them. The performances were not a simple mirror image of the cultural intent of the state which staged them as a supplement to economic and political policies. I have, thus, focused on a commemorative performance, now rare and infrequent, to dwell back on a cultural historical trajectory and address some of the debates in the field of post-colonial theatre studies. I do not cite the archive as a requiem of serious collaborative commemorations in the changing international-scape, but as a serious critical area of performance practices. Hobsbawm's classic work on invented traditions reminds us sharply that all these forms and genres of performance and dance, from the classical through the popular to the ritualistic, belong to invented traditions (Hobsbawm and Ranger, 2009). When their codes are modified, they actually reflect larger sociocultural trends. Today when the very traditions are making a sharp turn back to indigeneity, nativism, while being ruthlessly manipulated to create a neo-fascist distorted version, steeped in chauvinism of its own historical genre, the performance and the gathering bore witness to histories and the growing discrepancies in an actual performance manifestation. The process of institutionalization, which has allowed the continuity of these nations' invented traditions of the post-colonial world, remains a haunted memory that refuses to go away. It reminds us not only of a history of secular-democratized-cosmopolitan performance practices, but also of its inherent anomalies.

Notes

1. India, like Great Britain, adopted a parliamentary democracy with the leader of the largest party in Parliament as the prime minister. The president is a figurehead.
2. Initially four dance forms – Kathak, Bharatnatyam, Kathakali and Manipuri – were given classical status by the Sangeet Natak Akademy (SNA) in the late 1960s and 1970s. Odissi was the next entrant receiving recognition as a classical dance form. There are eight classical dance categories currently recognized by the SNA. The politics of recognition relating to classical dance has long been intertwined with processes of lobbying, networking and negotiating with the state and its institutions.
3. Interview of Sanjoy Roy (Teamwork Arts) on 28 June 2019 in Delhi.
4. The Gotipua is a semi-folk form from Orissa, often seen as one of the popular practising performance forms and a precursor to the Odissi reconstruction processes.
5. These are based on interviews of fifteen of the Indian performers taken between May and June 2019 in Delhi.

References

Bharucha, R. (1993), *Theatre and the World: Performance and the Politics of Culture*. London: Palgrave Macmillan.

Bharucha, R. (2000), *The Politics of Cultural Practice: Thinking through Theatre in an Age of Globalization*, Delhi: OUP.

Hobsbawm, E. (2009), 'Inventing Tradition', in E. Hobsbawm and T. Ranger (eds), *Inventing Traditions*, 1–14, London: Cambridge University Press.

Knowles, R. (2010), *Theatre and Interculturalism*, London: Palgrave Macmillan.

Mbembe, A. (2016), 'Africa in Theory', in B. Goldstone and J. Obarrio (eds), *African Futures: Essays on Crisis, Emergence and Possibility*, 211–30, Chicago: University of Chicago Press.

Nkrumah' in Martin Odei Ajei (ed.), *Disentangling Consciencism: Essays on Kwame Nkrumah's Philosophy*, 303–14, London: Lexington Books.

Prashad, V. (2007), *The Darker Nation, A People's History of the World*, New York: The New Press.

Roy, S. (Teamwork Arts) interviewed on 28 June 2019 in Delhi.

Index

Abbey Theatre 24, 112
   Peacock stage 112
   'Waking the Nation' 112
absence 69–70, 72, 75
   absent 71
accountability 67–8, 70
acculturation 58, 61
activism 42, 43, 68, 102
   activists 67
   protest 37–8, 41–3, 46, 47, 48
   riot police 42
affect 2, 6, 7, 9, 129, 133, 139
   affective 130, 133, 139
   affectively 14
Africa 161, 162
Agoşyan, Ardaşes 149, 151–3
Ahmed Adnan Saygun
   Özsoy 144
   Taşbebek 144
Akram Khan Company 51
Aleksić, Vladimir 42
Alexander, Peter 131, 132
alienation 59
ancestors 14, 84, 90–1
Anderson, Benedict 1, 2, 22, 52, 153
Anglo-Irish Agreement 24
anniversary 41
Antova, Minna 100
   DENK-MAL 99–100
Anu Productions (*see under* Bolger, David)
Arabs 87
   Arab 86, 90–2
   Arab-American 86
   Arab-Israeli War 87
   Arabic 88–91
   Islamophobia 91
   Muslims 88
archive 155, 164, 165
   bodies-of-archive (*see under* bodies)
   living archive 60
   sensory archive 132

Aristotle 12, 143
artists of colour 83
artist-citizen 164
Artscape Theatre 133
asylum 9
Atatürk Cultural Centre (AKM) 146
Attenborough, Michael 24
austerity 49
authenticity 55–6, 154
   authentic cultural experience 155
authoritarianism 43
autocracy 42

baby boomers 49
Balme, Christopher 3, 4
Bardot, Briggite 44
becoming 149, 153–4
Belfast Festival 28, 32
belonging 52–3, 59, 61, 153, 155
Benjamin, Walter 130, 135, 136
Bharucha, Rustom 167
Birmingham Repertory Theatre 23
bodies 58, 116, 118, 121–2
   abject bodies 23
   bodies-as-archives 10, 52, 57–60
   collective body 7
   corporeal
      acculturation 57–8
      dance archives 58
   embodiment 111, 118, 120, 122
   physical erasure 121
   physicality 30
   silenced bodies 23
Bolger, David 12, 114, 118–21, 122
   Falling Out of Standing 12, 111, 113–14, 118–19, 121–2
   These Rooms 113, 118–20
Bolsonaro, Jair 4
borders 27, 82, 89, 93, 153
   state 143
Boundary Commission 27

Brexit referendum 4
  EU withdrawal process 4
Breyne, Marike 132, 134, 136, 137
British Army 22, 118
  Shot at Dawn campaign 28
Büchner, Georg
  The Death of Danton 42
Burgtheater 104–5
Butler, Judith 7, 53

Carlson, Marvin 3
catharsis 135
censorship 143, 145–6, 150, 153
  silence narratives 65, 70
centenary 5
  centenary year 24
Cerberus Theatre 28
Cherkaoui, Sidi Larbi 51
Citizens Theatre 24
coercion 144
Cohn-Bendit, Daniel 46
CoisCéim Dance Theatre (*see under* Bolger, David)
Cold War 160, 163
  superpower politics 160
communalism 143
  communalist consciousness 145
commune
  Commune of 1830 48
  federated communes 143
Communism 40–1
  Communist 66
community 6, 44, 54, 56, 143–4, 146–8, 153–5
  affective 148
  building 148
  collective identity 27, 61
  communal 148, 155
    history 84
    identity 147
  dance 56
  diasporic 152
  Flemish 52
  imagined 1, 52, 56, 60, 153
  inoperative 13, 144, 154
  Kurdish 146, 148, 150, 153
  mnemonic (*see under* mnemonic)
  practice 143
  Slovak 56
  subaltern 144
  unmaking 144
  without community 149
Community Relations Council 24
conformism
  sexual conformism 49
Connerton, Paul 20, 38, 48
contradiction 1
Creet, Julia 53–4, 60
crisis 1, 3, 7, 65, 67, 70, 129
  migration (*see under* migration)
  point 70–1, 76
  refugee (*see under* refugee)
Critchley, Simon 135

Dans Centrum Jette Workspace 51
de Certeau, Michel 39
Decade of Centenaries (*see under* Ireland)
de Keersmaeker, Anne Teresa 51
  Rosas 51
Deleuze, Gilles 133
democracy 3, 40, 65–7, 69, 71, 76, 160, 164, 165
  democratic 67
  federation 152
  future 67
  society 75
Dersim massacre 150
de Smet, Sofie 132, 134, 136, 137
Diyarbakir City Theatre (*Amed Şehir Tiyatrosu*) 149
digitization 1
discrimination 3, 131
disenfranchized 46
disinterested contemplation 144
displacement 53–4, 59
diversity 165
  culturally diverse communities 54
  intercultural communities 148
  multicultural contexts 154
  multicultural identity 107
  multiculturalism 46
  multilingual performance 84
  multilingual play 93
  multilingualism 89
  multiracial 165
  transcultural 154
doubling 45
drama 55

de-melodramatize 45
dramatic
    action 71, 76
    conflict 65
    language 65
    space 66, 69
    structure 74
dramaturgy 37, 42–3, 45, 47, 49, 151
    dramaturgical 145, 150–1
    imagined dramaturgy 55
Drillet, Jonathan 42
Dubček, Alexander 40
Dutschke, Rudi 44, 45

Easter Rising (*see under* Ireland)
echo chamber 3
enactment 54–5, 61
    re-enactment 23
endurance 2
enemy 82–5, 88–9
    enemies 83–5
estrangement 65–6
Eurocentrism 40, 42, 49
European identity 60, 83
    European humanity 149
exile 9, 43, 54, 67, 151
    self-exile 51, 53

Fáil, Fianna 22
femininity 90–1, 114
    double feminine 91
    'fallen' women 115
    femme fatale 91
    misogyny 91
    vulnerable female 105
    woman of colour 91
feminist 2
Fenian 29
    Fenianism 25
fiction
    de-fictionalize 45
Firk, Michèle 45
First World War 19, 20–2, 24, 31, 106
    First World War centenary 31
Fischer, Joschka 46
Fischer-Lichte, Erika 6, 8
Fleishman, Mark 130, 134–5, 137, 139
folklore 54–6, 154
    circle dance 153

folk dance 51–2, 54–8, 60
folk stories 152
    halay 153–4
    harvest song 153
foreigner 82, 84
forgetting 69–70, 72–3, 75
fragmentation 1
Free State 22
    partitioned state 27
French Theatre of the National Arts Centre
    (Ottawa) 82

genocide 149–50
Gilbert, Helen 166
globalization 43
    anti-globalization 82
Golovchenko, Estela 11, 65–76
    Punto y Coma (Ready or Not) 11, 65–8,
    72, 74–6
Gomidas (Komitas Vartabed or Soghomon
    Soghomonian) 152
González, Camila Ymay
Gorbanevskaya, Natalya 45
governance 1
Grumbach, Tiennot 45
Guattari, Félix 133

Halbwachs, Maurice 21, 56, 148
Hamera, Judith 10, 51, 54, 56–8, 61
Hampstead Theatre 24
Hasan Uçarsa
    Sinan 146
Haughton, Miriam 12
haunting 72
Headlong and Liverpool Everyman &
    Playhouse 24
healing 99–101, 108, 129, 130
Hegel, Friedrich 85
    ethical pathos 85–6, 92
    ethos 87
    pathos 86–7, 93
    Romantic hero 86, 93
    Romantic tragedy 85, 87
    tragic character 87
hegemony 44, 47
Heritage 61
    Heritage Lottery Fund 24
    intangible cultural heritage 56
heroism 23, 30, 43

anti-heroism 29
heroic 23
　ideal 22
　masculinity 22
　narratives 31
　sacrifice 29
heroification 31
masculine heroic self-sacrifice 19
Hirsch, Marianne 13, 14
historiography 40, 44, 92, 115, 160
history 5, 6, 11, 12, 14, 51, 166
　a-historical 24
　communal (*see under* communal)
　embodied 160
　family 81
　historical
　　moments 169
　　past 159
　　turning point 131
　marginalized histories of exclusion 130
　personal 83
　private 81
Hobsbawn, Eric 2, 13, 169
　invented traditions 2, 52, 55, 57, 60, 169
Holdsworth, Nadine 7, 70, 138
Holocaust 13, 86–7, 102–3
　Auschwitz 102
homage 38
human rights violations 68, 76
Hutchison, Yvette 131

identity 51–4, 56, 60, 144, 148–9
　common imagined 144
　cultural 60
　formation 148
　heteronormative binary 26
　loss of 53
　national (*see under* nation)
　pan-Slavic 56
　relational 61
　sexual identity 26
　supra-ethnic identities 56
Ignatief, Michael 134
imaginary
　collective 25
　political imaginings 155
　re-imagining 146
imitation 45
India 159, 162

classical, traditional, modern and folk
　dance 161
Delhi 159
India-Africa Forum Summit 2015 13,
　159, 165, 167
Jawarhalal Nehru/Nehruvian vision 159
Non-Aligned Movement 159, 163, 164
Rashtrapati Bhavan (the president's
　palace) 160, 163
Vijay Prashad 163, 164, 166
integration 60
intersectionality 91
invasion 4
Ireland 111–16, 120–1
　1916 Rising (*see under* Easter Rising)
　A Fragment of 1916 History 118
　Decade of Centenaries 10, 12, 19, 24, 28,
　　32, 111, 113, 115–16
　Easter Rising 22, 111–13, 118–21
　General Post Office 120
　Irish
　　independence 111–12, 115
　　Literary Revival 111, 114
　　Republicans 21, 111
　　step dance 112
　　Volunteers 22
　North King Street massacre 118–20
　Sinn Féin 118
　Waking the Feminists (WTF) movement
　　112
Irish Arts Council 113
Irish Film Institute 113, 115
Israel 87–8
　Arab-Israeli War (*see under* Arabs)
　Hebrew 86, 89
　Israeli 88
　　army 87
　Israeli-Palestinian conflict (*see under*
　　Palestine)
Iziko Art Museum 136

Jew 86–8, 99
　anti-Semitism 102
　Holocaust-Mahnmal 99
　Jewish 84–7, 97, 98–100, 106–7
　　Austria 102
　　heritage 107
　　memorials 99
　　refugees 103

Jewishness 98, 105–8
Judenplatz 99
Nameless Library 99
non-Jewish 86, 101
Joyce, Lucia (*see under* Stapleton, Áine) 12
  Les Six de Rhythme et Couleur 114
Joyce, James 12, 113–15, 118
  A Portrait of the Artist as a Young Man 115
  Bloomsday 113, 115, 117
  Ulysses 113, 115
Judeo-Christian 46
Jung, Carl 115

Kehlmann, Daniel 102
  Die Reise der Verlorenen 97, 102–4
Kemalism
  Kemalist 143, 145
  Mustafa Kemal Atatürk 143–5
Knowles, Ric 166
Kurdish Question 12
  identity 145
  Kurds 143–5, 147, 149, 150–3, 155
    Zaza-speaking 150
  Kurdish
    dengbêj (tradition) 13, 145–6, 152, 154
    diaspora (*see under* migration)
    House of Dengbêj 154
    Kurdish Institute of Paris 147
    identity and memory culture 144
    identities 13
    liberation movement 13, 143, 151–2
    political history 151
    rebel leaders 150
    songs 152
    Women's Protection Units 151
  Kurdishness 152–3
  Kurdistan region 152
  Kurmanji (language) 13, 145–7, 149–50
  Mesopotamia 152
  Opening or Initiative 145

La Colline 82–4, 93
labour rights 49
legacy 4, 9, 75, 160
  colonial 160
legend 1, 3
Lefebvre, Henri 137

Lepecki, Andre 10, 52,
Les SlovaKs Dance Collective 10, 11, 51–5, 57–61
  Fragments 51
  Journey Home 10, 51–2, 54–5, 57–61
  Opening Night 51
Lessa, Francesca 67–8
Lessing, Gotthold Ephraim 85
  Enlightenment 85
  Nathan the Wise 85
lived experience 51
linearity
  linear
    evolution 46
    narrative 20
    retelling 114
    time 23, 46
LGBT+ 42, 46
Lo, Jacqueline and Gilbert, Helen 154, 166
Lothar, Ernst 102, 104, 106–7
  Der Engel mit der Posaune 102, 104
Lo, Jacqueline 166
Low, Polly; Oliver, Graham; Rhodes, P.J. 8, 9
Lowe, Louise (*see under* Bolger, David)
loyalism 25
  loyalist 22, 23
    Ulster culture 26
    Ulster loyalism 21–3, 28
Luther, Martin 46
Lynch, Martin 10, 19, 28–9
  Green Shoot production company 28
  Holding Hands at Paschendale 10, 19, 28
Lyric Theatre 24, 28

Macron, Emmanuel 10
Malle, Louis
  Viva Maria! 44–5, 47, 49
Maronite 81, 83
Martin, Carol 8, 37
  theatre of the real 37
masculinity 26, 112
  male identity 26
Mason, Patrick 24
Massumi, Brian 133
May 1968 38–41, 44, 47–9
  sexual liberation 42
Mbembe, Achille 164, 166, 167
Mbuli, Themba 133, 134, 135, 138

McCarthyism 3
McGuinness, Frank 10, 19, 22, 25, 27
  Observe the Sons of Ulster Marching towards the Somme 10, 19, 24–5, 29, 30, 31
mediatization 1
Meinhof, Ulrike 45
melancholy 52, 54
  melancholic impasse 58
  melancholy of no return 54
memory 5, 11, 14, 52, 65, 67, 69–73, 71–3, 76, 101–2, 107, 111, 113–15, 117, 119–20, 143–4, 148, 162
  architectural memorial structures 100
  body 114
  capitalistic 49
  collective 38, 53–5, 67, 84, 146, 149, 153–4
  co-memory 146
  common 48
  communal 38
  counter-memory 37–8, 43, 46, 49
  cultural 52, 148
  embodied 53
  haunted 169
  historical 106–7
  individual 38, 84
  lieu de mémoire (*see also* sites of memory) 10, 84, 91
  living 70
  mechanisms of 70
  memorial 97–100, 108, 119–20
    boom 38, 49
    culture 38–9, 114
    discourse 38
    fragments 46
    industry 41
  memorialization 22, 31, 120, 122
  mythical 44
  of protest 48
  official 38
  personal 41, 49, 65, 146
  remembrance
    politics of 147
    public 114
  remembering 46, 47, 98–9, 101
    shared 20
  sedimentation 120
  sites of 84–5, 97, 120

war memorials 10
métissage 52, 57
migration 83
  crisis 10
  diaspora 144, 153
  emigration 89
  emigratory experience 51–4, 59–61
  forced migration 53
  immigrant writer 88
  immigration 89
  immigrants 82–3, 93
  Lange Sommer der Migration 104
  mass 81
  migrant 53, 60
  migrating Europe 60
  migratory past 55
  post-migrant 52, 59–60
military code 29
Miller, Arthur 3
Milošević, Slobodan 42
mimesis 45, 47, 143
  mimetic 6, 14
  national (*see under* nation)
Mitrović, Sanja 10
  I Am Not Ashamed of My Communist Past 41
  My Revolution Is Better Than Yours 10, 37–8, 41, 44, 45, 47–9
Mkaza-Siboto, Cindy 134
  Iqhiya Emnyama 134, 138
mnemonic 153, 161
  community 143–6, 152–5
  practice 155
  socialization (*see under* Zerubavel)
  time 58
modernization 145
  modernist cultural project 145
Moleba, Eliot 132
  The Man in the Green Jacket 132–133
monument 9, 97, 99, 100–1, 119
monumental history 93
Moreau, Jeanne 44
Mouawad, Wajdi 11, 81–93
  Ciels 81
  Forêts 81
  Incendies 81, 88
  Le Pacte 83
  Le Sang des promesses 81
  Littoral 81

Ode à l'ennemi 82
Tous des oiseaux 11, 81–93
Mouffe, Chantal 61
mourning 72, 99, 100–1, 108, 129, 130, 138
   collective 135
   Mourning Walk 100
   ritual 133, 136
   unfinished 138–9
Mqomboti, Lidudumaʼlingani 129, 136, 139
multinationalism 160, 163, 165, 166, 167
   multinational allies 137
   multinational states 163
   principled multinationalism 163
   radical cosmopolitanism 166, 168
Munyai, Tebogo 133
   Doors of Gold by Tebogo Munyai 133, 135, 136, 137, 138
music theatre 144–9, 152, 154–5
myth(s) 1, 39, 41, 46, 49, 144, 153
   collective myth of blood sacrifice 25
   foundational 148
   interruption of 149
   mythical 49
      time 38, 41, 43–4, 46
   myth-making 148
   mythological function 23
   mythologization 23
   public mythologies 31
   totalizing mythology 28

Nancy, Jean-Luc 13, 144, 149, 154
Napoleon Bonaparte 150
   pro-Napoleon dissidents 151
narrative(s) (*see also* heroism, linearity, nation, nationalism) 71, 73, 147, 153, 155
   cognitive closure 147
   counter-narrative 25, 114
   disrupted 75
   family 69, 75–6
   focalization 151
   historical 111, 113–14, 119–20
      lineage 4, 8
      official 118, 122
   narration 144
   narrativity 147
   narrativization 147–8, 151
   narrativize 151
   narratological 147

national (*see under* nation)
oral 69
performative 92
personal 76
political 74
state 65, 76, 137, 146
storytelling 76, 81, 93
nation 6, 39, 49, 55, 67, 71, 129, 138, 161, 163, 166, 167,
   formation 164
   homeland 53
   lost national and cultural group 54
   nation-building 111, 122, 145
   nationhood 1, 5, 6, 14, 51, 55, 130, 138, 163
   nation state 10, 39, 162
   national 9, 55, 70, 73, 162
      belonging 166
      British narrative 24
      context 73, 75
      culture 165
      culture of commemoration 44
      discourse 49, 71
      history 7, 81, 153, 160
      identity 52, 56, 81, 111–12, 119, 121
      mimesis 82–3
      narrative 69, 71
      performance 4
      rebuilding 130, 132
      réconciliateur 39
      stereotype 29, 60
      struggle 160
      unity 4
   nationhood 5, 7, 8, 81, 88, 113, 122, 130, 132, 134, 139
   nationalism 21, 38, 29, 31, 52, 55, 81, 84, 143, 145–6, 165, 167
      hyper-nationalism 166
      nationalist 19, 106, 153–4, 163
         Catholic 22
         claims 20
         discourses 31
         heroic paradigms 19
         identity 55
         micro-nationalist fantasy 153
         mythologies 19
         narratives 7
         nostalgia 39
         paradigms 10

politics 52, 60
struggle 160
nativism 165, 169
patriotism (*see under* patriotism)
National Theatre 23
Nazi 42, 98–9, 103, 106
  myth 149
  Nationalsozialismus 98–9, 105–6
Necil Kazım Akses 145
  Bayönder 144
neoliberalism 38
  neo-liberal 41, 49, 83, 162
Northern Ireland 10, 19, 21, 23–5, 27, 28, 32
nostalgia 41, 159, 160
Nussbaum, Martha 135

opera 144–7, 150–5
oppression 43
  oppressed 150
Orange, William of 23, 32
  Battle of the Boyne 32
  Orange
    identity 23
    Order 32
    sashes 27
  Orangemen 27
  The Loyal Orange Institution 32
  Williamite War 32
Oriental 90–1
Other 58, 82–4, 88, 89, 92, 112–13
  alterity 113
  ethnic 83
  otherness 3, 61
  religious 83
Ottoman 145–6
  Empire 150, 152

Palach, Jan 45
Palestine 87, 91–2
  Israeli-Palestinian conflict 85
  Israel-Palestine controversies and conflicts 87
  Palestinian 86–8, 92
Paris Commune 43–4
P.A.R.T.S. (Performing Arts Research and Training Studios) 51
Passchendaele, the third battle of 28
patriarchal 2

chauvinism 169
patriotism 165
  cosmopolitan 92
Pavis, Patrice 71, 73, 76
Pavlović, Živojin 41
Peacock Stage 24
pedagogy 83
pedestrianism 98
  Path of Remembrance 98
  pedestrian
    performance 100, 108
    zone 99–100
  pedestrians 100
  urban pilgrimage 98
  walking 98–9, 100–1
perpetrator 3, 136
Pör, Gyorgy 45
post-apartheid 130
  history 130
  nationhood, citizenship and belonging 138
  neo-apartheid society 134
  present 131
  state 130, 138
  struggles 132
post-colonial 2, 13, 135, 159, 164, 166
  anti-colonial 160, 163
  colonialism 163
  colonial history 136
  imperial globalization 167
  League Against Imperialism 1927 162–3
  scholar 167
  theatre studies 169
  utopia 163
  violent dispossession 136
post-truth 3
  fake news 4
Prague Spring 42
propaganda 2, 81, 144
protest (*see under* activism)
Protestantism 25
  'Prod' 29
  Protestant 27, 29, 32
    Ascendancy 32
Provisional IRA 24, 32
Puccini, Giacomo 150, 155
  Tosca 12, 145, 149–54
Putin, Vladimir 4, 45

racism 82, 163
reconciliation 24, 30, 31, 68, 70–1, 75–6, 82–9, 90–3, 135
  dramaturgy of 84
  family 68
  personal 90
  social and political 84
Red Brigades 42
Red Faction 42
refuge 66
refugee 46, 49, 103, 150–1
  crisis 102, 104
religion 27
  religious
    affiliation 27
    debate 84
    fundamentalism 82
    sentiment 82
Remembrance Day 20, 22, 24
rencontre 83
representation 42–3, 45, 47, 48
repression
  political 67
  repressive 56
    acts of violence 75
    policies of ethnocide 150
    regime 66
  state 73
  victims of 69
residual power 67
resilience 4
revolution 41–9
  Glorious Revolution of England 46
  myth of 47, 49
  political 46
  Protestant Revolution 46
  revolutionary connotations 143
  sexual 40, 49
revolutionism 143
rewriting history 44
ritual 1, 2, 9, 37–8, 43–4, 46, 47, 133, 136, 143, 163
  embodied 162
  healing 161
  practice 46
  of protests 43
  re-enactment 3, 38, 43–7
  ritualistic 46, 47, 49
  rituality 3

tradition 163
Robespierre 41
role-playing 45
Rosińska, Zofia 52–5, 58
Ross, Kristin 40
Royal Field Artillery 28
Royal Inniskilling Fusiliers 21
Royal Irish Rifles 21
rupture 68, 70, 73

sacrifice 135
Sanguinetti, Julio María 67
Schechner, Richard xvi, 54
  scripts 54
Schneider, Rebecca 3, 21, 23, 47
Schnitzler, Arthur 104–6
  Professor Bernhardi 104–6
screendance works 111, 113–14, 118, 122
  choreography 111, 114, 116, 121
  dance performance 112–13, 122
Sechaba, Aubrey 132
  Marikana-the Musical 131, 132, 133, 136, 137, 138
sectarianism 27
  geographical separateness 27
  spatial segregation 27
secularism 6, 143, 160
  secularist 145
self 1, 6, 148, 164
  holistic 147
  selfhood 148
  self-in-process 149
sentimentality 23
Shakespeare
  Hamlet 145
simulation 45
Sindo, Mandisi 134, 136–8,
  Mari and Kana 30, 129, 134, 135–138
Sinn Féin (*see under* Ireland)
site-responsive 8
site-specific 26, 101, 119, 129, 133, 134, 137
slets (mass-choreographed festivals) 56
Small, Christopher 144, 147
  musicking 144, 147–9, 155
social
  equality 46
  fabric 1
  injustice 41, 73
  justice 68, 75

protest 45
struggle 41
solidarity 143
Somme 23, 25, 27, 28–9
Sontag, Susan 13
  pain of others 13
South Africa 129, 138
  African National Congress (ANC) 131
  Afrikaans 130
  African mourning play 130, 134, 135
  apartheid-era massacre 1961 131
  Cape Town 129, 136
  Company Gardens 129, 136
  Economic Freedom Front (EFF) 131
  Farlam Commission Inquiry 130
  Lonmin 130, 131
  Malema, Julius 131
  Marikana 132, 133, 134, 135
  Marikana Massacre 12, 129, 131, 132, 133, 134, 136, 138, 139
  Marikana mountain 130
    miners 130, 136
  mine unions 130
  National Arts Festival 132
  20/20 Vision 133
  Natural History Museum 136
  pass laws 131
  Ramaphosa, Cyril 130
  Rooikoopies 130
  Rustenburg 130
  Sharpeville 131
  Soweto student uprising 1976 131
  Truth and Reconciliation Commission 132
Soviet 41
spectacle(s) 1, 9, 130, 132, 160, 161, 165
speech act 89
stage design 45
Stalpaert, Christel 132, 134, 136, 137
Stapleton, Áine 12
  Medicated Milk 12
Stamenković-Herranz, Maria 42
Stapleton, Áine 111, 114–18, 119, 120, 122
  Medicated Milk 111, 113–18, 119, 120, 122 (*see also* Joyce, Lucia)
state (*see under* nation)
state-of-the-nation drama 107
statism 143
Stengs, Irene 137

stigmatization 3
strike 130, 131
Stroud, Christopher 138
Students' March 42
subjectivity 51, 53–4, 60–1
  interruption of 53, 60
  subject-positions 61
synecdoche 51, 54
systemic violence 29, 31

Taylor, Diana 72, 133
Taylor, Jane 6
Teatro Sin Fogón company 66
tellability 147
temporality
  linear time 46
  mnemonic time (*see under* mnemonic)
  mythical time (*see under* myth)
  tangled temporalities 3
terrorism 43, 86
testimony 47, 48
Theater in der Josefstadt 11, 97, 102–5
Théâtre de Loire-Atlantique de Nantes 82
theatrical canon 31
  national theatre 83
Theater Rast 12, 149
Tito 41
Toksöz, Celil 145, 149–51
Tommy 19, 22–5, 28, 31
  The Soldier's Pocket Book 22
totalitarianism
  totalitarian control 67
transnational 1, 5, 13, 40, 154, 160, 163
trauma 12, 20, 100, 111, 113, 116, 117, 119, 121–2, 129, 134
  'shadowing' 121–2
  studies 53
  survivors 117
  tourism 100
  traumatic
    conditions 53
    memories 113–15, 117–18, 121–2
    past 13, 14, 60
Trauerspiel 130, 134–7
Treaty of Sèvres 150
tropes 23, 28, 90–1
Trump, Donald J. 4
Tsvetkova, Olga 42
Turkey 12–13, 143–51, 153–4

Republic of 150
Turk 143
Turkish 145–6, 149–52
  Turkish-Kurdish 155
  (Turkish-)Armenian 149, 152, 155
  Turkishness 145
  contract 143
Turner, Victor 2
Twelfth of July 27, 32

Uhl, Peter 45, 46
Ulster 21, 25–8
  Division 21, 23, 25
  Protestant 23–4
  Ulstermen 22, 25
  Volunteer Force 21
Ulvi Cemal Erkin
  Ülkü Yolu 145
uncanniness 23
UNESCO 56
unionism
  British 21
Unmute Dance Company 133
Uruguay 65–9, 73, 75
  Uruguayan 65, 68–9, 71, 75–6
  dictatorship 65, 67–9, 72, 75–6
  Ley de Caducidad de la Pretensión Punitiva del Estado 68, 73, 75
  Movimiento de Liberación Nacional – Tupamaros 69
  Niños en Cautiverio Político (Children in Political Captivity) 75
  Parliament 66

post-dictatorship 65, 69, 75
referendums 73
resistance movement 69
society 69, 75–6

Vandekeybus, Wim 51
Verein Steine der Erinnerung 98
Verismo 150
  veristic 150, 155
Verstraete, Pieter 145–6, 149
victim 3, 11, 69, 75, 85–6, 88, 90–1, 98, 130–1, 136
victimization 106
Vietnam War 42, 46
Volkstheater Wien 102

Watkins, Peter
  La Commune (Paris 1871) 43
War of Independence 22
war memorial 23, 31
  War Memorial Garden 22
Weigel, Sigrid 135
We're Here Because We're Here 31
Werenskjold, Rolf 42
White Bear Theatre 28

xenophobia 82–3

Zelenskyy, Volodymyr 4
Zerubavel, Eviatar
  (mnemonic) socialization 144, 146–9, 152, 155
Žigon, Stevo 42, 45